URCHIN AT WAR

URCHIN AT WAR

The tale of a Leipzig rascal and his Lutheran
granny under bombs in Nazi Germany

Prologue by **Barbara Taylor Bradford**
Uwe Siemon-Netto

Urchin at War

© 2020 Uwe Siemon-Netto

All rights reserved. No part of this publication may be reproduced, distributed, or transmitted in any form or by any means, including photocopying, recording, or other electronic or mechanical methods, without the prior written permission of the publisher, except in the case of brief quotations embodied in critical reviews and certain other noncommercial uses permitted by copyright law. For permission requests, write to the publisher at the address below.

Published by:
1517 Publishing
PO Box 54032
Irvine, CA 92619-4032

Publisher's Cataloging-In-Publication Data
(Prepared by The Donohue Group, Inc.)

Names: Siemon-Netto, Uwe, author. | Bradford, Barbara Taylor, 1933– writer of supplementary textual content.
Title: Urchin at war : the tale of a Leipzig rascal and his Lutheran granny under bombs in Nazi Germany / by Uwe Siemon-Netto ; foreword by Barbara Taylor-Bradford.
Description: Irvine, CA : 1517 Publishing, [2021] | Series: [The urchin series] ; [1] | Includes bibliographical references.
Identifiers: ISBN 9781948969574 (hardcover) | ISBN 9781948969581 (softcover) | ISBN 9781948969598 (ebook)
Subjects: LCSH: Siemon-Netto, Uwe—Childhood and youth. | World War, 1939-1945—Personal narratives, German. | Journalists—Germany—Biography. | Grandparent and child—Germany—History—20th century. | Lutheran Church—Germany—History—20th century. | LCGFT: Autobiographies.
Classification: LCC D811.5.S534 A3 2021 (print) | LCC D811.5.S534 (ebook) | DDC 940.54/8243—dc23

Printed in the United States of America

Cover art by Brenton Clarke Little

For Gillian

In Memoriam

Clara Netto
(1888–1976)

Robert E. Bradford
(1927–2019)

Omi: the author's grandmother Clara Netto

Contents

Foreword by Barbara Taylor Bradford ix

Introduction: An Urchin Emeritus Remembers xv

Chapter 1. Urchin's Homecoming..1

Chapter 2. First Cheesecake, then the War 17

Chapter 3. Puddles of Green Fire.. 41

Chapter 4. Marzipan in Limbo 61

Chapter 5. Urchin, the Trolley Terrorist 85

Chapter 6. Theology 101, under Bombs.................................. 115

Chapter 7. The Scream..127

Chapter 8. Where Does the Urchin Belong?...........................149

Chapter 9. Auschwitz and Superstition 161

Chapter 10. Of Bravery, Bach, and the Guillotine 179

Chapter 11. Urchin's Defeats..191

Chapter 12. White Flags and Black Friends..............................199

Chapter 13. The Sunny American Interlude 219

Chapter 14. The Hungry Urchin's Russian Love 229

Chapter 15. Urchin's Farewell to Childhood 243

Chapter 16. Urchin's Journey into Exile...................................261

Postscript: Patience, Hope, and Faith................................ 285

Foreword
A Clever and Captivating Storyteller

Barbara Taylor Bradford

UWE SIEMON-NETTO IS A talented writer with a very special kind of flair. This shows itself in the way he uses odd words together; for a moment, they don't seem to fit, but then the reader gets a sudden image and smiles. At least I do, and sometimes I laugh.

Having been a journalist all his adult life, Uwe pays enormous attention to detail, and everything he sees around him is carefully noted and used to his advantage. He is a very clever and captivating storyteller with a true gift.

I have just finished reading this first book in a series of memoirs he has launched himself into. He tells us about growing up in Nazi Germany until the age of ten. Two more memoirs are planned, which continue his life story into adulthood.

I found *Urchin at War* amazing in that his memory of his childhood is so dear and, in parts, charmingly told. The entire book is captivating, and I had to keep reading to find out what happens next to my little urchin boy.

To refresh his memories of his childhood years, Uwe went back to the city of his birth, Leipzig, some months before starting the book.

FOREWORD

For several weeks, he wandered around that beautiful city looking for familiar places—where he had gone to school; the park he had played in; his family home; his grandmother's home, where he had also lived; and his favorite church.

Of course, he found all the buildings, streets, and shops he knew from long ago. But so many were new and, therefore, different. During the war, the Royal Air Force (RAF) of Great Britain and the Allies had bombed Leipzig heavily and constantly, and so much of the once elegant city had been rebuilt in a drab Communist style after its occupation by the Soviets in 1945.

The center of his life during his childhood was *Omi*, his grandmother. In a certain sense, she raised him and was the greatest influence in his young life. A lady raised by the refined standards of the late nineteenth century, she taught him manners, pluck, and how to have love and respect for people.

Through *Omi*, he knew of the values and elegance of a bygone world, was introduced to the Christian faith, and found true belief in God. Uwe learned from her that showing fear when the bombs dropped was "unmanly and unchristian." Better make the other people in the air-raid shelter smile with urchin-like cheek. *Omi* was somebody he could trust and look up to, and she has remained in his heart to this day.

Uwe writes about his parents with a reflective eye. *Vati* (father) was a damaged man from the First World War. His face was badly scarred and he was blind. But he was strong of mind and heart and moved determinedly back into civilian life. Karl-Heinz Siemon became a lawyer and eventually a prosecutor in the judicial system of the pre-Nazi Weimar Republic and was well respected in Leipzig.

FOREWORD

Mutti—Uwe's mother, Ruth—was twenty-one when he was born and had a fabulous mezzo-soprano voice. She became a professional singer and performed in oratorios and lieder concerts. He loved classical music through her, and it is still a great joy for him.

Uwe always smiled inwardly, apparently, when *Omi* referred to her daughter. This was when she merrily told him she was "scandalizing her persnickety progeny" with the things she said. There are many other comments he remembers that fell from his grandmother's lips, such as "Gentlemen don't stare, they just sneak a peek." In reference to *Vati*'s girlfriends, she called them "juicy nurses," and *Mutti*'s male friends were referred to as "uncles."

While Uwe received love and kindness at home, especially from *Omi*, life in Leipzig was difficult and hard. This beautiful city was now run by Nazi functionaries in brown uniforms matched in color by highly polished jackboots and by Gestapo goons in long black leather garments. They strutted around with arrogance. As Uwe's pert grandmother remarked, they were the only fat Germans then.

The unholy Third Reich ruled mercilessly. This writer describes the Nazis as atheists and neo-pagans. He had been brought up in a democratic royalist, non-Nazi home that despised the vulgar reign of Hitler's sycophants in Leipzig. The antipathy was mutual. The *Führer* loathed this large multicultural city in the center of Germany so much that he only paid it one brief visit during his twelve-year reign.

Leipzig's beloved mayor Carl Friedrich Goerdeler, who resigned shortly after Uwe was born, was the civilian leader of the German resistance against the Nazi regime, which hanged him on 2 February 1945. Decades later, Uwe made Goerdeler the central figure of his doctoral dissertation at Boston University.

FOREWORD

During the war, Uwe went to school every day when there was no air raid and played with his friends in the *Steinplatz*, a playground they occupied in their free time, and did so for the rest of the war. Somehow the bombs spared the chestnut, mulberry, and oak trees that grew there. And the children were safe.

Yet bombs did rain down from the RAF Lancaster and Halifax aircraft at night and from US planes at daytime. The Siemon-Nettos were bombed out and went to live with *Omi*. Food grew scarce; friends and family died in the raids. But like the other citizens of Leipzig, the Siemon-Nettos pushed on and made life work.

I liked the story Uwe tells of his schoolteacher who asked the class one day if they knew the first two bars of Beethoven's Fifth Symphony. "Which of you boys has heard this theme at home on the radio in the evening?" the teacher asked. The whole class raised their hands.

The teacher told them in a low voice to never do that again if they are asked that question. He was telling the children to pretend they didn't know anything at all about Beethoven's Fifth Symphony. *A warning.* And why?

Because those bars of Beethoven's Fifth were the call signal of the BBC from London, which was considered an enemy station by the Third Reich. Listening to it was considered a political crime and punishable. Senior civil servants passing on what they had heard on "enemy radio stations" even risked being decapitated.

Still, all the parents of the children in that classroom diligently listened to this particular BBC German program on their radios. They wanted to have the *real* news and not Nazi propaganda. The teacher was protecting them all.

FOREWORD

Bestseller author Barbara Taylor Bradford and her late husband, Bob

This lovely memoir of a young boy's life, growing up under the harsh, cruel, and unconscionable rules of the Nazis, is full of extraordinary stories, and Uwe tells them well. I have purposely told only a few anecdotes because I don't want to spoil the book for other readers.

When you pick it up and begin to read, I know you will be intrigued by the urchin boy and all the unique stories he has in a head full of memories. Some are lovely; others are sorrowful and sad. But that is life, and he tells it like it was for him. I say bravo to the writer, and I look forward to his second memoir.

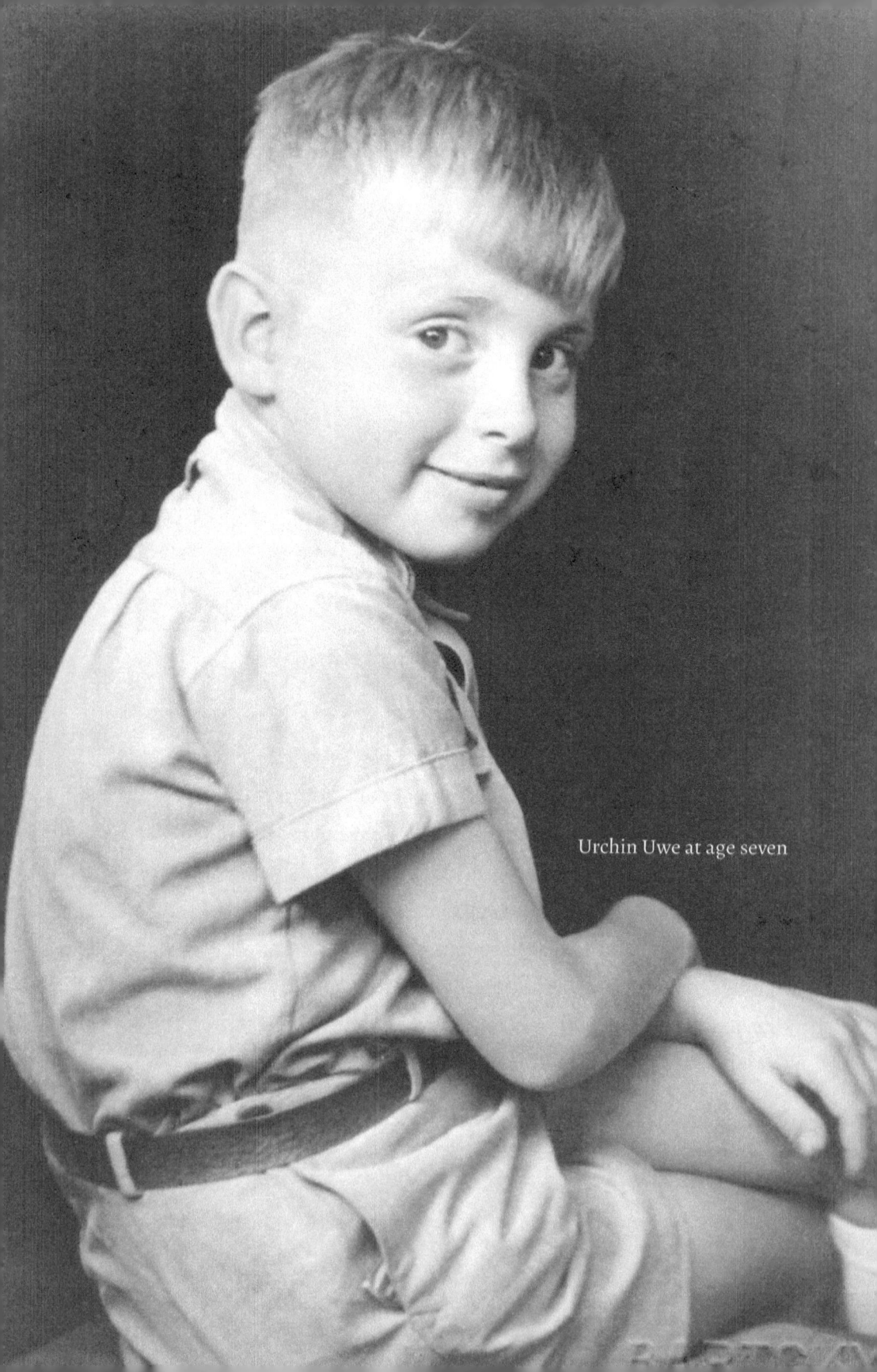

Urchin Uwe at age seven

Introduction
An Urchin Emeritus Remembers

"THIS IS THE IMAGE of an urchin!" exclaimed my wife, Gillian, when she first saw the photograph on the opposite page. "You have not really changed. You just look older," she continued. "You must use the word *urchin* in the title of your memoirs," decreed the novelist Barbara Taylor Bradford; Barbara and her Berlin-born husband, Robert Bradford, have been friends of ours for more than half a century.

The photograph was taken in Leipzig during World War II when I was about seven. My life then was marked by nightly air raids. Sometimes there were also daytime alarms. If not, I went to school in the morning and undertook exploratory expeditions into the smoking ruins of neighboring apartment houses in the afternoon. I played pranks on tram drivers and their passengers. I took music lessons from my mother and studied Martin Luther's Small Catechism and the history of the Saxon dynasty under my grandmother's guidance. Teaching her grandson to be a Christian and a monarchist was her way of shielding him against the all-pervasive National Socialist ideology.

I was born in Leipzig, where urchins are called *Griewatsch*. Like all urban urchins, we were impish and loudmouthed, but neither bombs, nor hunger, nor personal misfortune made us whimper. This

INTRODUCTION

is one key message of the present book: "A *document humain*, a little chronicle of the soul of more or less an entire generation," as historian Michael Stürmer wrote in his foreword to the German edition of my memoirs.

More precisely, it is a chronicle of a very small age group growing up in one of the most turbulent and bloody times in recorded history. We were born after Hitler came to power, or just before. We were on the receiving end of the war he had caused: bombs, starvation, and shame—all costs of his hideous crimes. We were only children but were keenly aware of what was happening to us and around us. Because of this, our childhood impressions were uncommonly incisive, if indeed it was a childhood at all.

I believe that, in my case, it was a childhood. I saw, heard, and experienced dreadful things, yet I played and laughed with other children in between air-raid alarms. I was taught the same Christian values as my ancestors but under more extreme circumstances, including the horrific discovery, at the age of seven, that the government of my country was murdering millions. Yes, some of us did hear about the Holocaust, even though we were so young!

Keeping a record of such strong recollections for the benefit of future generations in other parts of the world seems imperative to me now that I have entered the final stretch of my earthly life. Most educated Anglo-Saxons have received detailed reports about World War II from the perspectives of their own military, of German soldiers, of Holocaust survivors and perpetrators, of eminent scholars, and of former Nazis who grew rich writing contrite memoirs. With this book, I am adding one further angle—an urchin's eyewitness account.

INTRODUCTION

This account of an urchin emeritus might not be representative of all of Germany, since I was brought up in the city Hitler despised the most. Our mayor at the time of my birth, Carl Goerdeler, had been the civilian leader of the resistance against the National Socialist regime since it came to power and was ultimately hanged for this. More significantly in the context of my story, the *Führer* hated us for our racial imperfections. And there is something to this bias: We Leipzigers owe our reputation of being smart and crafty to the fact that we are mutts of varied provenance. Our ethnic blend has forged the Leipzig character: foxy, peripatetic, forever curious, and therefore mostly well-informed—traits that explain why it was in Leipzig, in 1650, that the world's first daily newspaper appeared and why it has spawned such a disproportionately large number of journalists, myself included.

Carl Goerdeler: ex-mayor of Leipzig, leader of Germany's resistance, hanged by the Nazis

We are mongrels because Leipzig lies at the crossroads of the Old World's two most important trade routes. Therefore, it became the venue of the world's oldest international trade fair more than 850 years ago. Every spring and every autumn, horse-drawn wagons from the east, west, north, and south, laden with all conceivable wares, rumbled into Leipzig's market square.

INTRODUCTION

Leipzig's cosmopolitan flair evolved thanks to the mélange of people these two trade routes brought into town, where they mingled merrily with the lustful locals, thus adding to the luscious looks of Leipzig's ladies. Portuguese, Spaniards, Italians, Venetians, and North Africans poured into Leipzig centuries ago. Soon that list grew to include French, British, Dutch, Scandinavian, Russian, and Polish traders, and then Turks, Persians, Chinese, and Jews, the latter turning the city into the world's leading transshipment center for furs until Hitler came to power.

As in the case of many of my fellow Leipzigers, people from scores of European villages seem to have added a branch to my family tree. Some came from the staid little town of Lage in the northwestern German principality of Lippe-Detmold, some from Annaberg in the Erzgebirge Mountains bordering what is now the Czech Republic, some from Holzminden near Hannover, and yet others from the Huguenot stronghold of Nîmes in southern France. Most significantly for my narrative, one branch hailed from Venice, if my mother's uncle, Hadrian Maria Netto (1885–1948), is to be believed.

Uncle Hadrian was a *Rittmeister*, or captain, in the Royal Saxon Cavalry. After his military career ended with Germany's defeat in 1918, he rose to modest fame as the author of dime novels and as a movie actor playing in forty films, including some directed by Fritz Lang. He also engaged in genealogical research. I can't vouch for his findings, but if they are correct, our branch of the Netto family was among the followers of Father Baldo Lupitano, the provincial of the Franciscan order in the Republic of Venice and a secret votary of Martin Luther.

In 1556, Lupitano was drowned as a heretic. This sent droves of Venetian Lutherans fleeing to the electorate of Saxony, my maternal

Family patriarch: Friedrich August Netto (1787–1861), the most famous scion of a dynasty of Saxon mining academics and clergymen. His father was a Lutheran pastor, as were many of his forebears.

INTRODUCTION

ancestors amongst them. The Netto clan in electoral Saxony produced many Lutheran pastors. Thus the Nettos have theology in their blood, presumably since Venetian days, and this has rubbed off on me.

By Uncle Hadrian's reckoning, then, the Nettos wound up in Leipzig for reasons of faith. The Siemons, on the other hand, were driven there by economic necessity. In the principality of Lippe-Detmold, they owned a lucrative distillery, producing a quintessentially Teutonic tipple: *Steinhäger*, a schnapps made from grain and the fermented must of juniper berries growing on the slopes of the Teutoburg Forest.

In the late nineteenth century, distilleries still distributed their liquor on horse-drawn wagons, most often driven by coachmen with a great fondness for their cargo. And so it came about that at the factory of my paternal grandfather, Carl Siemon, a driver reduced his employer from wealth to penury overnight. Returning from a delivery round, he gulped down too much of the potent liquid in the plant's warehouse, lit his pipe, and retired to the hayloft to sleep off his inebriation. Sparks from the pipe set the hayloft on fire. The whole business burned down, and my paternal grandfather lost everything.

The coachman's fate is not recorded, but *Opapa* (Grandpa) Siemon had to look for a new source of income to get rich again quickly. For this, the pulsating, booming kingdom of Saxony in the center of Germany was the most auspicious destination. So *Opapa* Siemon, a handsome, black-haired gentleman of Huguenot descent, moved his lissome, blonde wife, Anna Maria, and their children, Karl-Heinz, Oskar, Eduard, and Elisabeth, to Saxony, quickly prospering as a wholesale dealer in culinary delicacies; first in Zwickau and then in Leipzig, which had become Saxony's largest and liveliest city.

INTRODUCTION

Vinegar merchant Max Peter and his horse-drawn cart were a beloved feature in Uwe's neighborhood. Once, he took Uwe along on his delivery run.

Like all Saxons, Leipzigers have never embraced today's persnickety zeitgeist, which originated in the Victorian age and reached its zenith in the follies of today's political correctness. Saxons love to "let it rip," following a pattern Martin Luther might have set. He allegedly advised preachers to "hang their teats over the pulpit for the congregation to suckle on." Luther, a Saxon, was not a man of the understatement. He luxuriated in his own overstatements.

Crafting verbal abuse with the help of the distinctly German feature of composite words is one of the most hilarious Saxon art forms Luther taught his followers, including my eminently Lutheran maternal grandmother (*Omi*). Her name was Clara Netto. Her loose tongue mitigated the hardships the war inflicted on me. Once, in between two bombardments on Leipzig in 1944, she scolded me for stealing sugar from her larder with the unforgettable neologism

INTRODUCTION

Du Mistpfützenkrebs, meaning "You crab from the puddle around a manure heap." Even more refined Anglo-Saxon readers must admit that this is a masterpiece of word creation in addition to being an insult of a conciliatory nature. As *Omi* Netto was in the process of composing it, she had to burst out laughing in between *Mistpfützen* (puddle of a manure heap) and *krebs* (crab). We both laughed until the sirens summoned us again to seek cover in our basement.

My loving, funny, and cheeky yet deeply devout *Omi* Netto was the most influential figure of my childhood. It is to her memory and to my wife, Gillian, that I dedicate this volume, as well as to Barbara Taylor Bradford and her late husband, Robert (Lutz) Bradford. And I especially thank my friends Debi and Kurt Winrich, whose generosity has made this book, and the subsequent two volumes of my Urchin Trilogy, possible.

CHAPTER 1

Urchin's Homecoming

I AM BACK NOW where my life began eight decades ago. It's late spring. My windows in the Michaelis Hotel are wide open. The pungent fragrances of the morning air confirm that I am in Leipzig. This unique cocktail of smells has two ingredients: One is the bear leek growing in the *Auenwälder*, nearby forests rich in humus. The second constituent is the blossoms of the linden trees that gave Leipzig its Sorabic name, Lipsk (the Sorabs are a western Slavic tribe that originally had settled here).

I walk 150 steps from the hotel to the square where I was born on 25 October 1936 at 2:41 p.m. Before World War II, it was called *Sophienplatz*; after the war, it was renamed *Shakespeareplatz*. Giving birth must have been so strenuous for my mother that she devoured a big portion of roast hare with red cabbage after delivery. She found this experience so taxing she never repeated it; I remained her only child. A passion for babies—or pets—was not one of her many attributes.

Top left: Uwe and his mother, Ruth, outside their Leipzig home

Top right: Baby Uwe with his father, Karl-Heinz, and grandfather Carl Siemon

Center: Uwe in his snazzy pram with his parents

Bottom: Two years on: Ruth and Dr. Karl-Heinz Siemon with Uwe in a sailor's uniform, a bourgeois fashion in Europe then

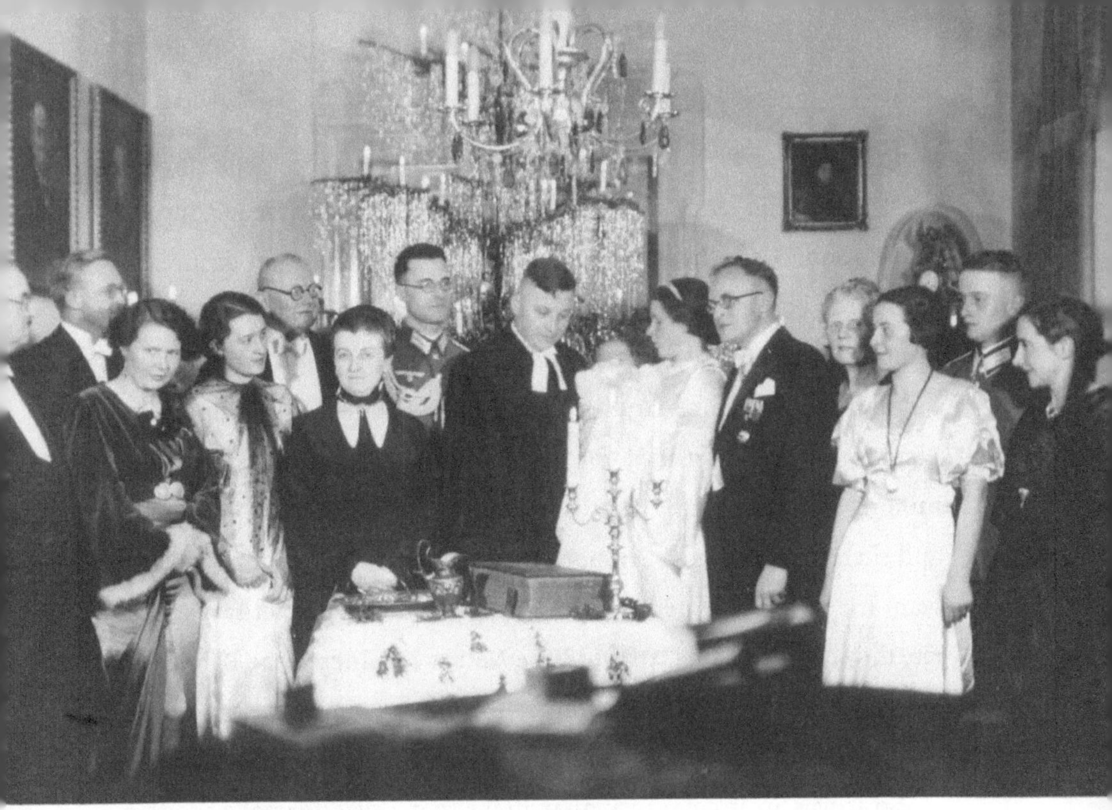

This elegant christening at home under the Christmas tree on New Year's Eve 1936 was arranged as a compromise to satisfy the Reformed and Lutheran branches of Uwe's family.

Uwe Siemon

Geboren am 25. Oktober 1936 um 14 45 Uhr

Geburtsort: Leipzig - C1 Geburtshaus: Sophienplatz 6 III r.

Gewicht: 3,695 kg Größe: 52 cm

Getauft am 31. Dezember 1936 von der ev.-ref. Kirche aus

zu Hause

Taufpaten sind Großmutter Netto, Fräulein Dr. Ch. Francke,
Fräulein L. Buchheim, Rechtsanwalt Dr. H. Reerink,
Stabsarzt Dr. Günther Friedrich, Herr William Siemon, U.S.A.

Bemerkungen über wichtige Ereignisse im Leben unseres Kindes:

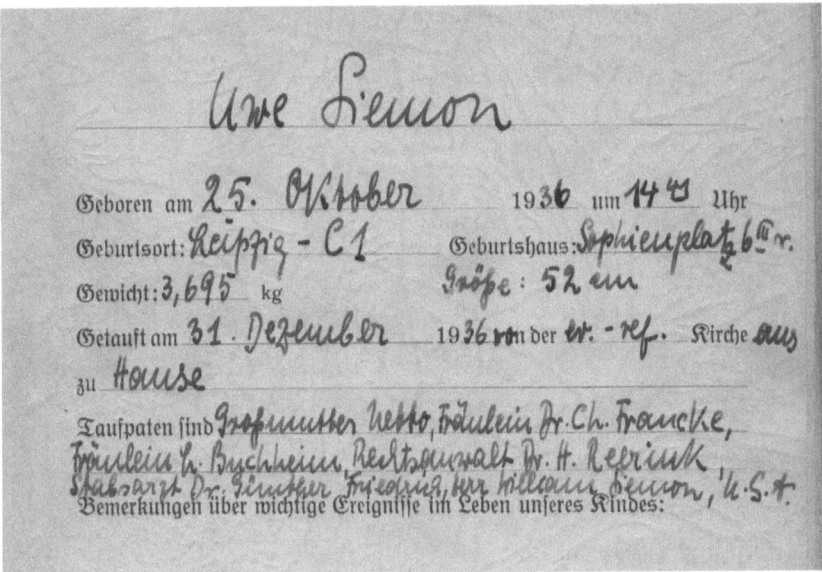

Uwe's baptismal certificate identifies him as a member of his father's Evangelical-Reformed Church. But his grandmother raised him a Lutheran.

Two months later, on New Year's Eve, I was christened in our music room. That this significant event in my life did not occur in a church, as baptisms usually do, was probably due to the denominational imbroglio between the two clans uniting that night at our family font by the light of live candles on a Christmas tree. My grandparents Siemon adhered to the Reformed branch of Protestantism, a tiny minority in Leipzig; the Nettos, on the other hand, were Lutherans and therefore part of the majority. I guess that the Siemons did not want me to be admitted to the Christian faith in a sanctuary and a rite they deemed "too Catholic." The Nettos considered the Reformed Church near the railway station far too stark a venue for the sacrament to be administered to their grandson.

So it was in my parents' apartment that I was formally made a Christian, witnessed by the portraits of my maternal ancestors—all Lutherans—covering its walls. Our seventeenth-century family Bible on the home altar is also Lutheran, of course. It survived the war, which started less than three years later.

Uwe leafing through the Netto family Bible that was rescued from the flames when his home was bombed out. With him are his goddaughters Charlotte and Clara Pankau.

Family photographs show that this baptism was an event of bourgeois elegance. The ladies were attired in fine evening gowns, the gentlemen in tailcoats or military dress uniforms. On my father's lapel I can make out his Iron Cross from World War I and the German equivalent of the Purple Heart. Across his chest he wears his *Couleurband*, or ribbon, identifying him as a member of his student corps. It bears the colors—black, white, and red—of *Thuringia Leipzig*, a fencing fraternity. My father never dueled because he lost his eyesight as a young officer cadet in France in 1917 before entering Leipzig's law school. The French grenade that wounded him had sufficiently scarred his face; it required none of the saber slashes proudly displayed by generations of German university graduates.

Thuringia Leipzig belonged to the "Black Circle" of fencing fraternities, a branch championing bourgeois values, especially parsimony, and stingy my father was indeed—so much so that when, in my teenage years, we stopped at a tavern for a glass of white wine after a twelve-mile walk along the shore of Lake Constance, he would not grant me to have a second ten-pfennig salt stick. Ten pfennigs were the equivalent of two-and-a-half US cents then.

"I am hungry, *Vati*," I protested.

"We'll have dinner soon," he replied.

Dinner at my father's house in Lindau was another twelve-mile walk away.

But my mind is wandering into the past prematurely. At this point in my narrative, I am moving like a phantom across the square where my life began three years before Hitler dragged us into yet another calamitous war that caused British bombers to destroy our home.

Uwe in front of *Sophienplatz* 6, where he was born. A modest family home now occupies the space of the belle epoque apartment house destroyed by phosphor bombs.

I am thinking, "This is what it must be like when one returns as a ghost to haunt his former house, now empty." Little that I could remember from my childhood is still there. I was born on *Sophienplatz* 6, and a building bearing that number still exists. But it designates a modest pink row house that has replaced the splendid art nouveau[1] edifice where I had spent my first seven years. It could have easily been rebuilt from the ruin. But the Communists tore it down; for decades a pile of coke[2] took its place.

On this sunny morning, I'm all by myself on *Sophienplatz* and almost can't recognize it. Once it was filled with laughing urchins from all social strata, some playing hopscotch, some cops and robbers,

---

1 In Germany, it is called *Jugendstil*.
2 Coke is a fuel made from coal.

others still Kurds and Bedouins, Apache and Sioux. More children bustled about on their tricycles, scooters, and handcarts. I find it a sad testimony to our soulless time that such joyous scenes have disappeared from big city streets because boys and girls now mindlessly sit at home playing computer games or fumbling with smartphones.

And whatever happened to that corner store where I bought ten-pfennig bags of lemonade powder to be traded against *Salmiakpastillen*, small, diamond-shaped licorice pastilles? We arranged these tiny lozenges to form a black star on the backs of our hands. Then we lined up in formation, one foot on the stone curb edge, the other on the cobblestoned street, and began limping in single file, chanting in Saxon dialect,

Hautse, hautse
Egal uff de Schnauze!

Clobber, clobber,
clobber them always on the snout!

In truth, we clobbered nobody. We Leipzig urchins were nonviolent. The first act of violence I personally experienced on *Sophienplatz* took place on 4 December 1943, when phosphor bombs rained on us from the sky. My quest for childhood relics is successful, though, as I spot the rusty cast-iron fence that once separated my stately place of birth from the rows of solid homes inhabited by our petit-bourgeois neighbors, the families of craftsmen, shopkeepers, bookkeepers, tramway drivers, and subaltern civil servants. Their children were my friends.

The sight of this fence makes me smile mischievously because it reminds me of the first naughtiness of my life. Before I entered elementary school, I had a pert little girlfriend who lived there. Hertha was the name of this freckle-faced master fitter's daughter. One morning she said to me in broad Leipzig jargon, referring to a mutual playmate of ours, "*Dä Baula behaupded bei Jung'n baumeld was zwischen dän Been'n. Schdimmd das? Zeich' mir mal Dein's* (Paula claims that there is something dangling between boys' legs. Is that true? Show me yours)."

I obliged. She led me behind a bush by the iron fence. We marveled at our anatomic differences. At lunch, when my father asked me about my morning's activities, as he always did, I eagerly reported my discovery in dialect: "*Bei d'r Herda, baumeld da und'n awwr iewerhaubt nüschd!* (Hertha has nothing at all dangling down there!)" As on most days, *Omi*, my maternal grandmother, was present, although she lived three miles away in another part of town. She covered her mouth with her left hand so as not to burst out laughing while eating her potato soup. My father grinned. But *Mutti*, my mother, admonished me: "Speak High German! Don't you realize that Hertha's father is not even *ein Akademiker* (a university graduate)?"

I was merely five years old!

Mutti, the classical singer[3] Ruth Siemon-Netto, was a beautiful and educated woman. She was also an exalted creature with a specific kind of conceitedness called *Akademikerfimmel* in German, a glorification of the professional class. It might have been rooted in the greatest disappointment of her youth. She had always dreamed of becoming the second woman in our family with a doctorate, following the example of her older cousin Charlotte Francke, the first female patent attorney in Germany. Auntie Lotte, as I called her, was my godmother. She earned her PhD in mathematics and physics.

---

3 Oratorios and lieder.

Four years before I was born, *Mutti* had graduated second in her class from *Gaudig-Schule*, the foremost classical high school for girls in Germany. She excelled in the liberal arts, especially in Latin, Greek, and Hebrew. This should have given her easy access to university, where she intended to study philosophy and theology, two disciplines requiring a solid knowledge of these languages. But no sooner had she left school than Hitler came to power, and almost instantly his sycophants took charge of the university administration.

They determined that *Mutti* lacked "National Socialist leadership qualities" and therefore was ineligible for admission. How they reached this conclusion, they kept to themselves. Perhaps they suspected the Netto family, with its Mediterranean features, of racial impurity. For whatever obscure reason, *Mutti* was denied access to higher education.

The next best thing to being an *Akademikerin* herself was to be an *Akademiker*'s wife. Hence *Mutti* bewitched a dashing lawyer she met at a *Thuringia Leipzig* fraternity ball. German student corps in those days maintained rosters of *Couleurdamen*, young local women whose social standing made them eligible to be invited to their balls and other festivities, and *Mutti* was one of those. The man she wooed was Karl-Heinz Siemon, a public prosecutor seventeen years her senior and one of *Thuringia*'s *alte Herren*, as postgraduate fraternity members were called.

Karl-Heinz Siemon was a "doctor of both laws" (canonical and secular), handsome, always suntanned, and dressed in tailor-made suits of the finest cloth. His dry, North German humor lured hosts of lovely females, though it was largely lost on *Mutti*'s narcissistic persona. On the other hand, he was a decorated veteran of World War I, where he sacrificed his eyes for the Fatherland. Shrapnel had entered his entire face and body during that battle in the French Vosges in 1917 and kept popping out of his skin in irregular intervals until shortly before his early death during a botched surgery when he was only sixty-two.

His traumatic head injury strangely distorted his musicality, rendering him incapable of playing the piano in a minor key. So he transposed every chord into a major key. This made my father an inadequate accompanist for my mother at her weekly house concerts. Somebody else had to take his place at her *Blüthner* grand piano, of which she was so proud.

Against the objection of her astute mother, but with the consent of her senile father, the twenty-year-old Ruth Netto married Dr. Karl-Heinz Siemon and thus became a *Frau Doktor* after all. The young couple took over her parents' spacious third-floor apartment on *Sophienplatz* 6, where their neighbors were a judge, an army colonel, a lawyer, a wealthy businessman, a corporate executive, and a privateer. My grandparents, meanwhile, moved to another building, two miles south of *Sophienplatz*, and into a ground-floor flat where my grandfather no longer needed to climb stairs.

As I meander across *Sophienplatz*, I shake my head at my mother's snobbery. It might, perhaps, have had its place in Leipzig's genteel *Gohlis* district, where she was born, or in the *Musikviertel* (music quarter), where every street was named after a composer and where my grandparents Siemon resided. But it was incongruous here on this square, as the joy of this place was that all classes lived side by side and interacted daily. I am still grateful for this experience because it conditioned me well for my future work as a reporter, which did not allow for any conceit.

This is the 1934 wedding photo of Uwe's parents. Ruth Netto was only twenty. The dress coat of blind Dr. Karl-Heinz Siemon shows his World War I decorations, including the Iron Cross. The ribbon across his chest marks him as an alumnus of his student fraternity.

We children never tormented each other for being a lawyer's son or a fitter's daughter, for having a traveling salesman or a waiter as a father. All of us had fun bombarding each other in the winter with snowballs and in the summer with horse manure left behind by the carthorses that were still plentiful in Leipzig's streets. If any of us had reason to be envious of the others, it was I, the bourgeois urchin. I could often have given my right arm to change places with my working-class playmates. So delicious were the smells wafting out of their parents' apartments—the mouthwatering odors of home-fried potatoes or stuffed cabbage! These scents would have never been tolerated in my hoity-toity home.

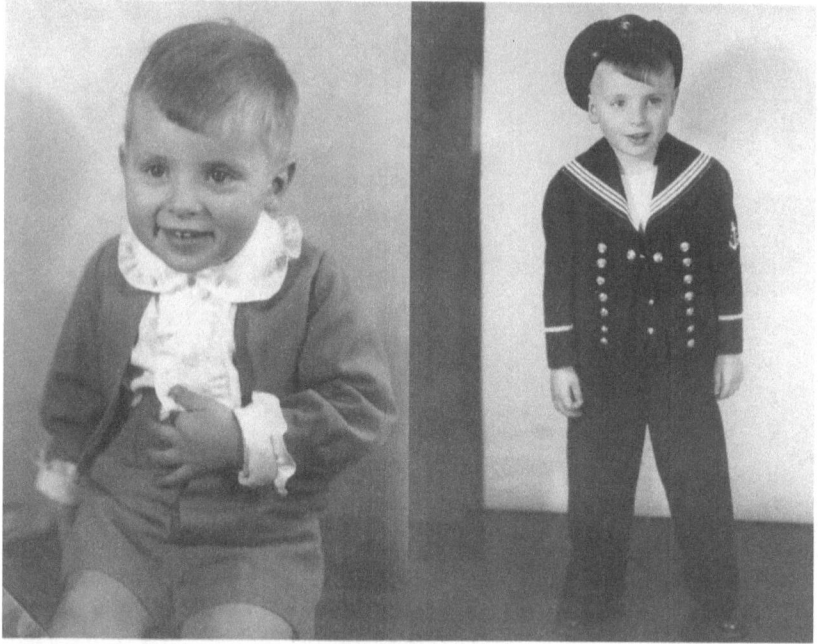

Tarted up urchin: Uwe in a frilly shirt at age two and, a year later, in a sailor's uniform, which was the fashion for boys in Europe then

My playmates pitied me for not dressing like a real street urchin. My father's sister, Auntie Elisabeth, told me later how sorry she always felt for me when she observed my mother sending me outside looking like a popinjay in a frilly shirt or a sailor's uniform. She clothed her children, my cousins Hans-Heinz and Elisabeth ("Mau") Reerink, in rough rags before dispatching them out into the backyard to play in their tree house, whereas I was always dressed as if I were about to appear at a princely palace bowing to the gentlemen and kissing their ladies' hands. Today, I am grateful to have been taught such gallant gestures properly at home; these social skills have served me well in later life, especially in France, my second home for many decades.

There I now stand, with my back against *Sophienplatz 6*, daydreaming about my childhood's woes and delights. I am dreaming it's Thursday. On Thursday afternoons, my mother belonged to me alone. This wasn't the case on other weekdays, when I saw *Mutti* only sporadically, except at lunch, which was a carefully formalized family event where I was not allowed to speak until spoken to. Come to think of it, this was not a bad discipline, especially as my father was a fair man who always addressed me early during every meal.

But *Mutti* and I led separate lives. She was not the type of mother who let her child cuddle up under her plumes every now and then. My parents' bedroom, way down at the northeastern end of our spacious apartment, was taboo to me. I remember sneaking a look at it once when *Vati* and *Mutti* were out and the maid was making their bed. I found their private quarters bleak and uninviting, unlike my sunny nursery at the southwestern end of the corridor.

Though I didn't see my mother much, I heard her all the time singing the scales in the music room for hours on end in order to train her voice. Up, up, and down again it went in thirds: "Wa-wa . . . wa-wa-wa . . . wa-wa-waaaaa," she sang, and "Now-nao-noi-noe-naeee." I loathed this noise, which my father was spared because he was in court then or else out drinking wine with his fraternity brothers in the *Harmonie Club* on *Königsplatz* (King's Square).

But Thursdays were different. On Thursday afternoons my mother belonged to me. Because of the dearth of motorized taxis during the war, a horse-drawn carriage pulled up for the two of us downstairs. First, we stopped at the local *Drogerie*, or drugstore, where I was allowed to replenish my supply of licorice pastilles. Then we continued to the city center. I can't remember ever being treated to cocoa or cakes in one of Leipzig's many elegant cafés. That was not my mother's style. Our Thursday carriage rides always had practical objectives. Once we drove off to have my palatine tonsils removed. But usually we went shopping. In the early war years, my crafty mother maintained useful contacts with stores keeping prerationing stocks of luxury goods—including rare clothes, toys, and footwear—for their regular customers. And so, I wound up with patent leather shoes, which *Mutti* made me wear when playing an Apache Indian on *Sophienplatz*.

This was embarrassing. I remember my playmates staring at me aghast as I mingled with them like a peacock amongst barnyard chickens. But they never teased me about this, much less beat me up. This might have had a variety of reasons. For one thing, being musical, I excelled in the most vulgar street Saxon, a hideous idiom strictly forbidden in my home. For another thing, I was as brash as these other rascals. Thirdly, I owned a Bordeaux-red pedal car, which I allowed everyone to use. And finally, it took me mere minutes to dirty my frilly shirt and patent leather shoes, winning their respect while making my mother wonder if I would ever amount to anything in life.

Sundays were different, though. On Sundays, even many working-class street urchins dressed up for the children's service in the *Peterskirche*, whose slender spire is still visible through a gap in the northeastern corner of *Sophienplatz*. I often went there hand in hand with Hertha, the master fitter's daughter. This is where my enduring love for the Lutheran chorale began early in my childhood. I don't know if my playmates still sing these hymns as I do. They gave me comfort in difficult times in later life, especially during the Vietnam War, which I covered as a reporter. In heavy combat, I hummed these songs in my head. My favorite was an early seventeenth-century tune. Its German first lines have indelibly remained in my head:

Ach, bleib mir Deiner Gnade
Bei uns, Herr Jesu Christ,
Dass uns hinfort nicht schade
des bösen Feindes List.

The English translation is equally beautiful:

Abide, O dearest Jesus,
Among us with Thy Grace,
That Satan may not harm us,
Nor we to sin give place.

Saddened by the emptiness of *Sophienplatz* today, I stroll around the corner to the former *Sophienstraße*, now *Shakespearestraße*. The large storage space of a construction firm by the name of Wolff & Müller yawns on the spot where once the legendary *Schauspielhaus*, a private theater I first visited at the age of six, stood. Gazing at this bleak piece of industrial real estate, another piquant anecdote of my past comes to mind.

I must have been in my late teens when, in the industrial city of Hagen in Westphalia, I met the ringmaster of a circus. He told me that before I was born, he was a penniless *Schauspielhaus* actor rooming in the servants' quarters of our apartment, which was then still occupied by my grandparents and their adolescent daughter, Ruth, who later became my mother.

"Your mother always thought I fancied her," the ringmaster said with a chuckle, "but she was *so* wrong! I was her mother's lover. Late every morning, your *Omi* came up to my room with a steaming pot of pea or lentil soup and sausages. As soon as I finished eating, we fell into each other's arms."

I loved that story. It meshed so well with *Omi*'s delicious character. More than any other member of my family, *Omi* fit Martin Luther's definition of a Christian: *simul iustus et peccator*, at the same time justified (before God, by grace alone) and sinner. I joyfully apply this central doctrinal statement of the Lutheran Church to my own identity.

Simul iustus et peccator: I have decreed that these words will one day be displayed on my gravestone.

CHAPTER 2

First Cheesecake, then the War

As I meander around the empty *Sophienplatz*, I try to think back to the sunny part of my childhood, before flames engulfed my home and turned the surface of that square into a lake of fire, putting an end to that brief, beautiful period of my life. In my mind, I project the lovely art nouveau facade of that slain house against the bland, modern, one-family dwelling now bearing the number 6.

I see myself coming out of its iron gates, once again dressed in a frilly white shirt, not to play this time, but to embark on my first long journey. A horse-drawn taxi was waiting for us. My mother, my father, my nanny Martha, and I took our seats while the driver loaded our hand luggage. The heavy trunks for a four-week stay at the swank Baltic Sea resort of Swinemünde had been sent ahead a few days earlier. Swinemünde was once a favorite vacation spot of Kaiser Wilhelm II; today it is part of Poland and has been renamed Świnoujście.

For half an hour or more, the carriage rumbled over cobblestone streets to the *Hauptbahnhof*, Leipzig's central station, then the largest in Germany. We took a *D-Zug*—a corridor train, as this comfortable form of transportation was once called in England. Its cars were dark green. They were pulled by a huge, black steam engine, which puffed and thumped impatiently, emitting exciting aromas of burning coal and smoke.

I remember my apprehension when, barely after our arrival at the station, *Mutti* unexpectedly gave me a quick embrace and briskly guided my blind father to a seemingly distant carriage, leaving me with Martha standing where we were. Martha reassured me, "Don't worry! We will arrive in Swinemünde at the same time, but your parents travel first class, and we don't." In later voyages, I found out that first-class compartments were very posh. They had large, mahogany-paneled compartments with only four well-upholstered seats.

Martha and I were relegated to seats of brown wooden slats in third class. At lunchtime, a steward with a gong walked from car to car, summoning smartly clad passengers like *Vati* and *Mutti* to the dining car. Martha, meanwhile, unpacked our liverwurst and blood sausage sandwiches, popped open bottles of sparkling water, and unscrewed two thermos flasks, one filled with coffee for her, the other with cocoa for me. Oblivious to the class difference dividing my family, I hugely enjoyed this trip, especially as the locomotive's black smoke kept wafting in through the open window, quickly darkening my frilly shirt.

Most of the other passengers in our carriage were soldiers. Martha explained that they were Wehrmacht conscripts, corporals, and sergeants. "These poor men must feel hot in their thick, gray cloth uniforms," she said. There were also seamen returning to their ships from home leave. Their white linen uniforms seemed more comfortable. I decided that if I ever joined the military, I would definitely become a sailor.

Ruth and Dr. Karl-Heinz Siemon on their last summer holiday in Swinemünde before the war. Even at the seaside, Uwe's father always wore elegant tailor-made suits.

This decision was reinforced a few days later when I boarded, in Swinemünde, the *Albert Leo Schlageter*, a three-mast training vessel of the German *Kriegsmarine*. Sea cadets took me below deck to feed me cheesecake from the tall ship's galley. Then they ushered me to the deck again to play with the crew's mascot, a tortoise.

The taste of the cake has remained on my tongue till this very day, but my encounter with an armored reptile must have slipped into my subconscious mind until I discovered a photograph of me holding the

Left: Uwe on board the *Albert Leo Schlageter*, a three-mast training vessel of the German Navy, playing with its mascot, a tortoise. Right: The family in a covered beach chair.

beast. Strangely, though, I yearned to have a tortoise as a pet throughout my childhood. I was fifteen when I finally managed to buy one. Inanely, I named my tortoise *Eulalia* because she was of Greek origin. Having learned Greek in high school, I should have known better. *Eulalia* means "well-spoken," yet I never elicited a single sound from this otherwise affectionate creature.

My most vivid memory of Swinemünde was riding on the right arm of a kindly gentleman speaking German with a strange accent. Later I learned that he was the Reverend William A. Ashby of the Lordship Lane Baptist Church in East Dulwich, a district of the London borough of Southwalk. On first sight, Pastor Ashby seemed to be a harbinger of the type of well-meaning clergyman belittled as "Peaceniks" during the Vietnam War era.

He accompanied a party of blinded British World War I veterans on a tour across Germany at the invitation of the German Association of War-Blinded Soldiers. My father was one of the German veterans with whom he had long conversations. I am certain that *Vati* was one of those who assured Pastor Ashby of their desire for peace with Great Britain.

In the arms of English pastor William Ashby weeks before the war.

Vati was a steadfast Anglophile who risked life and freedom listening to the German-language program of the BBC every day, a seditious act in the eyes of the Nazi government. Such was his love for England that a few years later, at the height of World War II, he impressed upon me not to think of that nation as my enemy.

At a time when British airplanes unloaded blockbuster bombs over Leipzig at night, my elementary school class was taken to a *Volkssturm* (people's militia) barracks to celebrate the *Tag der Wehrmacht* (Armed Forces Day). As my father had foreseen, we were taught to aim air guns at so-called *Pappkameraden*. These were cardboard silhouettes representing Franklin D. Roosevelt, Winston Churchill, and Joseph Stalin. "Shoot Roosevelt and Stalin if you must," he admonished me, "but do spare the fat guy with the cigar [Churchill]."

On *Sophienplatz*, I find myself in front of the former corner store where we urchins used to buy our lemonade powder. Its door and shop window were bricked up when it was converted into an apartment.

Wistfully, I pause before the store that is no more. I imagine walking in as I so often did with my father.

"*Heil Hitler, Herr Doktor*," its owner greeted *Vati*, as the political etiquette of that period required.

"*Heil Hitler, Herr Doktor*," echoed the other customers who knew the blind Dr. Karl-Heinz Siemon by sight.

"*Guten Tag*," answered my father in the traditional German manner, provoking an eerie silence, as if he had spoken a four-letter word.

Nobody in our family said "*Heil Hitler*," in public or at home. Granted, this did not amount to a heroic act of resistance against the Nazi tyranny, but a modest form of resistance it was nonetheless.

My father was an avowed constitutional monarchist. He considered Hitler a vulgar, brutish usurper of power, an illegitimate ruler. In the Weimar Republic, *Vati* had voted for the liberal National People's Party. My mother was too young to participate in prewar Germany's last election in 1933, which resulted in Hitler's takeover as chancellor of Germany. Like all members of our family, and most of our friends, she was fiercely loyal to the nine-hundred-year old *Wettiner* dynasty of Frederick Augustus III (1865–1932), the hugely popular last king of Saxony, who is said to have uttered his raunchy farewell words in Saxon when forced to abdicate in 1918 at the insistence of the victorious allies.

"*Machd Eiern Dregg alleene* (Go do your dirty work yourselves)," he allegedly told Richard Lipinski, the Social Democrat chairman of the People's Council of Saxony, when leaving his throne on 13 November 1918.

In her teenage years, my mother corresponded with the former king, then living on his estate, Sibyllenort Castle in Silesia, where he died in 1932. Once, she showed me his letters—before they were lost when our apartment burned out after an air raid in 1943. I inherited tinges of my family's monarchism, at least to the extent that I keep a small photograph of Frederick Augustus III on our music chest in Laguna Woods, California.

Reverend Ashby's peace mission failed, as I found out on 3 September 1939. I remember that balmy Sunday in almost every detail. I recall the warm, late-summer sun. I remember Martha taking me to the children's service in the *Peterskirche*. I remember my father's oddly somber demeanor at lunch. I remember wondering, "What's wrong with *Vati*?" He usually became a lighthearted conversationalist after his first glass of wine! Today, I know why he was so solemn during that meal: Two days earlier, the German army had invaded Poland. *Vati* knew that World War II was now imminent.

In the afternoon, my mother set the coffee table on our loggia with our blue-and-white Meissen china. There was a coffee pot for my parents, next to a smaller jar with my cocoa, to accompany the three kinds of pastry we Leipzigers consider our basic staple: streusel cake, cheesecake, and poppy-seed cake. A bunch of late-summer flowers adorned the table.

I will never forget my father's grim, battle-scarred face as he came out of his study, where he had just listened to the BBC news on his *Blaupunkt* radio, which was sensitive enough to receive foreign broadcasts. "London announced that England and France have declared war on us," he said.

My twenty-three-year-old mother's answer was so breathtakingly childish that she herself mocked it in her diary: "*Ach, Karl-Heinz*, as long as we have such beautiful flowers . . ." *Vati* just shook his eyeless head and said nothing.

I was allowed to finish my cocoa and eat a piece of cheesecake before being sent down to drive around *Sophienplatz* in my Bordeaux-red pedal car while my mother filled our bathtub with water, expecting the Royal Air Force to bomb us any minute. The RAF did not show up for another four years, but her naïveté was not at all unique. Twenty-three years later I learned that, at the same hour 740 miles west of Leipzig, a little brown-haired girl by the name of Gillian Ackers drove her pedal car up and down Brownell Avenue in Southampton, England. Gillian's car was also red but a little brighter than mine, more like a fire engine. Meanwhile, Gillian's mother, Ethel, filled her bathtub, just like *Mutti*.

Gillian and I have been married fifty-eight years at the time of this writing. She is not with me on my brief sentimental journey home to *Sophienplatz*. But as I think back to our many discussions about our experiences on the first day of the war, uncanny parallels in our respective childhoods in two warring nations emerge. Like my mother, Ethel Ackers was a professional musician with a preference for the works of Johann Sebastian Bach, except that she wasn't a singer but a pianist. Like us, the Ackers family was bombed out, but just as my father revered Churchill, my mother-in-law admired German Field Marshal Erwin Rommel. Not that Ethel Ackers was a clandestine Nazi sympathizer; she just thought of Rommel as the most glamorous of all World War II generals on either side.

While Gillian and her parents lost their home early in the war, it barely affected us at first, except that the fathers, uncles, and elder brothers of my playmates were called up, and *Mutti* evacuated me for a few months to the children's home *Urihof* in Bad Kohlgrub in the Bavarian Alps, a seemingly irrational act that did nothing to enhance my safety but did much for the beauty of her voice. In my absence, she sang her "Wa-wa . . . wa-wa-wa . . . *wa-wa-waaaaa*" and her "*Now-nao-noi-noe-naeee*" so assiduously that she was able to give her first important concert soon after my return.

In retrospect, I bear her no resentment for sending me away for the sake of her musical career, using the war as an excuse. On the contrary: I consider my love of music the greatest legacy she left me with. For this I am deeply grateful to her. The Bach chorales she implanted in my heart helped me overcome my fear in moments of grave peril—for instance, in combat when I was a war reporter in Vietnam. The stark mathematical beauty of the *Art of the Fugue* still marvelously orders my mind even today when I am in distress, especially when a writer's block hits me.

Now that I am in my eighty-fourth year, I rank my knowledge of music as the most precious gift I have received that allows me to enjoy my life even at times of adversity, alongside my faith and my marriage of fifty-five years thus far. Gillian and I spend our summer months in southwestern France, in whose empty Romanesque churches stirring sermons and an uplifting liturgy are even scarcer than priests or worshippers. So, every Sunday morning before lunch, we sit down in our spacious, eighteenth-century drawing room, which is marvelously suffused with light and overlooks two magnificent mulberry trees, and there we listen to the Bach cantata written for that particular day in the church year. This might not be the perfect substitute for divine service, for it lacks Holy Communion, one of the two means of grace (the other being the word of God). But as Gillian says time and again, it is infinitely more enriching than a mediocre homily. It is in these moments of bliss that both of us remember our mothers thankfully. They taught us to understand Bach, a rare treasure indeed!

Standing now in the middle of *Sophienplatz*, I can't help chuckling at the irony of being banished to Bavaria, ostensibly for my own safety, but really for the sake of music. My deportation didn't last long, though. I was back here on *Sophienplatz* well before the first "enemy planes" dropped phosphor on us.

But we are not there just yet. Before I learned what war was really like, benign martial paraphernalia from before World War I showed up in my nursery next to the kitchen. One day a handyman, presumably on my mother's orders, brought Grandfather Curt Netto's uniform case down from the attic and deposited it among the white, matte-lacquered furniture in my room, next to my teddy bear, which had wheels and was tall enough for me to ride on.

Curt Netto died of heart failure a few months before I was born. Still, in my early childhood, his military exploits became a significant factor in one of my favorite family squabbles. *Mutti* was the archetypal *fille à papa*. The intensity with which she idolized her father struck her mother as odious. As long as we were living on *Sophienplatz*, my mother often evoked, with misty eyes, his valor in World War I as she watched me strutting up and down the corridor carrying his officer's epee or when I opened his uniform case in her presence and she saw grandfather's *Pickelhaube*, the resplendent epaulets of his parade uniform, his sword knot with its silver tassel, and his decorations, which I still keep to my daily bemusement in a display case affixed to the wall right behind my office chair in California.

I say bemusement because these decorations were the subject of hilarious skirmishes I frequently initiated between my mawkish *Mutti* and my mischievous *Omi*, who was every inch the Saxon equivalent of the pert Lady Violet in the British television series *Downton Abbey*.

The subject of these recurring tussles was Curt Netto's first and only combat experience. Curt Netto, an officer in the Royal Saxon Army Reserves and a partner of Netto & Klepzig, a passement[1] manufacturing business in Leipzig, was called to arms on 3 August 1914 at the age of forty-six.

Mutti and *Omi* did agree on what happened when he first faced the enemy in the Vosges mountains: his saber drawn, Captain Netto charged a wooded hill ahead of his company in an intrepid style more befitting eighteenth-century combat tactics than was prudent in the industrial killing of men that was the mark of World War I. On the peak of the hill, a French machine gun awaited him. It opened fire. *Rat-a-tat-tat*. Grandpa Netto dropped from his saddle and lay motionless on the forest floor.

"Captain Netto is dead, our good captain is dead!" sobbed his soldiers, according to his batman.[2] But Grandpa wasn't dead. He had suffered a heart attack. Up to this point, my mother's and my grandmother's narratives were in accord.

---

1 An ornamental braid or decorative trimming resembling lace and made of gold, silver, or silk threads.

2 A soldier assigned to a commissioned officer as a personal servant.

But then commenced their tiff. It pertained to the state of his breeches as he lay there, unconscious.

"His pants were full," said *Omi*, looking sheepish like Maggie Smith after her pungent comments in her *Downton Abbey* role as the Dowager Countess.

"Oh, Mother, you are so awful!" protested *Mutti*, who started bawling. "He was a brave officer! Just look at his decorations clasp!"

"His breeches were full," insisted *Omi*, then shifting into higher gear: "They were brown *inside*. Brown! Your father's batman told me."

At this turn of the conversation, *Mutti* normally left the room in tears, whilst *Omi* just sat there, gurgling. For my impish tastes, this scene was so delicious that I couldn't help triggering it every time I had the two women together, almost up until *Omi*'s death at age eighty-seven in 1976.

"Please, please talk to me one more time about Grandpa's adventure in the Vosges," I begged them. It always worked and never failed, entertaining me enormously.

King Frederick Augustus III thought more than *Omi* of Curt Netto's pluck. His Majesty put more medals on Grandpa's chest and promoted him to major but, cognizant of Curt Netto's bad heart, did not have him sent back to the front. Instead, Major Netto, once out of the field hospital, was reassigned to an influential position with the Leipzig draft board. This significantly lifted the esteem in which my grandfather was held in Leipzig society beyond the war years.

This appointment turned out to be a blessing for the family beyond my grandfather's death. For instance, one of his many acts of benevolence to well-born young men of draft age resulted in a lasting friendship with Alfred Seltmann, a member of the landed gentry and owner of a farm with a sweet rococo castle in Dölzig, at the outskirts of Leipzig.

Uncle Alfred, as I called him, was a borderline case of mental retardation. It lay in Grandpa Netto's purview to have him exempted from conscription or sent to his certain death at the front. Curt Netto chose the former, and the appreciative lord of the Dölzig manor reciprocated faithfully right until the end of World War II.

When his farmhands slaughtered a sow, chickens, ducks, or geese, he sent farm-fresh meat and sausages to us in the city along with vegetables, apples, pears, peaches, gooseberries, and red and black currants. Often *Omi*, my parents, and I spent weekends at this enchanting manor house, situated sufficiently far away from the city not to be targeted by the RAF at night.

Late on Friday afternoons, we would take the number 17 tram to its Lindenau terminal where, in the summer, Uncle Alfred's barouche—and, in snowy winters, his horse-drawn sleigh—waited for us to take us to Dölzig. I was allowed to sit next to the coachman, where the horses' massive flatulence caused me immense merriment while *Omi*, *Mutti*, and *Vati* sat in the back, kept warm by furs in the cold season.

Once, Uncle Alfred invited us shortly after we were bombed out in the Advent season of 1943 and we had moved in with *Omi*. Suddenly, as soon as we had pulled away from the tram stop, the whole sky behind us lit up with "Christmas trees," as we called the flares RAF bombers dropped on their urban targets before an air raid. Soon it boomed, banged, and thundered, and the snowy ground under the sleigh seemed to shake. As the coachman whipped his horses to race toward the safety of Uncle Alfred's village, we could not help turning around to watch in awe the sinister spectacle of one of the worst attacks on Leipzig, fretting if *Omi*'s apartment would still be there when we returned on Sunday afternoon. It was.

Once again, I have jumped ahead of myself. We are still on *Sophienplatz*, of which much has yet to be told. I stand before the pink row house that now bears the number 6. In my mind, I am trying to project upon its unexciting facade the graceful *Jugendstil* building that once stood there but get no farther than the basement flat where our most disagreeable neighbor lived. Let's just call him "*Herr* Kretzschmar" because I have forgotten his real name. All I knew at the time was that he was the air-raid warden and Nazi Party watchdog. "Like so many Nazi functionaries and their Communist successors, this pudgy little fellow was filled with class hatred, which he directed against the tenants," my mother explained to me decades later.

My first noteworthy encounter with *Herr* Kretzschmar occurred on 20 April 1942 at about one o'clock in the afternoon. *Vati* had just returned from his office at the *Landgericht für Strafsachen* (criminal court), where his workload as prosecutor of juvenile delinquents had been greatly lightened by the fact that young men were now being disciplined by drill sergeants in military barracks to be sent to the front.

We had just sat down for lunch, served by Martha's successor, a young Frenchwoman from Amiens named Raymonde; she doubled as my nursemaid and as our servant. Unusual for this time of the day, the doorbell rang. "Go open the door, please," *Mutti* asked me. "As you can see, Raymonde is busy."

Kretzschmar was at the door, his face distorted with rage.

"I must talk to your father," he snarled in vulgar Saxon.

"I'm sorry, but you can't," I answered, "because we are having lunch."

"I don't give a damn," Kretzschmar bellowed. "Tell him to come out here now! It is about a matter of greatest patriotic importance."

I brought my father out from the dining room and witnessed a dialogue with Kretzschmar that would become a fixed part of the oral histories of both the Siemon and Netto clans, even after my father and my mother had parted ways.

Kretzschmar went immediately on the attack: "*Sie sinn m'r ä gomischer Badriode!* (You are some funny sort of patriot!)" he said in Saxon.

Vati pointed to his dead eyes and his wounded veteran's pin in gold in his left lapel. "What's so funny about the patriotism of a man who sacrificed his eyesight for his fatherland?" he asked Kretzschmar.

"That's not what I'm talking about," stuttered Kretzschmar. "Really, now, don't you know what day it is?"

"Monday, the twentieth of April 1942."

"A-n-d?"

"And what?" my father asked back impatiently because his food was getting cold.

"The twentieth of April is the *Führer*'s birthday. Every patriot should know that!" Kretzschmar said.

"How nice for the *Führer*. Please relay my best wishes to him. But why must I let my lunch get cold for that?"

"Because of the flag, *Herr Doktor*—on the *Führer*'s birthday, all of us must fly our flags, even you, *Herr Doktor*!"

"What's this nonsense?" retorted my father, restraining his anger. "Only this morning I ordered our maid to raise the flag from our tower room. Is it not there?"

"It's the wrong flag, *Herr Doktor*," said our Nazi minder. "The flag dangling from your tower room is black, white, and red. It's invalid now."

"Why should this be the wrong flag? Are black, white, and red not the colors of the German Reich? Was I not sent to war under these colors?"

"Sure, sure, they still are," answered Kretzschmar, now squirming. "But now only the swastika flag is valid. It's the law!"

"Listen now: I am blind because I was sent to war under the colors black, white, and red. That's enough, do you hear me?" said *Vati*. "Now kindly let me eat my lunch."

"Then I will have to report you at once, *Herr Doktor!*" shouted Kretzschmar.

"You do that," my father replied, ending the discussion with a mocking smile. "You best write to the office of prosecutions at the criminal court building, *Elisenstraße* 64, fourth floor, third door to the right."

It was the address of my father's place of work.

With that, my father closed the door. We heard the air-raid warden shout, "*Heil Hitler!*" and then trudge down the stairs. Over lunch, my parents decided, nonetheless, that it would be prudent to acquire a swastika flag, but a small one, to be displayed every twentieth of April alongside the large, imperial German black, white, and red banner, which would envelop it at the slightest breeze.

This it did only once before British bombers came and destroyed it along with the rest of our home. As it burned, the air-raid warden moved his own furniture to the courtyard but refused to help us extinguish the fire or rescue our valuables. Neighbors overheard him say, "I have brought my stuff to safety, but now the fire has reached Dr. Siemon's flat. He deserves losing everything because he is no patriot."

A similar incident upset my family much more, though. To tell this story well I may be forgiven for providing some background and amplifying its particulars. So now, while *Mutti* was in her music room training her voice with *"wa-wa . . . wa-wa-wa . . . wa-wa-waaaaa"* and *"mimi-mimi-niniiii,"* and while my father, according to her, spent more time with pretty secretaries in his court's casino than behind his desk, three other women busied themselves in the rest of the apartment.

One was the most beloved person in my young life: my strict, God-fearing yet cheeky *Omi* Netto. She walked two miles every morning to be with us most of the day before taking the tram home in the evening. The second was Raymonde, a contract laborer from German-occupied France whom my parents had hired as a domestic with the additional task of teaching me the rudiments of her language. And the third was Auntie Emma.

Let's start with Raymonde. I found it easy to learn French because I really liked this young woman. One Sunday, when Raymonde left the house after lunch, she became the object of one of *Omi*'s salacious observations that I always relished, while they caused my mother embarrassment.

"Have you noticed," *Omi* asked the rest of us, "that on Sunday [her afternoons off] Raymonde always leaves the house in a white skirt and always comes back in a green skirt at night?"

By this she assumed, probably correctly, that Raymonde made merry with a member of the opposite sex, doubtless a fellow French laborer, in the rich grass along the banks of the Pleiße river. After all, these foreigners didn't live far from us. They were lodged in the

Volkshaus, a trade union building, just around the corner from us. They would turn out to be a big blessing for our family, as my next chapter will show.

Auntie Emma, the third member of the trio, also inspired my grandmother's wit with a conspicuous feature south of her hips: her bowed legs. They were so spectacular that *Omi* once commented after dessert, "It's astounding how Emma is equipped with the perfect chassis for her chosen profession."

"*Mutti!*" her daughter—my mother—cried out in disgust.

Once again, *Omi* gurgled gleefully, for she had again succeeded in scandalizing her persnickety progeny. I laughed without understanding the context of this exchange. My father remained silent.

Emma was no real aunt of mine. Actually, she was a former prostitute from Bohemia. Her husband, "Uncle" Adolf Bodenstein, was the scion of an ancient dynasty of Leipzig wine merchants. In the 1920s he had bought Emma out of a *Puff* (brothel) in *Goldhahngäßchen*, the preferred red-light district for Leipzig's lower middle classes. This turned out to be a disastrous move, for it helped drive Bodenstein to bankruptcy.

As a last resort, he turned to his faithful former customer, my grandfather Curt Netto who, in those days, lived with his wife and daughter in our spacious belle epoque townhouse, next to Netto & Klepzig, his passement manufacturing business. According to *Omi*, the two men came to terms quickly after the following interview:

"What was your wife's profession before choosing her, *ahem*, current line of work?" Curt Netto asked Adolf Bodenstein.

"In Bohemia, she was a hairdresser, *Herr Major*," Bodenstein replied.

"Good, good," said Grandpa Netto. "In that case, your wife will do my wife's hair every morning. As for you, I will take you on as my factotum to look after our property. Tomorrow you may move into our attic."

And so Uncle Adolf and Auntie Emma entered our family's service, where they remained even after Curt Netto was forced to give up his stake at Netto & Klepzig following the world economic crisis of 1929 and moved from his town house to the rental apartment on *Sophienplatz* 6. Adolf and Emma Bodenstein followed the Netto family and took a smaller flat on the fourth floor of the same building.

Then came the time when Grandfather Netto's heart condition forced him and *Omi* to move into a ground-floor suite two miles away. My parents inherited the apartment at *Sophienplatz*—and the Bodensteins as well. From now on, Emma cleaned house for us and cooked wonderful Bohemian dishes. Adolf did nothing and grew fat.

I loved Auntie Emma for the same reason I loved *Omi*. Although the two were very different, they had one thing in common: they were always there to hug me or be hugged. Sometimes Emma Bodenstein embraced me, pressed me hard against herself and—inexplicably for me at first—cried the biggest tears I'd ever seen from anyone in our house. Years later, *Omi* explained why. "Poor Emma had become so sad," *Omi* told me. "She kept lamenting about 'my Adi' [Adolf] and his Nazis and how they had changed him. All of a sudden, Bodenstein had become a vicious, brutalizing bully."

Adolf Bodenstein had joined the SA, the paramilitary wing of the National Socialist Party. During my nostalgic visit to Leipzig, I am spending days in the city archives trying to find out more about the lives of the people I was close to in my childhood. Auntie Emma's husband, Adolf Bodenstein, was one of them. There isn't much I can find about him, except that he wasn't even a Nazi big shot, just an *Amtsgehilfe*, or lowly gofer, in the party bureaucracy.

Nevertheless, he was *somebody* now. After years of dependence on my grandfather's magnanimity, Adolf Bodenstein held a regular position. When I visited Auntie Emma at home, he sat ostentatiously at his living room table, clad in well-polished brown jackboots and a brown uniform, listening to a broadcast of Nazi marching music and speeches by Hitler and other party leaders. A broad leather strap running from the top left rear of his breeches, over his right shoulder, to the top left front of his trousers held his imposing beer belly in place. Later in the war, I would meet many more fat men in brown uniforms; my readers will encounter them in chapter five.

One day, Uncle Adolf showed up uninvited at our front door. My father was at court, my mother had gone out shopping, and *Omi* wasn't there either. Bodenstein rang the bell. Raymonde opened the door. I stood behind her. "Adi" was dressed in a freshly ironed brown shirt and glistening jackboots. In his right hand, he carried a large bunch of flowers.

"Give me Uwe!" he growled.

"I am sorry, *monsieur*," answered Raymonde. "I am not allowed to do that. Madame Siemon-Netto has given me strict instructions—"

"Get out of my way, you French *Schlampe* (slut)!" Bodenstein roared, pushing Raymonde against the wall with his left arm. With a cry, Raymonde collapsed to the floor. Her cry was so loud that Auntie Emma, busying herself on the kitchen balcony, must have heard her—though she pretended not to.

Then Adolf Bodenstein grabbed me by the arm and dragged me down three flights of stairs and across *Sophienplatz* without letting go of me. At the next corner, he turned right onto *Sophienstraße*, his fat left fingers still pressing into my flesh. He turned left onto *Adolf-Hitler-Straße*, where a huge crowd noisily greeted a convoy of large, open cars moving slowly toward the city center.

In a huge cabriolet stood a stout, uniformed man, his right arm stretched forward, Hitler-style. Uncle Adolf forced himself through the crowd, dragging me with him. He handed me his flowers and literally threw me toward the saluting big shot in the open car. The man grabbed me and kissed me. I remember his wet, pudgy face and his body odor; he reeked of sweat.

For decades I regaled my friends with this story, claiming to have been kissed by Hitler. Now, in the city archives, I discover that the *Führer* only once visited Leipzig, which he loathed, and this happened long before I was born. Today I suspect that the smelly VIP in the cabriolet was *Gauleiter* Martin Mutschmann, Hitler's murderous vice-regent in Saxony, whose denizens mocked him as *König Mu* (King Moo).

When I was back home, *Vati* queried me at lunch about my morning, as he usually did. I said, "*Vati, der Führer stinkt* (Daddy, the *Führer* stinks)."

"How do you know?" my father asked. I told him what had happened. *Vati* called for Raymonde, who was still in shock.

"Poor Raymonde! You have a huge hematoma on your face. What has happened to you?" shouted my mother.

Raymonde confirmed my report: that Adolf Bodenstein had thrown her against the wall and called her a French *Schlampe*. My father called for Auntie Emma to come out of the kitchen at once, and said, "I want to see your husband—now!"

When Adolf Bodenstein walked into our dining room, he was still glowing from his experience that morning. But his expression swiftly changed into sheer hatred when he heard my father say, "*Herr* Bodenstein, you are never to set foot in our apartment again! Did you hear me? Never!"

Bodenstein obeyed my father with a vengeance in the true sense of the word. When the house at *Sophienstraße* 6 burned down one year later, he acted like Kretzschmar, the air-raid warden. "Uncle Adi" rescued his own belongings from the flames and left the site telling bystanders that we were not patriots. In other words, our family, which had sustained him and Emma for many years, deserved no help.

Omi and I saw the Bodensteins one more time in the hunger years immediately after the war in Auerbach's Keller, the sixteenth-century restaurant that owes its worldwide reputation to Goethe's play, *Faust*, as it's the first place Mephistopheles takes Faust on their travels. Auntie Emma worked there as a cook, Adolf as a dishwasher. He had retained his corpulence. I, by contrast, was as thin as a rail and had almost died of tuberculosis because the Soviets rationed the Germans in their zone of occupation to seven hundred calories a day.

Raymonde remained not much longer with us on *Sophienplatz*. In the summer of 1943, my parents gave her home leave. She took the train to Amiens and never came back. This is as much as I knew until my father told me the whole story fifteen years later.

"You know how I hated the French because they had treated me so abominably when I, a blind German soldier, was their prisoner of war?" he asked. "This is why I never spoke French with Raymonde. Others might think of this language as beautiful, and they are probably right. But it made me sick listening to it."

"But?" I asked.

"But I did not wish this young girl harm. So when Field Marshal Paulus's Sixth Army lost the Battle of Stalingrad, I called Raymonde into my study and told her in French—in French, Uwe, in French!—'*Mademoiselle*, with the loss of Stalingrad, we Germans have lost the war. I don't know who is going to occupy us in one year or two. Whoever it will be, if you are caught here, you won't be treated mercifully. Use your home leave to disappear somewhere in the French countryside, and don't reappear until this madness is over.' Evidently, Raymonde did just that."

In the early summer of 1945, when Leipzig was temporarily occupied by the Americans before being handed over to the Soviet Red Army, my mother received a postcard from abroad.

It bore only two words: "Merci! Raymonde."

Uwe's father downed two bottles of wine a day, usually at the *Harmonie*, a club founded in 1776, where he tippled just hours before he was bombed out.

CHAPTER 3

Puddles of Green Fire

IT'S TIME TO END my meanderings around *Sophienplatz*. Staring at its cobblestones evokes dark reminiscences of the fiery night that abruptly terminated my sunny childhood, which destroyed my home and eventually led to the breakup of my family.

As happened often, *Mutti* had just returned from a concert. *Vati* had come home mildly inebriated from the *Gesellschaft Harmonie*, a club founded in 1776 by merchants, scholars, senior civil servants, and artists, where he was in the habit of imbibing impressive amounts of wine. My mother objected to many of his habits, but never to his Bacchanalian passion because, as she said, he was such a pleasant drunk. With one or two bottles of wine inside him, he was merry, witty, and loving, quite in contrast to his sober moments, when he tended to take his overwhelming grief over his blindness out on us.

The *Harmonie* society owned a stately clubhouse on *Roßplatz*, close to where we lived. As always, two fraternity brothers had guided my father home, arm in arm, all three of them swaying, singing

"*Gaudeamus igitur*" (Therefore, Let Us Be Joyous), the centuries-old student song. Its first stanza runs as follows:

Gaudeamus igitur
iuvenes dum sumus
post iucundam iuventutem,
post molestam senectutem,
nos habebit humus!

Let us therefore rejoice,
While we are young;
After our youth,
After a troublesome old age
The ground will hold us!

By the time *Vati* opened the front door, he had progressed to the ominous part of this hymn, which every German high-school graduate knew by heart. Decades later I brought it up with my mother: "*Mutti*, I remember that in the night we were bombed out, *Vati* came home singing the '*Gaudeamus igitur*.' Not that I recognized the lyrics, but I knew the melody because he came home singing it at least once a week. On that evening, though, you chimed in from your dressing room. Do you remember at which point you began singing along?"

"I do! *Vita nostra brevis est, brevi finietur,*" she said, with tears welling up in her eyes. "It was spooky!"

My mother was quoting the first line of the third stanza, which says,

Vita nostra brevis est,
Brevi finietur;
Venit mors velociter,

Rapit nos atrociter;
Nemini parcetur.

Our life is brief,
It will shortly end;
Death comes quickly,
Cruelly snatches us;
No one is spared.

Still humming, my father went into his study and turned on the *Blaupunkt* to find out where the RAF bomber formations were heading that evening. Leipzig had not been bombed very heavily until that point, but Berlin was pummeled in the nights leading up to the fourth of December. Now, again, a large number of enemy aircraft were reported heading toward the German capital. What we did not know at this point was that almost the entire Leipzig fire brigade was on its way to Berlin, leaving only four trucks behind to protect a city of eight hundred thousand people. What we also didn't know was that the direction the planes took was a deceitful act. In truth, once the British bombers reached the outskirts of Berlin, they took a sharp turn south. The real target was my hometown.

For *Mutti*, the timing of this attack came entirely unexpected. She was already in the pre-Christmas spirit. The first Sunday in Advent lay behind us. *Mutti* had convinced herself that nothing horrible would happen in this holy season. "The Allies will have their hands full with Berlin," she pronounced. "Surely they won't bother us for now."

So she temporarily had all our valuables brought back from our weekend home in Bad Lausick, a charming spa twenty-five miles southeast of Leipzig. All our silverware and Meissen china had been evacuated there, in addition to precious oil paintings of *Mutti*'s ancestors that used to hang in the salon, her music room. Her jewelry and my Christmas presents also were removed from the safety of this gem of a small Saxon town, and so was a Märklin toy railroad *Mutti* had bought in 1939 anticipating that the coming war would result in a scarcity of playthings in addition to much harsher shortages, of course.

Mutti planned a series of house concerts, and so her salon had to look truly festive, with her paternal forebears looking down mildly on musicians and audience alike. When it came to the Netto genealogy, as *Omi* observed unkindly, *Mutti* had *einen Furz im Kopf*—a fart in her head. "Let's celebrate Christmas once more like in peacetime," *Mutti* had decreed. I never found out what my father thought of that.

Mutti never forgave herself for guessing wrong. After midnight, the sirens wailed. Immediately after the *Voralarm* intending to warn us of the approaching fleet of airplanes, we heard the first detonations and the barks of the antiaircraft guns. As it turned out, four hundred RAF bombers attacked Leipzig for two hours in three waves, killing 1,815 people and wounding 4,000, including forced laborers from countries occupied by the *Wehrmacht*. By the time they left, 140,000 Leipzigers, one-fifth of the population, had lost their homes, including the Siemon-Netto family.

Since the first, relatively harmless British raid on Leipzig in August, we took the precaution of bathing after supper and going to bed already half-clothed. *Notkoffer* (emergency suitcases) were lined up in the corridor, already packed and ready to go. As soon as we heard the sirens, we jumped up and threw on trousers and jackets. We grabbed the bags and locked the door to prevent pilferers from cleaning out the apartment during the air raid, as happened often, even though this was a capital crime punishable by decapitation.

We rushed downstairs to the basement, where benches and wooden bunk beds with straw bags were set up between the coal and potato compartments. My father took a seat by the outer wall and pressed his right ear against it; in his left ear he was deaf since being wounded in combat in World War I.

"We have taken a hit," *Vati* shouted. "I can hear something pouring down this wall.[1] This can only be phosphor. We must leave this basement!" Having listened to German and British broadcasts diligently, *Vati* knew about these things. We left the basement. The attic was already burning. *Mutti* rushed upstairs and returned with our overcoats, hats, and gloves, which we had forgotten in our haste.

"Uwe, take *Vati* to *Omi*," she said.

"What about you?" I asked.

"I'll stay here to try to extinguish the flames when they reach our apartment."

Mutti ran upstairs again, followed by our new maid, Gerda, Raymonde's successor. I remember *Mutti* handing the young woman keys to our neighbor's apartment. They were a twenty-nine-year-old army colonel and his very pretty wife. He was on furlough and had taken her for a couple of weeks of R&R—rest and recuperation—to the Bavarian Alps a few days before the air raid. The colonel's wife was heavily pregnant, as was Gerda who was expecting a child from a corporal serving, like the colonel, at the eastern front.

Mutti told me later that after the air raid, she instructed Gerda to bring the neighbor's baby linens to safety and come straight back

---

1 The RAF Lancaster planes shown on the cover of this volume were among the very bombers that attacked Leipzig on 4 December 1943. That raid killed 1,815 residents, severely wounded 806 more, and made 114,000 Leipzigers homeless.

to help her extinguish the fire, for it was already burning in several of our rooms.

Vati and I left our burning building as soon as the sirens sounded the "all clear." The *Sophienplatz* was covered with puddles of green fire, some large, some small, but all close together.

"The flames are green, *Vati!*" I shouted.

"Phosphor," he said. "They will take some time to burn out. Let's get a move on."

The green fires on the streets contrasted unnervingly with the fiery red sky. The air was filled with the biting odor of burning beams dropping from roofs to the street.

Scores of urchins from neighboring houses, my playmates, jumped over the phosphorous fires like demented dervishes. Some did this friskily, some screamed in terror as the flames lurched up their trouser legs and began to engulf their mothers' skirts. Awed by this sight, I forgot for a minute that my father's left hand was clutching my right upper arm.

"Let's go!" *Vati* urged me on.

"*Dann wärschde awwr hubbn missn* (But then you'll have to hop)," I answered unwittingly in street Saxon, the idiom of all these other urchins who were my friends and whom I would never see again.

"Speak High German!" *Vati* commanded.

We started jumping. But I was the one in command now, not he, because I could see and he couldn't. So I stubbornly continued in Saxon, the dialect that offended his North German sensitivities.

"*Hubbe weid, Vadi. Un' chetzd awwr ganz gurz hubbn. So, nu ä bissel nach rächsd, und nu widdr nach links* (Jump far, Daddy, but now do a very short hop, now a bit to the right, now again to the left)."

He followed my commands, uncomplaining, because he was far too busy concentrating on the precision of our zigzagging hops over a total distance of two kilometers.

It helped to be blessed with a sardonic sense of humor, even as a child, to digest the absurdity of the scene in which I was an actor, and which unfolded around us. Here an urchin leapfrogged wildly with his blind father over puddles of green flames, jumping a little to the left, a little to the right, taking a short hop here and a long one there, with the bravery it requires to jump across the St. John's Day bonfires. And all around, shadowy figures whirled about, irradiated by blazes sticking their huge, fiery tongues out of every window of the apartment buildings lining the burning streets.

A woman burning like a human torch ran in circles in the middle of *Sophienstraße* outside the blazing *Schauspielhaus*, the private theater from which one of the actors had been my grandmother's lover. Around, around, and around she ran, screaming, until two boys not much older than I threw a blanket around her, extinguishing the flames. Where did they find a blanket in this chaos? I don't know. Perhaps one of them had worn it to protect himself against the December cold. I remember that it seemed of military issue and was olive drab, which provided an eerie disparity to the red flames on the woman's body and the green flames on the street.

Halfway to *Omi*'s apartment, we passed my elementary school, the *Vierte Volksschule*. It was already a smoldering ruin. Across the street stood *Vati*'s courthouse.

"I don't have to go to school Monday," I told my father jubilantly. "It is no longer there."

"Selfish lout!" he chided me. "What about my office?"

Karl-Heinz Siemon's place of work: the *Landgericht* (regional court). His offices on the top floor burned out. Uwe's school was across the road.

I looked up to the fourth floor of the criminal court and saw tongues of fire shooting out of its windows.

"Your office is also burning, *Vati*. You don't have to go to work on Monday either."

A grim grin crossed my father's scarred face. He hated being a lawyer and loathed being a prosecutor of juvenile delinquents. As a young boy and adolescent, he had dreamed of becoming a physician, but as a blind man, he could not study medicine. Only two academic fields were thus open to him, law or theology, but he was even less suited for the ordained ministry than for jurisprudence. Too profound was his quarrel with God.

We stopped. My joy over not having to go to school on Monday evaporated within minutes. I had actually loved my first two years at the *Vierte Volksschule*. It was the only one of the fourteen schools I attended in my childhood and adolescence that I enjoyed. From that fourth of December on, through the war, Germany's collapse, and my subsequent escape from the Soviet zone of occupation to the west, I was forced to change schools and educational systems like shoes. The first wasn't poisoned with Nazi ideology; the next ones were. Then I had private teachers for a few months until I was forced into a Communist school. Three Rudolf Steiner schools followed and, in the end, a traditional German *Gymnasium*.[2] This didn't help my grades. No wonder I didn't earn my doctorate until I was fifty-five and had a long career in journalism behind me.

My first two years at school, though, were wonderful and gave me enough self-confidence to last a lifetime. At a breathtaking speed that astounded my parents, I learned the most important skills for my future vocation as a journalist: to read and to write. This I owed to my unforgettable class teacher, *Herr* Born, who was neither a political fanatic nor one of those soft modern types too wimpy to discipline their pupils.

Paul Born was one of those marvelous royal Saxon *Steißtrommler* (butt drummers) who enriched Germany and the rest of the world with educated, cultured, and well-mannered young people. He was a wiry man in his early sixties, kindhearted but swift with the cane, which we boys never held against him. To us, *Herr* Born seemed an archaic creature with his glistening manorial long boots, his well-trimmed mustache, and a pair of pince-nez enhancing the twinkle in his eyes. When *Mutti* first met him, she remarked, "Looking at *Herr*

---

2 The *Gymnasium* is the most advanced of the three types of German secondary schools, the others being *Realschule* and *Hauptschule*.

Born gives me one more reason to regret the monarchy." Every morning, he prayed the Lord's Prayer with us, which was highly unusual in the Third Reich ruled by atheists or neo-pagans.

One day, in first grade, he asked five of us boys who were his favorites to stay behind for a brief while after class. All five of us were friends and hailed from similar royalist, non-Nazi homes. *Herr* Born had brought along his portable gramophone. He cranked it up and put on a record, which I now know was Beethoven's Fifth Symphony. He played only the first two opening bars: three short eighth notes in G#, followed by a long D#. He lifted the needle and asked us, "Which of you boys has heard this theme at home on the radio in the evening?" All of us raised our right arms.

"Listen, boys," he warned us. "Next week, men in brown shirts will pay our class a visit. They also will bring along a gramophone to play these two bars. They will ask you the same question. For God's sake, do not raise your arms! Do *not* raise your arms! If you do, you might never see your parents again. And please keep this to yourselves! Just do as I say, please!"

Beethoven's *Schicksalsmotiv* was the call signal of the BBC. Listening to it, and especially passing on information broadcast by an "enemy station," as the Nazis called it, was considered a political crime, punishable by years at hard labor or even, in the case of senior civil servants as my father was, by death under the guillotine.

In my first elementary school years, I picked up my father from his office every day to take him home for lunch. On the day *Herr* Born made us stay behind to listen to his warning, I was a little late.

"What happened?" *Vati* asked.

I began telling him. He cut me short.

"Shush," he warned me. "Wait until we are home."

At lunch, we continued our conversation as soon as the maid had left the dining room.

"Your teacher is a very brave man," *Vati* said. "He has risked his life for us." From that day on, he turned down his *Blaupunkt* to a point where I could barely hear it in my nursery room, which was next to his study.

It seems that I paused far too long in front of my burning school, lost in doleful thoughts about my teacher Paul Born, whom I knew I would never see again. "Let's move on!" my father urged me. Most of the green flames on the street had, by now, burned out. Taking normal steps, we proceeded south on *Elisenstraße*. We passed *Steinplatz*, a charming playground where I would spend much of my free time for the rest of the war and the first two postwar years. The bombs had spared its chestnut, buckeye, hornbeam, and oak trees.

We turned left onto *Fichtestraße* and then right onto *Bayerische Straße*, where several multistory homes were ablaze, spewing burning beams onto the tracks of the number 14 and 16 tramlines. A day or two later, I would join the urchins of that neighborhood, treasure-hunting the still-smoking ruins of these buildings. We came across a fully intact wine cellar. I helped myself to one bottle and brought it to *Vati*. He popped it and found its contents undrinkable.

The windows of *Omi*'s bedroom, living room, and narrow maid's chamber faced *Bayerische Straße*, although the entrance to the elegant *Jugendstil* house where she occupied one of the three ground-floor flats was around the corner on *Kaiserin-Augusta-Straße*. *Mutti* had called her from our burning apartment to announce our arrival. When *Omi* saw us coming, she tied an apron around her waist, rushed into the kitchen, and did what one expected of a Saxon granny under such circumstances: she grated potatoes for potato pancakes. Their taste has remained on my pallet until this very day.

Then *Omi* lit her coal-burning copper bath boiler for me. While its water was heating up for my bath, *Vati* took a cold shower. As he dried himself, he ordered the whole family, *Omi* included, to forthwith do the same; he explained that his nose was too sensitive to bear the odor of unwashed people, and our severely curtailed coal rations would not allow for a warm bath every day.

As soon as I was washed and had eaten my pancakes, *Omi* bedded me on the sofa in her drawing room, covering me with a thick blue-and-gray wool blanket she had knitted herself. This blanket became my faithful companion in *Omi*'s basement during air raids and is still with me. Though gravely tattered, it now has its place of honor on a couch in the library of my summer home in France.

Omi sat down beside me and read from the *Herrnhuter Losungen*, known in English as Daily Watchwords, a globally distributed publication that was started in 1728 and is now available in fifty languages, making it the oldest and most widely read daily devotional work in the world. Next, she launched into a long intercessional prayer, first for my mother, who was, at that time, wrestling with the flames in our apartment on *Sophienplatz*, and then for a swift end of the darkness enveloping the German people and the world.

Vati listened silently but attentively. I never really figured out his faith, as little as I learned any details about the nightmares he suffered in World War I. He did not attend church services and kept quiet when his family prayed. Yet he showed no dislike of our devotions. He was a strange man. Decades later, when he lived in Lindau on the shores of Lake Constance, he surprised me by tuning into *Radio Vorarlberg* in nearby Austria every Sunday morning for the brilliant sermons of a Dominican father.

"Why are you listening to a Catholic priest and not to a Protestant pastor?" I asked him.

"Because he is an excellent preacher worth listening to, which is what I expect from a Dominican. After all, he belongs to an order known for good homilies," he answered. And that was that. He offered no further explanation.

Omi now said the Lord's Prayer and, curiously, asked me to sing with her the hymn "Now Thank We All Our God." I was stunned. Why would *Omi* want me to thank God as our home was burning down and I could not even be sure that *Mutti* would escape the fire? It took me many decades to discover the answer: a pastor by the name of Martin Rinckart wrote the lyrics of this song at the height of the Thirty-Years War (1618–48) when his town, Eilenburg, near Leipzig, lay under Swedish siege, the plague ravaged its population, and he had to bury an average of fifty people every day.

It wasn't for these miseries that Rinckart thanked God; he thanked the Creator for the gift of life, for all the blessings He bestowed on people, and, most importantly, for the grace by which the people Rinckart accompanied to their graves every day were saved through their faith in Christ's vicarious suffering on the cross and His resurrection. This was pure Lutheran theology, which my grandmother understood so well and passed on to me.

When *Omi* and I finished singing, we waited in silence, and we waited, and waited, and waited. Though exhausted, I dozed off for brief spells but could not really sleep. It was beginning to get dark. After four o'clock in the afternoon, four Frenchmen showed up at the front door of *Kaiserin-Augusta-Straße* 53 where *Omi* lived. They had come with a wooden apple cart of the type street hawkers still used in my childhood. On this two-wheeled cart lay *Mutti*, unconscious and clutching our seventeenth-century family *Kurfürstenbibel* against her chest. This rare and large leather-bound Bible owed its name to the images of eleven Protestant electors (*Kurfürsten*). It was printed in Nuremberg on the command of the sovereign of Saxony and, at the end of the book, includes the three creeds of the Christian Church[3] and the major confessions of the Lutheran Church[4].

Gently, the Frenchmen carried my mother to the couch in *Omi*'s living room, where I had just lain. *Mutti* woke up, whispering to my father, "Now I am blind too. What a fine pair we are, *nicht wahr, Karl-Heinz?*" Then she fainted again.

"This will pass. It's just smoke poisoning," said my grandmother. She hurried into the kitchen, came back with lukewarm water, and washed out her eyes.

"What happened?" *Omi* asked the Frenchmen. They didn't speak German. My father still sat there in silence, but the French I had learned from Raymonde was enough for me to translate, which is why I remember their story so well. It is one of the most moving tales of human decency I had heard in this indecent war.

These four men were foreign laborers, more or less forcibly recruited by the German occupation authorities in France to make

---

3 The Apostles' Creed, the Nicene Creed, and the longer Athanasian Creed, which Lutherans recite on Trinity Sunday.

4 Including Luther's Small Catechism, which my grandmother made me study, using this *Kurfürstenbibel*, which had been in the Netto family for many generations.

up for the shortage of workers in the Reich. They were quartered in the *Volkshaus*, a massive former trade union building on *Adolf-Hitler-Straße*, only a few steps from *Sophienplatz*. During the bombing, they voluntarily left their shelter to help German civilians fight the flames and escape from their burning homes.

Why they came to *Sophienplatz* 6 and risked their lives running up the burning stairs to our third-floor apartment to save an enemy woman must remain a matter of speculation. I suspect that at least one of them was the lover responsible for changing the color of Raymonde's skirt from white to green on Sunday afternoons. Perhaps before returning to Amiens earlier that year, Raymonde had urged her friends to keep an eye on us should my father's dire prediction of the impending catastrophe come true. Who else but Raymonde could have given them *Omi*'s address on *Kaiserin-Augusta-Straße*? *Mutti* told me later that in her semicomatose state, she would have been unable to tell them where her mother lived.

"We rushed from room to burning room and found this young lady in the salon under her grand piano, clutching the Bible," one Frenchman told me. "The fire had already reached that room as well. We noticed how the flames were consuming the paintings of your ancestors. It was too late to save them."

"Well, bless you, *Messieurs*, you saved what is most precious to us, my daughter!" *Omi* made me tell them in French. "Please, go on. What happened next?"

"Something extraordinary, Madame," he answered. "We said, '*Courage, Madame, il est fort temps de partir* (Have courage, Madam, it's high time to go).' But you know what she replied? '*Mais d'abord il faut que je nous fasse un café* (But first I must make us coffee).'"

According to the Frenchmen, she boiled up bottled mineral water with an immersion heater because there was no longer any running water in the apartment, while amazingly, the electricity had not yet been cut off. But the Franco-German *Kaffeeklatsch* never happened.

"Before we could drink, part of the ceiling collapsed, and your mother fainted. We found a blanket, wrapped it around her. My big friend here threw her over his shoulders," he continued, pointing at the tallest man in the group. "Then we raced down the blazing staircase and requisitioned the apple cart we found on *Sophienplatz*."

"May I offer you some refreshments?" *Omi* asked.

"*Peut-être une pomme* (Perhaps an apple)," their spokesman replied, nodding at *Omi*'s *Adventsteller*, the seasonal Advent plate filled with fruit, marzipan, biscuits, almonds, and nuts that is customary in German homes. Then the four of them left.

There was no air raid that night. In the morning, *Mutti*'s eyesight had returned. She was anxious about her young neighbor's baby linens. Our maid, Gerda, did not take them to my grandmother's place as *Mutti* had told her to; neither did Gerda return to *Sophienplatz* to help her. The doorbell rang. The Frenchmen were back, wanting to see how *Mutti* was.

"I must find out what happened to my neighbor's baby linens," my mother said absent-mindedly. "Gerda must have them at her parents' home. Uwe, you know where they live. Let us go there. *Messieurs*, would you be so kind as to accompany us? We might need your help."

I guided *Mutti* and the Frenchmen to Gerda's parental home in the suburb of Connewitz, about half an hour's walk from *Omi*'s apartment. Gerda had taken me there to meet her mother earlier that year. *Mutti* rang the bell. Gerda opened the door.

"Where are my neighbor's baby linens?" *Mutti* asked her. "Why have you not taken them to my mother, as I had asked you to? Why have you not returned to *Sophienplatz* to give me a hand?"

"I have nothing further to do with you," Gerda said sullenly. "You have no home for me to go to anymore. So we are quits." I explained the situation to the Frenchmen—they were aghast.

Mutti shoved Gerda aside and walked into her eat-in kitchen, and there, under the table, she saw our neighbors' two cases. *Mutti* whirled around and slapped Gerda's face forcefully, saying, "You are a despicable human being who looted another pregnant woman's home after an air raid!"

That same day Gerda went to the police to press charges against my mother. *Mutti* was called to the local precinct. She could have explained herself. She could have told the cops what Gerda had done. Pilfering at wartime was a capital crime. Gerda would have been allowed to remain alive in prison until her baby's delivery. But after that she would not have escaped the guillotine. The death penalty was compulsory for this offense, not only in Germany.

That's why *Mutti* refrained from giving the real reasons for her behavior. "Gerda was a thievish swine," she told me later. "But I didn't want her to be decapitated just for being a thievish porker."

"I did this because I was at the end of my tether. I was under severe stress," *Mutti* said at the station. She could have received long prison terms for abusing a subordinate physically, especially as Germany was a National Socialist state then with a strong bias in favor of the working classes. My father had very little influence in the prosecutor's office in those days, but he did manage to finagle a 150-mark fine for his wife, representing one-tenth of his monthly salary.

The Frenchmen accompanied *Mutti* with the apple cart to our burned-out home on *Sophienplatz*. There was nothing more to rescue than the coals in the basement. They packed three-hundred-weight of briquettes on the cart and pulled it to *Omi*'s place on *Kaiserin-Augusta-Straße*.

"Take some more fruit. Take some sweets. Take all you want," *Omi* urged them. "After all, it's Advent in France too, is it not?" They nodded, took a few cookies, wished us well, and left.

"It gives you pause," *Mutti* said later, "that four Frenchmen were ready to sacrifice their lives for an 'enemy,' while Germans who were once very close to us behaved like pigs. Think of Adolf Bodenstein who owed so much to our family. Think of the air-raid warden whose duty it would have been to help me extinguish the flames, especially as there were not enough fire engines in Leipzig on that fourth of December. Think of Gerda, who, as our maid, was a member of our household. I shall never forget this, and neither should you, Uwe."

For centuries, we Saxons have been lovers of France, especially we Leipzigers. "I praise my Leipzig! It is a small Paris and educates its people," wrote Johann Wolfgang von Goethe in *Faust*. We understood ourselves as the cultural soulmates of the French, as we had a common foe: the stark Prussians. We thought them less refined.

We were proud that one of us, Count Moritz of Saxony (1696–1750), became one of the most celebrated marshals in French military history and that the French novelist George Sand was his granddaughter, never mind that the charmless Friedrich Nietzsche, also a Saxon, belittled her as a "milking cow with a fine style." Count Moritz was one of the countless illegitimate sons of the immensely cultured and manful Augustus the Strong (1670–1733), king of Poland and elector of Saxony, whose insatiable libido was the favorite topic of *Omi*'s seemingly limitless yarn.

On the fourth of October 1943 and the subsequent days, I became fully aware of my love for France. It began with Raymonde and has lasted until this very day. As for my Francophile mother, it didn't take her a week after the loss of her home to resume her house concerts. Accompanied by a friend on her mother's Feurich upright piano, she gave a *Liederabend* (lieder concert), which she began with the French chanson, "*Plaîsir d'Amour*" (Pleasure of Love), an eighteenth-century song by the Franco-German composer Jean-Paul-Égide Martini (1741–1816), who was born under the name of Johann Paul Aegidius Schwarzendorf in the Bavarian region of Upper Franconia.

For centuries, Leipzig has been Francophile. Since German reunification, the French are slowly returning. Among them is Alexandra, co-owner of the café La Chocolaterie.

My encounter with Alexandra and Isabelle, two agreeable young women from Normandy, fanned my hopes. They have opened La Chocolaterie, a small café on *Waldstraße*, one of Leipzig's smartest streets, where they sell their homemade French confectionary. I ask Alexandra Picouays, "How Francophile is Leipzig still—or again?"

"All I can tell you is that I have always been welcomed with open arms wherever I went in this town," she replied.

"That sounds vague . . ."

"Perhaps," Alexandra retorted, "but there are seven hundred French people living in *Little Paris*. I know many of them personally, and none of them has expressed unhappiness about being here."

It's not much for a city with Leipzig's traditions. Still, it's a start.

CHAPTER 4

Marzipan in Limbo

IT WAS TIME TO stop lingering around *Sophienplatz*. I am now retracing my steps on the streets where my father and I had hopped over green flames after we were bombed out on 4 December 1943. Now I am sauntering south to the art nouveau building that was my home for the rest of the war and the two years beyond. *Omi* lived on the ground floor.

When I last saw this house, decades ago in Communist times, it was still pockmarked by bomb shrapnel from the Second World War. Today, its

Kaiserin-Augusta-Straße 53, where Uwe lived with his Omi after he lost his home

facade is repaired and painted in bright yellow. Still earlier, when I was seven or eight, many of its window frames were filled with cardboard instead of glass panes for many weeks at a time after air raids. In *Omi*'s apartment, this was never so for long. She had befriended an elderly

• 61 •

master glazier whose journeymen were serving at the front. With hundreds of desperate customers in our neighborhood begging him to repair their windows, he could not keep up with the demand, although he always had a good supply of glass, despite the wartime shortage of almost everything.

A friend of my mother's, a young officer on furlough, taught me how to cut this glass and fit it with putty into the frames. This way we enjoyed the light of the day until the shock wave of yet another RAF attack shut it off by shattering the windows, which forced us to replace them provisionally with cardboard until I was able to get to work with the glass cutter the master glazier had given me.

Until the end of the war, *Omi*'s address was *Kaiserin-Augusta-Straße* 53. This was changed to *Richard-Lehmann-Straße* soon after the Soviet Red Army had marched into Leipzig in the summer of 1945. Viennese-born Richard Lehmann (1900–1945), an admirable Social Democrat and a journalist, was an audacious resistance fighter beheaded by the Nazis. "At least he wasn't a Communist," *Omi* said.

Still, the name change saddened her. The beloved Empress Augusta was the wife of Kaiser Wilhelm I, who died in 1888 and was succeeded in the same year by his son Friedrich III and then Wilhelm II, the last of Germany's monarchs of the house of Hohenzollern. *Omi* often reminded us that she was born in 1888, known to Germans as the *Dreikaiserjahr*, the year of the three emperors. This, in addition to her sturdy Lutheran faith, her common sense, and her earthy Saxon humor, defined her persona. She was a creature of the cultured late nineteenth century and tried to mold me in that spirit. In that sense, I span three centuries—born in the twentieth, brought up with the values of the nineteenth, and winding up my life in the twenty-first.

Wistfully, I wander around the building where I spent the happiest years of my childhood, being fully aware of the probability of being killed by a bomb any given night. I turn the corner onto a street called *Bayerische Straße* in my childhood, and later *Arthur-Hoffmann-Straße*, named after another anti-Nazi martyr. Three windows of *Omi*'s apartment faced that north-south thoroughfare. The first of these belonged to the former maid's room, which *Omi* and I shared since my parents and I had moved in. It was a narrow chamber with just enough space for two single beds, lined up head-to-foot against the wall, with *Omi*'s bed facing the window and mine facing the door.

Beneath my bed, next to the chamber pot, I had stored my school satchel holding notebooks, schoolbooks, and pens. There was also my little library, of which I loved most the *Leatherstocking Tales* by the nineteenth-century American novelist James Fenimore Cooper. The German edition of the *Leatherstocking Tales* was a Christmas present from my godmother, the patent attorney Charlotte Francke, and became my invaluable guide for playing Indians and trappers with the other urchins in my new neighborhood after school and homework and in between the daytime attacks by the US Army Air Force and the nightly raids by RAF planes.

There was a little table in that bedroom. It doubled as my desk and as *Omi*'s altar for her morning and evening devotions. There were two chairs, a commode, and, best of all, a coal-fired tiled stove, which kept this little chamber wonderfully warm and made it a popular room for the whole family on the coldest winter days.

Some might call this abode my personal foretaste of hell, considering the terrifying things I witnessed while living there. But to me it did not seem hellish at all. Given that I faced death all the time, it definitely wasn't Heaven either. Let's call it a "limbo" then, fiddling a little with speculative eschatology. It was a secure place where I was allowed to crawl under *Omi*'s duvet for a while following the "all clear" after the nightly bombardments.

Mutti never allowed me to do that. Abiding love for children, whether born or unborn, was not the mark of my mother; besides, she didn't care for pets either. To her, dogs, cats, or babies were annoying competitors in the pursuit of people's attention. Witnessing the metastasis of feminist narcissism in America in the 1960s has convinced me that I was actually the progeny of a trailblazer of postmodern womanhood.

"Why do I have no brothers or sisters?" I asked *Mutti* late in her life.

"I tried to prevent pregnancies," she answered nonchalantly.

"How?"

"After every intercourse, I called in a midwife to massage my uterus. When that didn't work, I had an abortion."

"Are you telling me that I had the privilege of being the sole exception—that you actually *wanted* me to live?"

"You slipped through, Uwe. Your will to live was very strong! But now I am glad you are here."

". . . !"

My grandmother was altogether different. *Omi* was a level-headed grande dame brought up in the style of Saxony's cultured monarchy. At a time of mortal danger, she mastered the art of nurturing a child with a beautiful blend of sternness and soothing love. As soon as the RAF bombers had left the Leipzig airspace, allowing us to return to her apartment, *Omi* let me to slip into her bed. She held me tight and caressed my head until I stopped shaking. But woe if I moaned about my fate! Then her right hand would land on my left cheek with sharp swiftness. In *Omi*'s world, whining evidenced a lack of faith in God and an inferior upbringing. "In *my* family, one does not whine," she admonished me and resumed stroking my head softly.

Standing on the sidewalk below this tube-like room, a train of the number 16 tramline rumbles by. It is blue and yellow and shrieks metallically as it turns left to proceed toward its southern terminus, a housing settlement with the enchanting name of *Märchenwiese*, meaning "fairy-tale meadow."

This piercing sound is music to me, for it echoes the trams I had known in my childhood when streetcars in Leipzig were red and yellow with windows painted dark blue so as not to attract the attention of British reconnaissance planes in the evenings. Only narrow, horizontal strips were left unpainted for the drivers to look ahead and for passengers to check when to get off. Sometimes, after heavy air raids, trams had no glass windows at all, just cardboard panes with small holes in them. That they ran at all, though waddling like ducks along tracks warped by wear, rubble, and burning debris, was testimony to a brilliantly managed municipal transit system.

All this was part of my reality in the winter of 1943 to 1944; what seems more unreal in retrospect is my parents' attempt to make our lives appear normal for just a while longer during our first months in *Omi*'s apartment. I already mentioned that my mother resumed her house concerts less than a week after we were bombed out. Twenty or more people, dressed elegantly, as if we were in deepest peacetime, filled *Omi*'s living room. My father wore an impeccable dark-gray suit from the extensive wardrobe he had stored in our weekend flat in Bad Lausick (and had not allowed my mother to repatriate for Christmas). Though not normally generous, he did bestow his dinner jacket and trousers to *Mutti*. She had this suit retailored into the semiformal costume she wore at her afternoon performances.

The concert began at four o'clock in the afternoon and ended two hours later, to give the guests time to get home before the nightly air-raid alarm. *Omi* had baked Advent cookies for the event. Tea with rum was served, as was *Glühwein* with cinnamon sticks and lemon slices. I spotted my uncle Felix among the audience. He was a tall gentleman whose elegant posture fitted his title of baron, although his nobility was of recent vintage. Frederick Augustus III, the last king of Saxony, had awarded him his title not long before the monarchy in Germany was abolished, following its defeat in World War I.

Uncle Felix usually arrived late, sat unnoticed by most others in the back of the room, and left early, always keeping his overcoat on, although the room was well heated.

"Why did Uncle Felix do that?" I asked *Mutti* decades after the war.

"He was *ein Halbjude*, the baptized son of a Christian mother and a Jewish father," she said. "Uncle Felix tried to avoid being recognized before, during, and after the concert."

"Did you know this all along, *Mutti*?"

"Of course, and so did *Omi* and *Vati*," said my mother.

"But why did Uncle Felix stop coming all of a sudden?" I pressed on. "What happened to him?"

"Relatives smuggled him out of Leipzig to the Mecklenburg countryside where landowners hid him, dressed as a farmhand, in a barn."

"That was brave of them," I said.

"Very!" *Mutti* agreed.

Uncle Alfred Seltmann, the lord of the rococo manor house in Dölzig, also contributed to the appearance of normalcy in our household. One morning, his coachman drove a horse-drawn wagon through the ravines of Leipzig's ruins with provisions for us. He brought potted meats, vegetables, potatoes, apples, and most importantly, our Christmas goose.

Christmas Eve 1943 confirmed to me that I had been spared the worst for the time being. The RAF bombers stayed on their bases until after the second Christmas Day, called Boxing Day in the UK. I could not accompany *Mutti* to church because I had the flu. But on Christmas Eve, I was called out of bed and dressed. The chime of a glass bell beckoned me into the festively adorned living room I had not been allowed to enter on the previous two days while *Mutti* and *Omi* decorated the tree and arranged the gifts beneath it. The candlelit room was redolent with incense and the fragrance of *Omi*'s freshly baked pastries.

I knew that my Christmas presents, including a model railway, had been destroyed on the fourth of December. But there were marvelous substitutes, notably big portions of marzipan from two different and incongruous sources, both worth a lengthy description because they are romantic nuggets in my family history.

The first load of almond paste sweetening my wartime life in limbo came from my grandfather Siemon, a strange, scholarly character whose knack for making money, and whose Mediterranean looks, earned him the nickname "White Jew." Decades later I learned that this alone prompted Gestapo officers in long leather coats to raid his luxurious apartment on *Beethoven-Straße* behind the German Supreme Court during the war.

But *Opapa*, as we grandchildren called him, was neither a Nazi nor a Jew, just a descendant of French Huguenots with a dark complexion and stunning black hair, although by the time I came around, he sported a shining bald pate, to which photographs of my baptism attest.

I always thought that *Opapa* was independently well-to-do and had no idea that this scholarly gentleman made sweets while Leipzig was ablaze. How it came to that was a lovely, labyrinthine story originating in the late nineteenth century.

The tale begins in the summer of 1894, when "Red" Fritz Moritz, the wealthy opposition leader in the parliament of the principality of Lippe-Detmold in northwestern Germany, gave a fair for the people of the town of Lage, his constituency. "Red" was his nickname primarily because of the color of his hair, but his rebellious temper might have contributed to this cognomen. His shouting matches with his prince during their walks through the Detmold city park were legendary.

According to my father, two medical students from Hannover, fully dressed in their fraternity garb, happened across the fields during their term break and cheerfully mingled with the Lage revelers. One of the two was Carl Siemon. He felt instantly attracted Red Moritz's daughter. She was lissome and very blond. The two danced until late in the evening. By the time the band played the closing waltz, the two were seriously in love. That same evening, Carl Siemon bowed suavely before Red Moritz and asked, "May I ask His Excellency for his daughter's hand in marriage?"

"What does he do for his living?" asked Red Moritz, scowling at Siemon's fraternity gear.

"I am a medical student in the last semester, Your Excellency."

"I don't need a quack in my family!"

"What does His Excellency require?"

"A manager and businessman. I have thirteen children. Each of them will inherit a business. To Annemarie I intend to leave a still."

"If His Excellency will kindly train me as a manager and a businessman, I am ready to give up my studies."

And thus, Carl Siemon received a sound education in management and soon skillfully ran a distillery producing *Steinhäger*, a local schnapps, delivered throughout the principality in horse-drawn trucks. My father could still remember the horses, their stables, the stacks of hay, and a permanently inebriated, pipe-puffing coachman. One evening, he fell asleep in the hayrick, his pipe still lit. The hay caught fire, and soon the hayrick, the stables, the still, and the entire estate, including *Opapa*'s house, were ablaze.

I could never find out whether the drunken coachman survived. All I know is that *Opapa*, Annemarie, my father Karl-Heinz, and his sister Elisabeth were now homeless and penniless. *Opapa* decided to emigrate. There were two places a German with his entrepreneurial skills could move his family to. One was America, but that was far away; the other was the flourishing kingdom of Saxony in the center of Germany. *Opapa* opted for the pretty, small city of Zwickau but soon moved to bustling and cultured Leipzig, site of the world's oldest international trade fair, where he established assorted enterprises, one being the manufacture of marzipan.

According to my father, my grandfather never voiced any regret over having sacrificed a medical career so as to be allowed to marry my grandmother. "But I know that he always wanted to be a physician rather than a businessman. That's why, since my early childhood, he urged me to become a doctor," *Vati* told me years after World War II. "And now look what has become of me: an eyeless lawyer loathing his profession."

The second load of almond paste I found on my table of Christmas presents in 1943 came from an anonymous donor in the *Generalgouvernement*, as the German zone of occupation in Poland was called. Only two decades later did I discover my benefactor's identity: he was Professor Wiktor Kemula, a renowned Polish electrochemist who paid my wife and me a visit in our apartment in New York where I worked as a foreign correspondent.

Dr. Kemula was my mother's first heartthrob when she was a teenager and became her last lover late in her life. After the war, she had tried for twenty years to find out what had happened to him, enlisting Jewish classmates who had fled from Leipzig early in the Nazi period.

Her best friend at school was Alice Dimenstein, née Levin, a wealthy dentist's daughter. She lived on Central Park West, a half-hour's walk from my apartment on East Fifty-Fifth Street. One morning, Alice called me excitedly, saying, "Have you read today's *New York Times*? There is a short article about a conference on electrical chemistry presided by Dr. Wiktor Kemula, vice-rector of Warsaw University. This must be our man."

I found him by telephone in his hotel in Chelsea. Immediately he took a cab uptown, eager to hear about my mother, who, he said, had been the love of his life. Wiktor wasn't very tall but was an elegantly dressed gentleman with sparkling eyes, a hilarious sense of humor, and a command of eight languages. He was also a brilliant pianist. "What a charmer!" my wife, Gillian, whispered into my ear.

No sooner had he sat down than he asked me, "How did you like the marzipan I sent you during the war?"

"I remember the marzipan from the *Generalgouvernement* well. They came from some factory in Lemberg, but without a sender's address. We had no idea who had ordered them. By the way, how did you even find us? My mother was no longer *Fräulein* Netto but *Frau* Siemon!"

"Well, as you Germans say, *vee heff our vays* . . ."

Then Wiktor Kemula proceeded to tell me one of the most unusual wartime stories I had ever heard.

It began one Sunday afternoon, probably in 1929, four years before Hitler came to power. The doorbell of the Netto household rang. Grandfather Curt opened the door in a jolly mood, a champagne glass in his left hand, and saw Wiktor Kemula bowing to him in a courtly manner, holding a gorgeous bunch of flowers in one hand and an expensive box of pralines in the other.

"I am a postdoctoral student from Poland. The international welcome service of Leipzig University sent me," he explained.

Professor Wiktor Kemúla and Uwe's mother: a love revived after fifty years

"*Ach so!*" said Grandfather Netto, as if this visit by a stranger were an everyday occurrence on a Sunday afternoon.

For centuries, the upper bourgeois families of Leipzig had the tradition of opening their homes to foreign students as well as to merchants visiting the international trade fair.

"Make yourself at home," my grandfather said, according to Wiktor. "You have chosen a wonderful moment to come here. You see, we are celebrating my daughter's confirmation. Follow me into our salon and enjoy some champagne with us."

My mother was only fifteen years old then, and Wiktor was twenty-eight. They instantly fell for each other, taking long walks together, conversing sometimes in Latin or classical Greek, French, and German. *Mutti* even learned some Polish from her beau until, after two years, Wiktor had to return to Poland.

Before saying farewell to my family, he asked Grandpa Netto boldly, "I know that Ruth is still young, but we love each other; would you please give me her hand in marriage?"

"Young man," Curt Netto responded sternly, "I can happily overlook the fact that you are a Pole. I can even forgive you for being a Roman Catholic. But what I find unforgivable is that you want to yank Ruth away from her *Abitur* (high school diploma). Return to Poland and come back in about two years' time, and then we shall see."

Wiktor went. *Mutti* stayed in Leipzig and pined for him. The two exchanged some love letters, but then their correspondence dried up, presumably because Wiktor had found and married another woman, and then, of course, Hitler's Germany invaded Poland, triggering World War II.

"What happened to you?" I asked him over dinner in my New York apartment.

"I became a professor at the University of Lemberg. Do you know Lemberg? It belonged to the Austro-Hungarian Empire before World War I. It was a beautiful city. We Poles call it Lwów. Its Ukrainian name is Lviv."

But soon the Germans occupied this city from the west, while the Soviets took its eastern part, not without first abducting members of the elite from what became the German sector. In this turmoil, Wiktor lost his position at the university and was forced to feed his wife and himself by selling off his substantial library of German books to a secondhand store specializing in foreign literature, where he encountered an immaculately dressed German.

"Your German is wonderful," he told Wiktor. "Where did you study?"

"In Leipzig."

"So did I! May I pay you a visit?"

"Well, I don't know if that's appropriate. I am Polish; you are German..."

"Please let me come. I mean no harm."

Reluctantly, Wiktor gave the stranger his address. On the following Sunday, the German, resplendent in the uniform of a ranking *Generalgouvernement* official rang Wiktor's doorbell, saying, "Don't be afraid, and please hear me out: when we occupied Lemberg, we inherited a marzipan factory with all its workers but none of its executives, who were all nabbed by the Red Army before we arrived and presumably taken to the gulags. Why don't you run the factory for us?"

"I am an academic, not an executive!" said Wiktor.

"But you are a chemist. Making marzipan involves chemistry."

"But..."

"But what? You have many books to sell but not enough to feed your family for many years until you find a teaching position again."

Thus it came about that in 1943, I found a lump of almond paste from occupied Poland under *Omi*'s Christmas tree, sender unknown until twenty years later.

When Wiktor came to our New York apartment, we telephoned my mother in Frankfurt. She had just married the music professor

Hans Bäppler, having divorced my father in 1946 and also having stood up her second husband, whom she found inadequate because he had only been a sergeant-major in the *Wehrmacht* and not a commissioned officer like her father, prompting *Omi* to tell her to her face, "Ruth, you have gone through life with a fart in your head."

The Bäpplers and the Kemulas became close friends, visiting each other regularly until Wiktor's wife and *Mutti*'s husband died within days. And now Wiktor and my mother were an item again, spending part of the year in Warsaw, part of the year in Frankfurt, and occasionally driving to my house in the Dordogne. In 1985, Wiktor collapsed from a heart attack as he entered Warsaw Cathedral a few minutes late. Still, he died a beautiful death with the *Kyrie* of Mozart's *Requiem* in his ears. This happened more than half a century after he and *Mutti* had met on the day of her confirmation.

After this long excursion to strange romantic features in my parents' life, I must return to my Christmas in *Omi*'s apartment after we had lost our home in an air raid.

Apart from the marzipan, my favorite gift under *Omi*'s pine tree, decorated with silver tinsel shimmering in the light of live candles, was a wooden sleigh. Non-Leipzigers might wonder how we could derive joy from the huge amounts of snow falling on our city in the war years. What winter pleasures could there be in a part of Germany so relentlessly flat that it makes the surface of American breakfast pancakes look like a pleasantly undulated landscape by comparison?

Granted, there was one area of elevation in our city. It was man-made and no more than sixty feet high. We called it *Monte Scherbelino* (debris mount) because it consisted of sixty thousand horse cartloads of rubble and household garbage dumped there between 1887 and 1896. Leipzig's city fathers were so proud of this ridiculous hump that they crowned it with a lookout, which British bombers knocked off in the night of that fateful fourth of December 1943.

However, the mildly elevated *Steinplatz*, a mere five blocks north of *Omi*'s home, provided a little slope for winter sports in our neighborhood. *Steinplatz* was a playground of national fame. It was lined by poplars and a rare species of horse chestnut trees whose bright red blossoms attracted gawkers from all over Germany in springtime.

Steinplatz was a miniature *Monte Scherbelino*, only ten feet high, if that. But for us urchins, it was the Leipzig Alps. Every snowy winter's day, when we weren't at school or being bombed, we pulled our sleighs up to the top of this playground scores of times, threw ourselves on them belly-first, and then whooshed down our slope in less than three seconds.

In retrospect, I still marvel at our steering skills. Not once did I see a child collide with a tram passing our slope that ended on the sidewalk, just short of the tracks on *Bayerische Straße*. In my experience, urban urchins of my generation were remarkably circumspect.

My parents had a less pedestrian notion of relief from the nightly bombing. They preferred traveling to *Schloß Elmau* in the Bavarian Alps, a glamorous resort frequented by Germany's cultured elite of the 1920s and '30s. It featured nightly chamber concerts, ballroom dances, and highbrow lecture series. Some of the world's most celebrated musicians performed in Elmau—usually works by Mozart, Beethoven, and Franz Schubert.

After World War II, Elmau resumed this tradition. It also became a member of the *Leading Hotels in the World* consortium. In 2015,

Chancellor Angela Merkel hosted the G-7 summit in this resort, starring US president Barack Obama.

Omi objected to wasting time and money in this Alpine resort as a way of escaping British bombs. She thought Elmau's principal proprietor odious. His name was Johannes Müller. He was a theologian of the type that gave our Lutheran faith a bad name. In one of his most nauseating statements, Müller called Hitler "a repository and organ of God's reign emitting eternal radiance."

Mutti agreed with her mother. Educated in Germany's best classical high school for girls before Hitler's ascent to power, *Mutti* was well grounded in Lutheran doctrine. She knew how much Luther had thundered against "false preachers and rebellious spirits cooking and brewing . . . the two kingdoms together," meaning the secular realm and Christ's reign of grace: preachers mixing politics and religion do the Devil's work, Luther said.

Mutti considered Johannes Müller's Elmau blend of Christian speculation and National Socialist ideology so obnoxious that she walked out of his second lecture and never returned. My father didn't attend in the first place. He found it more rewarding to deftly pick the brains of senior combat officers on R&R about how the war was going.

I had no wish to leave Leipzig and would have much rather stayed with *Omi* and gone to Heaven with her if that was God's will. But *Vati* and *Mutti* decided otherwise. One evening in January 1944, a cab pulled up at the front door of *Kaiserin-Augusta-Straße* 53 to drive us to the *Hauptbahnhof*, the central station. The cab was a closed, horse-drawn carriage because most privately owned cars were drafted into military service and gasoline was severely rationed. I was allowed to sit next to the coachman while my parents sat behind us in the unheated cabin covered with thick blankets.

We rumbled through black canyons of apartment blocks, some burned out, some badly damaged, some still apparently intact. As we crossed *Augustusplatz*, once one of the largest and most elegant squares in Germany, I saw for the first time the horrific extent of the damage this air raid had caused. I still shudder at the memory of the dark, dead facades of the beautiful classicistic buildings that flanked this plaza on all four sides: the university, the opera, the central post office, and the Fine Arts Museum. It occurred to me that all of them looked like eyeless war victims, just like my father.

I heard the traffic around us but could not see it; I heard the *cluck-cluck-cluck* of horses' hooves, the clutter of the carts and carriages they dragged, and the shrieks and whines of the trolleys that stopped here: the tram lines 10, 11, and 28 on the western side and 14, 16, and doubtless many others on the eastern flank of the square. There was the odd purr of an official limousine and the rattle of a diesel truck. All this was spookily invisible, except for tiny bits of light shining almost imperceptibly from thin slits in headlamps that were otherwise covered.

The *Hauptbahnhof*, a short drive north of the *Augustusplatz*, had been spared serious bomb damage thus far. When we traveled to Bavaria the year before, long-distance trains still had wood-paneled dining cars serving fine meals that could be bought with ration cards. Now the ministry of transport had discontinued dining cars.

Sleeper trains, too, would soon disappear. But for our journey to Bavaria, my father's secretary had still managed to book a spacious suite with three beds on train D-70. It didn't leave Leipzig for Munich

Leipzig's *Hauptbahnhof*, the largest rail station in Europe. From here, Uwe traveled to Bavaria and the Baltic Sea. It was badly bombed but has been beautifully rebuilt.

until 10:34 p.m., giving us time to have supper in a station dining room. *Vati* loved this place because it used to be one of the finest French restaurants before the war in central Germany and still had a fine cuisine and an admirably stocked wine cellar.

With uncharacteristic generosity, *Vati* splurged ration coupons and Reichsmarks, which made *Mutti* happy. She knew that getting him tipsy would make the start of our journey harmonious. *Vati* was in a merry mood as we headed for the Munich-bound train.

As a severely wounded veteran, *Vati* enjoyed special privileges, such as having an elderly railway official assigned to us to guide us through the enormous, blacked-out station to our carriage. I heard the hissing and wheezing of steam engines, the whistles of the station masters, and the rumble of incoming and departing trains, but saw no more than their big silhouettes.

Inside our car, the light was on but window shades and curtains prevented it from radiating out, lest British fighter bombers spot us on our way south. I was first to put on my pajamas and crawl into my bed. *Mutti* sat down by my side. Together we said the Lord's Prayer and asked God to protect *Omi* in her apartment on *Kaiserin-Augusta-Straße*.

We still prayed when the train left Leipzig and gathered speed, whilst *Vati*, filled with wine, stood leaning against the compartment's door with a benign smile, whistling a tune I often heard him sing to himself.

"What was it that *Vati* whistled that night on the train to Munich?" I asked *Mutti* years later.

"'The *Kaiserwalzer*' (Emperor's Waltz) by Johann Strauss," she said. "It was his favorite piece of music."

I fell asleep but was awakened three or four hours later by a weird cacophony of noises. I heard an aircraft engine, machine-gun fire, and the anguished cries of women and children in the neighboring compartments. Our carriage lurched alarmingly, its wheels squealing as the train hurried faster and faster. "Phew, are we speeding!" remarked *Vati*. In wartime Germany, long-distance trains were pulled by steam locomotives that were authorized to travel at eighty miles per hour. This time the engineer took his machine to its limits in an attempt to shirk off the RAF fighter plane or at least make it difficult for its pilot to score a hit.

The door to our compartment flew open.

"*Tiefflieger!* (Strafers!)" yelled the sleeping car attendant. "Everybody drop to the floor!" My mother and I threw ourselves down, but my father didn't.

"You too, *Herr Doktor!*" the attendant shouted. *Vati* ignored him.

I looked up to *Vati*. He lay on his upper bunk with an enigmatic smile I had not noticed on him before but that would haunt me from that moment on. I saw it often in the remaining months of the war; he smiled that way every time the sirens howled to warn us of an impending air raid.

It took me decades to decipher this smile. It conveyed his hope of being delivered from his life in darkness; from his unhappy existence at the side of an exquisite young socialite who did not love him anymore; from his work in the profession he hated; from his marred sense of music from which a French hand grenade had excised the softness of the minor key; from his gloomy daily drudge of which only nightly inebriation and loveless sexual encounters with the nurses in a veterans' clinic, or the wives of friends serving at the front, relieved him temporarily.

In the end, this smile adorned his refined but battle-scarred features as he lay in his coffin after a botched gallbladder operation killed him at age sixty-two. When I saw him for the last time before his sarcophagus was closed, I was certain that this beautiful expression reflected the bliss of being released from his grim fate on earth.

The train screeched to a sudden halt. All we could hear now was the locomotive's sonorous sigh of relief—*chomp-chomp, chomp-chomp*—echoing all around us. The sleeping-car attendant went from compartment to compartment, announcing jubilantly, "We are in a tunnel; you are safe for now! Sleep well! We'll be here for quite a long time." We indeed slept well and long because the train remained stationary in the tunnel for many hours while the damage inflicted on the tracks beyond its southern end by RAF aircraft was being repaired.

"The *Reichsbahn* (national railroad) has placed spare rails all along the major trunk lines," our sleeping car attendant explained. "When enemy bombers damage or destroy the tracks, repair crews move in quickly to fix them."

"Where does the *Reichsbahn* find workmen when every able-bodied German man is at the front?" *Vati* asked.

"These are prisoners of war or foreign laborers from occupied countries," the attendant answered.

We arrived in Nuremberg five hours later. On the track opposite ours stood a train with large red crosses on white fields marking the sides of each car. I described it to *Vati*.

"*Lazarettzug*," he said. "This is a hospital train, bringing wounded soldiers home from the front."

"One man is waving at me with only half an arm," I reported. "The other half is missing. And there's a soldier with his head completely bandaged. How can he look out?"

"He can't," my father answered. "He is probably blind. I looked like that when a train just like that one brought me back to Leipzig from Switzerland in 1917."

"From Switzerland? Why Switzerland?"

"France and Germany exchanged their severely wounded POWs through Switzerland. A French *Lazarettzug* took us to a Swiss station where Red Cross workers transferred us to a German *Lazarettzug* that took us home."

With that, *Vati* fell silent. He did not speak a word until we reached Munich. *Mutti* put her fingers over her lips, signaling me not to interrupt my father's gloomy thoughts with my childish prattle.

In Munich, we transferred to a local train for a two-hour journey to Klais, the rural station closest to *Schloß Elmau*, where I had my most hilarious, and therefore noteworthy, experience of the entire trip. Outside this snow-covered *Bahnhof*, a vehicle, the likes of which I had never seen before, was waiting for us. It was a large, black, luxury limousine with eight leather-covered seats. Perhaps it was a Mercedes, perhaps a Maybach. The trademark by which I could have identified it was no longer there because its entire front, including the engine and the radiator bonnet, had been removed. A drawbar, to which a heavy draft horse was hitched, had taken its place. Like the funnel of the train's locomotive, its nostrils spewed out clouds of warm air.

Schloß Elmau in the Bavarian Alps—today, Germany's most elegant resort: Uwe and his parents spent their winter vacation here after losing their home to Allied bombing.

The coachman was a spectacular character. He wore a big, bushy beard and spoke an almost incomprehensible dialect. A felt hat with a tuft of chamois covered his head, and a *Loden* coat covered his beer belly. His paunch was so copious that it made his legs, in leather breeches, look almost spindly. He gallantly opened the car door for my parents and covered their laps with thick blankets. I rode next to him. The car no longer had a steering wheel. Instead, leather reins coupled driver and horse through two openings in the windshield. These holes were so large that the pong of equine farts filled the inside of our cabin in short intervals all the way up to *Schloß Elmau*.

To me, this immensely entertaining scene was the best part of our winter holiday in the Alps. The next noteworthy and joyful event was my return to *Omi*'s arms a few weeks later, knowing all too well that the stark realities of World War II were awaiting me.

CHAPTER 5

Urchin, the Trolley Terrorist

NONE OF THE NAMES at the door of *Richard-Lehmann-Straße 53* read familiar. The name *Netto* disappeared half a century ago when *Omi* moved into a Protestant retirement home near Frankfurt in West Germany. There is no trace of the family of Otto Grüner, *Omi*'s kindly landlord. *Herr* Grüner occupied a luxurious apartment with a balcony facing south on the belétage—the first floor (second by American counting).

As the head butcher at Leipzig's central slaughterhouse only a few

Uwe at the controls of a 1908 tram, the kind he used to terrorize

blocks up the street, he was a wealthy man. Shortly before World War II broke out, he bought a new, dark-green Mercedes in which he proudly chauffeured *Omi* about. Soon the *Wehrmacht* drafted his

· 85 ·

Mercedes, as it conscripted almost all privately owned automobiles in Germany. The military issued *Herr* Grüner a voucher promising that the Mercedes would be returned to him after victory. "A worthless piece of paper!" he grumbled. Grüner was a realist; he didn't trust the words of the regime he hadn't elected. He also told *Omi* that victory was a false illusion. "Adolf is a car thief!" he whispered into *Omi*'s ear.

When meat rations became scarce, *Herr* Grüner supplied *Omi* with the odd slab of beef liver, or a kidney, or a pig's knuckle for her pea soups, whenever he could. But as the war drew to a close, agents of the Reich food ministry controlled the slaughterhouse so scrupulously that *Herr* Grüner only seldom dared to smuggle out even a little meat for his friends, lest he risk being beheaded by guillotine.

I am eager to see what *Omi*'s apartment looks like now. So, I linger around the front door for a while until a young man comes out. I quickly slip in behind him before the glass door closes again. The beautiful green tiles in its entrance hall are still there.

In my childhood, there were two flats on the right-hand side of the ground floor, one facing south and east while *Omi*'s apartment faced north, east, and west. With a mere five rooms, hers was a modest dwelling by the standards of that time, but it has now been subdivided into two small units. Her and my former bedroom, the living room, the dining room, *Mutti*'s artistic boudoir, and, presumably, our bathroom with its coal-fired copper boiler, were sliced off and regrouped into what must now look like an awkward, linear railroad flat, although that's purely speculative because there was nobody around to let me in.

I would have loved to have seen the bathroom of which I had mixed memories. Was the copper boiler still there? *Omi* used to polish it so lovingly that it shone almost like gold. Of course, she couldn't use it often because coal was strictly rationed. Only on Saturday evenings *Omi* fired up the boiler for bathwater. On all other days, even in the winter, every family member was obliged to take a cold shower at my father's insistence. He claimed that, as compensation for his blindness, nature had fine-tuned his nose to such a degree that the slightest body odor became intolerable for him.

There is nobody home in this larger section of what used to be *Omi*'s home. But I am allowed into the remaining part, which is now a studio apartment consisting of her sunny kitchen and the adjoining room, where my father lived after we were bombed out in 1943. I had disagreeable memories of this room. It was here that *Vati* caned me execution-style until *Omi* stopped him, and it was in that same chamber that I languished for many months with tuberculosis after my parents' divorce in 1946. *Omi* blamed the low food rations in the Soviet zone of occupation—seven hundred calories per day—for my illness, and she was probably right.

The tenant of this studio is Ulrike, a lissome blonde. Born decades after the war, she listens to my childhood reminiscences of her flat as if they were tales from an alien universe.

"Where your front door is now was my grandmother's larder," I say. "It was the main battlefield between her and me in our war of wits over sugar."

"Over sugar?" she replies, shaking her head. "Why would anybody fight over sugar?"

Indeed, why? Belly cramps from hunger were my constant companion in the declining months of the war and even more so afterward, when fruit, vegetables, eggs, and poultry stopped coming from Uncle Alfred, the lord of the Dölzig manor. The German Communist

A beautiful window adorned the staircase in *Omi*'s house.

enforcers of Soviet rule blew up his rococo castle, divided his land among his former farmhands, and confined him to a room in what used to be his gardener's cottage, which they placed under permanent surveillance to stop neighbors from bringing him food. Within two months, dear old Uncle Alfred, a simple-minded man with a kind heart, was dead of starvation.

My craving for food was such that *Omi* soon stopped sending me to the bakery for our weekly bread ration because by the time I came home, I had gnawed off the crust on both sides of the three-pound loaf, reducing it by a third and drenching it with my spittle.

My most effective way to accommodate my yen for carbohydrates was to attack our monthly sugar supply, which *Omi* kept in a mason jar in her larder. In the vain hope of keeping it out of my reach, she placed this jar on the top shelf, just under the ceiling. But I figured out how to get to it. I moved a stool on which she normally sat when peeling potatoes into the larder. On top of the stool I placed our seventeenth-century family Bible, a fat, beautifully illustrated book bound in leather. Together, the stool and the Bible made me just tall enough to get to the sugar, whose surface *Omi* had marked with a rune.

As soon as *Omi* was out, I sneaked into the larder and helped myself to three or more tablespoons of sugar. Then I evened its surface by shaking the jar and marked it with a perfect copy of *Omi*'s rune. In the days that followed, *Omi* designed ever-more intricate runes, which I unfailingly counterfeited. This went on until the jar was less than a quarter full, prompting *Omi* to give me an unforgettable dressing-down.

One day at lunch, after reading the quotidian watchword from her *Losungen*, as the Moravian Daily Texts are called in German, she lowered her lorgnette, gave me a cold, gray-eyed stare, and a let loose a string of Saxon invectives that would have made Luther proud and initiated my abiding love for the lithe beauty of German composite nouns. "*Du schäbiger Gartenzwerg!* (You despicable garden dwarf!) What makes you think that you have a first right on our sugar, while the rest of us must make do with salt!" she hissed, immediately shifting into higher gear. "*Du erbärmlicher Wustzippel!* (You wretched end of a sausage!) *Du nichtsnütziger Stechkahnheizer!* (You useless coal stoker on a punt boat!) *Du Mistpfützenkrebs!* (You dirty crab from a puddle of slurry at the bottom of a dung heap!)"

My straitlaced mother stared into space, consternate, as *Omi* accelerated her attack: "How dare you insult my intelligence, you little fart!" she went on. "I will outfox you anytime! You will never catch up with me! Never! I am smarter than you ever will be. Before you lowered your smelly feet on our sacred Saxon ground, I had been around for almost half a century!"

I pinched my thighs under the table so as not to laugh, but I also saw her point. *Omi's* outburst was so funny it made me love her even more; hence I stopped stealing the family sugar.

Ulrike gives me a perplexed smile. "I have never met a grandmother like that," she says.

"Grannies like mine are an endangered species," I reply. "My grandmother was my mighty fortress in dangerous times. She was the one family member I trusted unconditionally. When she chewed me out or boxed my ears, I understood that this was her way of teaching me to recognize, receive, and give love. My mother and father, for all their other merits, were far too self-involved to do that. I was never really convinced they loved me. With *Omi* I could be absolutely certain."

By now Ulrike and I had moved to the spot where *Omi*'s coal- and gas-fired kitchen stove stood. I regale Ulrike with stories about the wholesome dishes my grandmother created on this massive device: her glorious Christmas goose with red cabbage and potato dumplings, her *Rouladen* (beef rolls), her goulash with potato dumplings, her onion gravy on meager days when we had run out of our meat rations, served with potato dumplings, her rabbit stew, or her sauerbraten with potato dumplings. In short, we had dumplings with almost every meat course.

I describe to Ulrike one of my favorite memories of my childhood: the scene of *Omi* sitting for hours on her stool by the kitchen window grating more potatoes than needed for one family lunch because dumplings are, if anything even more delicious when sliced and fried the following day, perhaps with an egg on top. Often bits of skin from my grandmother's fingers wound up in the dumplings as well. "You cannibals, you are eating my flesh," *Omi* would say with a thin smile, showing us her bandaged right hand.

Ulrike's eyes widen as I launch into a convoluted Saxon narrative about what happened at this stove during the times of famine, a condition that had existed in Germany four decades before her birth. I describe how my grandmother made home-fried potatoes with onions and caraway seeds, browning them with ersatz coffee, a vile-tasting brew made from malt and chicory, instead of with butter, oil, or lard, which we lacked.

Ulrike invites me to sit down on her sofa and regale her with more anecdotes involving my grandmother's stove. We are both staring at the spot where it once stood.

"Right there, Ulrike, I witnessed an explosion that was more memorable than all the bombs detonating around us. It was my grandmother herself who exploded. But that's a long, long, shaggy-dog story. Do you have time, Ulrike? How is your attention span?"

"I love shaggy-dog stories. Go on!" Ulrike commanded.

"Well, first I must introduce you to the terminology of that era of famine," I continue. "As we Germans like to say, '*Die Not macht erfinderisch* (Adversity makes one resourceful).' Marvelous words were born in the 1940s—for example, the verb *fringsen*. It describes, in two syllables, an activity that otherwise would require a whole paragraph to explain."

"I have never heard it."

"The winters were very cold in Germany then, and coal was strictly rationed, especially in the years immediately following the war. So German urchins jumped from railway bridges onto the tenders behind steam locomotives throwing as much coal on the ground as they could. Other brats ran alongside the trains with handcarts to pick up the stolen goods and take them to rendezvous points where they divided up the spoils with the little coal thieves. We called this *fringsen*."

"Why *fringsen*?" asks Ulrike.

"Because Cardinal Josef Frings, then the Roman Catholic archbishop of Cologne, had told the faithful in a sermon that this form of self-defense did not violate the seventh commandment."

"That's really funny!"

"Apropos my grandmother's stove, I must teach you another word born of adversity: *hamstern*. It derives from the noun *Hamster*, the name of the rodent with great stockpiling propensities. In the last years of the war, and in the immediate postwar period, German urbanites ventured to nearby farms in order to trade their family china or silver against victuals." I then tell Ulrike about *Omi*'s *Hamsterfahrten* (stockpiling outings) to Dölkau, a village just beyond the demarcation line between the former kingdom, now free state, of Saxony and the former Prussian province of the same name, which today is known as Saxony-Anhalt.

I often accompanied her on these trips, as did my mother occasionally, although her assignment was really an activity called *organisieren* (to organize), meaning scrounging from famous Leipzig shops whatever they had squirreled away for their regular customers. *Mutti* was very good at that, notably as she, being the quintessential "daddy's girl," felt a great affinity for elegant, elderly gentlemen, such as Dr. Beckmann, the owner of a once-famous department store. Dr. Beckmann was a faithful Roman Catholic with strong anti-Nazi feelings, which he aired liberally when he took *Mutti* on excursions in his two-tone Adler convertible. It was beige and had chocolate-brown wings. That this beautiful automobile was not confiscated—and that Dr. Beckmann was even given a concomitant gasoline ration card—was one mystery that baffled and pleased us at the same time.

My father, on the other hand, neither went *hamstern*, nor did he indulge in *organisieren*, claiming that, as a prosecutor, he must not be caught committing unlawful acts. This excuse infuriated my grandmother. "You contemptible hypocrite," she snarled. "You don't want to be seen carrying food illegally into our house, but you cheerfully eat it when it's put under your nose, don't you?"

Dölkau, *Omi*'s favorite destination, was the home of Hermann and Friedchen Reiche, a good-hearted couple of rural Lutherans with a small farm of barely fifty acres. The Reiches refused to accept any valuables from urban residents who had thus far been spared the fate of being bombed out. "That would be unchristian," they said.

When *Omi* came to see them, they picked her up at the Dölkau station by horse and cart and fed her opulently. The first time I accompanied her, I was made to witness the fate of a chicken from the moment of its death at Friedchen Reiche's hands to its resurrection, roasted, on a plate in front of me. Never squeamish, I watched with fascination as Friedchen caught the hapless bird by hand and decapitated it with an ax, and how it then ran idiotically around the farmyard, seemingly unaware that its head had gone missing, which persuaded me that it had no brain in the first place. This insight, combined with my hunger, freed me from any compunction to eat one of its legs and part of its breast with great gusto at the Reiche's kitchen table.

Before we left, the Reiches filled our rucksacks with homemade liver and blood sausages, a freshly slaughtered rabbit, ham, eggs, pots of goose grease or lard, and whatever vegetables were in season. They also filled two milk cans *Omi* had brought along. On one occasion, the Reiches gave *Omi* seventy pounds of sugar beets before driving her back to the station. I wasn't with her when that happened, which is why she had to carry all this weight from Leipzig's *Hauptbahnhof* to the number 16 trolley line, which stopped outside *Omi*'s home.

Omi's most cumbrous work took place in her kitchen, however. First, she cleaned and skinned the beets; then she cut them into slices, which she boiled in water in three ten-liter aluminum pots. Gradually, an evil smell permeated the entire apartment. It would linger well into the night.

Once the sugar beets were cooked, *Omi* transferred them into burlap bags and poured away the water. Groaning, she squeezed the burlap with her tiny but immensely powerful hands. Beet juice dripped into the now empty pots, which *Omi* put back on the stove, where it would cook on a low flame all night. "By breakfast time it will have thickened to molasses," my grandmother said, as she readied a battery of glass jars into which she intended to transfer this sweet but sticky brown substance the next morning.

"Used as a spread, molasses was our standard source of carbohydrates during the war and in the years of famine that followed," I tell Ulrike.

Exhausted, *Omi* nevertheless prepared a supper of liverwurst and blood sausage sandwiches with pickles for us, downed a generous shot of caraway seed liqueur, a favorite Saxon tipple, said her prayers, and went to sleep, only to be awakened three hours later. We heard a redoubtable thump in the kitchen, followed by my father's screams of agony.

Omi and I jumped out of bed, as did my mother, who slept in a separate room. The kitchen presented a sight I found hugely entertaining. There was *Vati* in his fancy silk pajamas, his feet glued to the sea of semithickened molasses that had spread over the kitchen's dark-red linoleum floor. From his yelps we could tell that he had burns all over the lower part of his body, which earned him no sympathy from my grandmother.

"What happened?" Ulrike asks me, giggling.

"Well, my father had tiptoed into the kitchen in the middle of the night to pinch some of the condensing beet juice. Being blind, he clumsily tipped over two of the three pots, thus depriving the family of most of our molasses ration for the winter."

"What did your grandmother say?" Ulrike asks.

"She flew into a memorable rage."

"You useless turd," she hissed at my father. "You were too snooty to be seen helping me carry sugar beets or clean them, but then you don't mind stealing food from your child's mouth—and your wife's and mine! You nauseate me, Karl-Heinz! Haven't they taught you at cadet school that no gentleman would ever do this?"

"But Clara . . . ," he whimpered.

"Quiet!" she commanded coldly. "Get out of my sight while I clean up this mess, which will take days. The next time you must nibble at something that doesn't belong to you, help yourself to a juicy nurse or two in a veterans' recreation center. Off you go, Karl-Heinz. Tomorrow you're out of here—and please don't hurry back!"

Omi could not stand my father, not so much because he was an ardent philanderer; in that respect, he was no worse than my mother. Both considered the sixth commandment optional, a stance they unfortunately passed on to me, as I now realize in my dotage with remorse.

No, my grandmother had no time for magpies. To her, *Vati* fit the cliché of the selfish, penny-pinching Calvinist; his parsimony was incompatible with her far more generous Lutheran tenets. In short, she considered him ungentlemanly, his fine lineage, good looks, doctoral degree, and respectable position notwithstanding. To be fair to both, *Omi* could not possibly imagine how much my father's blindness and other brain injuries might have changed his character; the condition now known as post-traumatic stress disorder, or PTSD, had not even been identified back then, much less treated. Of course, *Omi* would never slap him the way she often cuffed me and even her daughter; one doesn't hit an eyeless man. She simply threw him out.

My father welcomed his marching orders, as did his superiors at court. His office had burned out in the bombardment of 4 December 1943, so there was no place for him to sit other than in the company of his secretary, at the well-stocked courthouse bar. Moreover, there wasn't anything for him to do. Juvenile delinquency and breach of contract, his two prosecutorial specialties, had nearly ceased to ail big-city life in wartime Germany.

So his boss, the *Oberstaatsanwalt* (district attorney), gladly granted *Vati* an extended leave of absence, and before the next wave of RAF bombers reached Leipzig the following evening, he had boarded, at taxpayers' expense, a first-class compartment of a train to a mountain resort for severely wounded veterans, where comely nurses were all too willing to give comfort to this elegant and witty *Herr Doktor* from Leipzig, just as *Omi* had imagined. By the time he returned, well fed and tanned, he had missed a dozen air raids.

I doubt that Ulrike really gets the point of my tale. How could she? What does a young woman in twenty-first-century Germany know about famine, except that it seems to be some phenomenon peculiarly afflicting black people in Africa? Does she even know what sugar beets are and that molasses is something sweet and edible? I decide to stop troubling her with further musings on this topic.

I look out of her living room window that used to be my grandmother's kitchen window into the backyard. Nothing had changed there since my childhood.

"Look at that garage," I tell Ulrike. "This is where *Herr* Michael kept his delivery truck."

"Who was *Herr* Michael?" she wants to know.

Herr Michael was our grocer. He owned a shop on *Kaiserin-Augusta-Straße*, across the street from this building. He drove a Tempo, a three-wheeled vehicle with a feeble two-stroke engine. My friend Heini, another neighborhood urchin, and I tried to steal it many times. We didn't have its key, but *Herr* Michael never locked his truck's doors and always kept the garage open. We knew how to step on the clutch and put the machine in reverse gear.

One evening, after supper, we pressed the starter, which by itself did not trigger the ignition of the Tempo but made the vehicle hop backward a foot out of the garage. We kept pressing the starter again and again. The Tempo jerked closer and closer to the cast-iron gate separating the courtyard from the sidewalk and the number 14 and 16 tramline tracks. The gate was always locked. In the end, we crashed into the gate with a God-awful thump, loud enough that *Herr* Michael could hear it in his grocery store across the road.

Bending with laughter, Ulrike asks, "How did *Herr* Michael react?"

"He was furious, of course. Many times he had tried in vain to start his truck in the early morning hours to drive it to the *Kohlrabizirkus* (kohlrabi circus), as Leipzigers called their wholesale market because of its architectural style. He couldn't because Heini and I had rendered his battery flat."

Herr Michael knew who the culprits were; all too often he had seen us linger around his garage. This time, he had had enough. He ran across *Kaiserin-Augusta-Straße*, barged through our front door, and came out the other end. We saw him entering the courtyard, so we jumped onto the Tempo's loading space, trying to hurl ourselves over the cast-iron gate.

URCHIN, THE TROLLEY TERRORIST

The gate on which Uwe spiked his privates. His granny predicted that from this moment on, he would sing soprano for the rest of his life. She was wrong: he grew into a baritone.

Heini made it across, but I slipped, spiking my family jewels on one of the portal's evil jags. *Omi* heard my screams, came calmly out of her apartment, and stated coolly, "From now on, you will be a lifelong soprano."

When my mother heard this story later that day, she corrected *Omi* pedantically. "Not soprano! Really now! Uwe is a mezzo-soprano, and if your prognostications are right, he'll remain a mezzo-soprano." In the end, both *Mutti* and *Omi* proved mistaken; when my voice broke a few years later, I turned into a baritone, as most young mezzo-sopranos do.

Inspecting my pierced testes, *Omi* did not compound my agony by boxing my ears, as I fully expected her to. She asked *Herr* Michael

Uwe's caricature of Dr. Heinrich Firnhaber, who treated his testes

to drive me to Dr. Heinrich Firnhaber, our family physician, who had delivered me seven years earlier. Dr. Firnhaber gave me a tetanus shot and sent me home with the stirring information that the serum was taken from a horse. On the way back, I asked *Omi*, "Why did you not box my ears this time?"

"Because God had already punished you. That was enough. I am a fair woman," she answered, chuckling evilly at the thought that when I reached adulthood, I might just chirrup like a girl.

Later she explained to the rest of the family why she had been so lenient in this case: "I wouldn't want a *Schlappschwanz* (wimp) for a grandson. I am glad that Uwe is a real Leipzig *Griewatsch* (urchin), and *Griewatsche* pull pranks."

Omi said this during a row with my father about how I was to be disciplined. Their dispute took place in her living room and became so loud that I had no trouble hearing it next door in my bedroom.

Omi, *Mutti*, and *Vati* punished me in greatly different ways, the distinctions of which were clear to me even at age seven. I never held it against *Omi* when she cuffed me. I knew that this was a normal reaction by my caring grandmother to some folly of mine. It was an expression of love. There was no need for *Omi* to tell me all the time how much she loved me. I just *knew* she did.

My mother hit me rarely, but when she did, it was always erratic and seldom prompted by any particular misdemeanor on my part. I simply ignored her slaps to my face, knowing that they merely reflected some inexplicable hiccup in the narcissistic imperative guiding her behavior.

My father, on the other hand, was a sadist who caned me ritualistically, execution-style. He ordered me to hand him the cane and count out each strike. I often knew how to defend myself, though, boldly taking advantage of his blindness. Once I protected my bottom by cushioning it with exercise books stuck into the back of my trousers. When *Vati* discovered this, he caned me even more harshly.

Next, I shoved the big teddy bear I had inherited from my maternal grandfather between *Vati*'s legs and, lying beside it, screamed in vicarious agony. By the time my father realized that he was brutalizing a Steiff animal and not his son, I had fled his bedroom and run into the kitchen, prompting *Omi* to lay down the law.

"Karl-Heinz," she said coldly, "this is my home and I will not have you turn it into a torture chamber."

It was this incident to which *Omi* referred during the family council about the means of disciplining me. She told my father, "I expect you to remove your cane from my apartment, Karl-Heinz! From now on, I am the only one here permitted to discipline Uwe."

With that she rose, came to our bedroom, and kissed me goodnight.

Ulrike seems bewildered. "I don't get it! You are glorifying that old lady who kept boxing your ears. This is nuts."

"But it does make sense, Ulrike! My grandmother never beat me up; she never dispensed more than one quick slap at a time. To her generation of mature women, cuffing an unruly urchin was meant to be a warning and nothing more. It was as humane as disciplining a puppy by grabbing it by the scruff of its neck and shaking it. We wartime children weren't snowflakes. We had to be tough to make it through nightly bombings, starvation, tapeworms and intestinal helminths, whooping cough, measles, and tuberculosis, through Nazi terror followed by Communist terror, with teachers trying to indoctrinate us against our parents and our Christian faith and pry into our family lives. True, hardly a day went by without *Omi* cuffing me for one act of mischief or another. Once in a while, she even slapped her own daughter, a woman over thirty, especially when she whined. 'In our family, we don't whine,' *Omi* told her. When *Mutti* complained, she received another cuff.

"As far as I was concerned, I didn't mind *Omi*'s punishments because, even at age seven, I knew her to be right. I understood that she wanted to protect me. I loved her all the more for that."

Ulrike looks at me blankly. I wonder if, at this point, she even understands the incongruity of our encounter. Here, in what used to be my grandmother's kitchen, this lovely millennial, altogether a creature of the twenty-first century, tries to make sense of the tales and frame of mind of an old man rooted in the values and standards of the nineteenth century and marked by the bloody revulsions of the twentieth.

Never mind—I resume my narrative.

One day, after a night without an air raid, I rummaged through, with a few urchin friends, the still-smoking ruin of a neighboring apartment building where we built the wartime equivalent of a treehouse from its beams and rubble. We furnished it with the charred remnants of a sofa and a table we created from half-burned timbers.

We leaned back on the sofa, playing homeowners, and popped a bottle of wine we had found in the ruin's basement. Suddenly we were enveloped by a horrific stink, which our experiences from previous air raids had conditioned us to identify as the smell of a putrefying body.

At home, I told *Omi*, "There is a body buried under the rubble. It stinks!" *Omi* immediately telephoned the fire department, then turned around and cuffed me.

"Ouch! Why are you boxing my ears this time, *Omi*?" I asked her.

"You did right in telling me this because corpses must be recovered quickly and buried," she answered, "but I punished you for playing in a ruin. A wall might have collapsed on top of you. You might have unwittingly rekindled the fire and burned to death. A dud bomb could have detonated and torn you to shreds. Uwe, promise never to enter a ruin again! By all means, enjoy monkey business, but don't risk your life. It's horrible enough that you must spend your childhood in a war, but don't make matters worse by acting like an idiot. Promise?"

"I promise, *Omi*!"

"Handshake?"

"Handshake!"

I kept my word. From then on, I eschewed ruins until the war was over, but next my mind focused mischievously on the *Trümmerbahnen*, the narrow-gauge railways with tipping wagons carting away most of the 247 million cubic feet of air-raid rubble from the sites of ten thousand bombed-out houses and twenty-six thousand severely

Much of Leipzig was covered by tracks for rubble trains, which removed the debris of bombed-out buildings. Urchins like Uwe stole them. In the background is the *Thomaskirche*.

damaged buildings. The rest of the rubble was removed by freight trains using Leipzig's extensive network of tramway tracks.

There were three miniature *Trümmerbahn* lines in Leipzig then: the *Nordbahn* in the northern part of the city, the *Zentrumsbahn* in downtown, and the *Südbahn* in the south, where we lived. Observing steam and diesel locomotives pulling long trains of tipping cars on the sidewalk opposite *Omi*'s apartment made my urchin's brain go into high gear. Surely an opportunity for some heavy-duty tomfoolery presented itself here!

I called a powwow of five local urchins on *Steinplatz*—the Leipzig Alps, as we called it—because that was where we sleighed in the winter. All agreed that stealing a locomotive after dark would be a glorious accomplishment, but it would require a lot of vigilance. At the end of each workday, the locomotives would normally be driven to their depot in the city center. Occasionally, one of the diesel engines was left in our neighborhood overnight, but they were of no use to us. Like cars, they could only be started with ignition keys, but I can't recall the engineers ever forgetting to take their keys with them at quitting time.

Steam locomotives were a different matter. Their engines could not be stopped by turning a key, which is why the workmen almost never left one of these marvelous machines behind—almost! One evening after supper, though, there was a frantic knock at *Omi*'s door.

"Uwe, Uwe, *schnell, schnell* (quick, quick)," said Werner, one of our gang of urchins. "We have found a complete rubble train with a steam engine near the corner of *Kronprinzenstraße*. The locomotive is still under steam. It gurgles *harrumph, tshtshtsh, harrumph, tshtshtsh*. We can seize, it, Uwe, I promise!"

We hopped on the running board of a northbound number 16 tram and jumped off four or five blocks later, before the ticket collector could reach us.

There, next to the northern sidewalk of *Bayerische Straße*, it stood: a dark-green locomotive emitting stertorous puffs of smoke from its funnel, just as Werner had said: "*Harrumph, tshtsch, tshtsch, harrumph, tshtsch, tshtsch.*"

"What a beautiful beast! It's alive!" I cried, "What happened here? Where is its engineer?"

"The engineer is an older woman. We have observed her all afternoon until two younger women came in a gray, Opel P4 limousine and drove away with her."

"Arrest?"

"I don't think so," said Werner. "These girls looked more like junior colleagues of the engineer, seeking her advice. They seemed very friendly but in a hurry. Something might have gone wrong with another train. Anyway, they did not return, and now we have a real live steam engine waiting for us to drive it away."

Two more urchins joined us from across the street. The four of us squeezed into the locomotive driver's cabin. Werner seemed to know something about steam locomotives. He opened the fire door.

"Feed her!" he commanded.

I grabbed a shovel and transferred coke from the tender to the firebox. Werner released the brake and opened the throttle. "*Shtsh, shtsh, shtchtchtchtch,*" hissed the engine, and the train lurched forward, more energetically than Werner had intended. Seconds later, it shook violently, derailed, and ground to a halt, making a God-awful metallic noise that drew the attention of the passengers of a passing streetcar to our predicament. This was getting dangerous.

"Let's run!" commanded Werner.

We jumped off the steam locomotive, hopped a southbound trolley, and then slunk nonchalantly into our apartments.

"You are home early," remarked *Omi*.

"Yeah, it was boring out there today," said I. "I don't know why, but it was boring!"

Ulrike threw me a skeptical smile. "Come on now. You didn't really do this during the war, did you?"

"Not during the war, Ulrike! Immediately after the war! During the war, we subjected much more significant vehicles to our pranks."

"Automobiles?"

"No, not automobiles! They didn't interest us wartime children. There were too few private cars around, and those few were usually ridiculous-looking vehicles with bags of wood piled on the roofs, big, ungainly gadgets looking like old-fashioned bath boilers protruding from their trunks, and tubes running over their roofs all the way from the rear to the engine."

"What were those?" asks Ulrike.

"These were limousines converted to run on gasified wood instead of gasoline. They were hideous. If you wanted to drive off at eight o'clock in the morning, you would have to get up at four, often immediately after an air raid, and fire up those stove-like contraptions called pyrolizers. If you were lucky, they would be ready to go four hours later. But even then, you would have to stop after relatively short distances, put more wood in the stove, and make sure not to kill the fire in the process lest you sit there for another four hours, waiting for the pyrolizer to produce more gas."

"So what were your favorite targets?" Ulrike wants to know.

"Trams."

All Leipzig urchins loved trolleys and had their impish fun with them. We knew exactly how to drive streetcars. Whenever possible, we stood to the left of the motorman, observing him at his work. Many different kinds of trams rumbled through Leipzig. They ranged from smart, mahogany-paneled, low-floor tramcars with leather seats, brass doorknobs, and veritable cockpits for the motormen, to hilarious little veteran trolleys the transit authority had recalled from retirement after much of its contemporary rolling stock had been depleted by British and American bombs.

These venerable vehicles, built between 1900 and 1907, were our favorites because they made us laugh. They were short and waddled like ducks on worn-out tracks, their archaic engines emitting howls reminding me of one particularly vexing set of my mother's vocal exercises: *nui-nui-nui-nui-nui*.

Best of all, they had open-air control stands on both ends of each car, which were equipped with old-fashioned trolley poles as current collectors instead of the sturdy, diamond-shaped pantographs on the roofs of more contemporary trams. The top end of each of these poles featured a steel wheel running along the overhead cable, which jumped easily—notably, when prompted to do so by urchins like us.

This was easy. We just pulled on a rope dangling from the top of the pole down to the unmanned rear control stand. Deprived of electricity, the train stopped until the ticket collector, usually a middle-aged woman, had reconnected the rod with the overhead cable, which was a fiddley exercise, giving us ample time to run away.

One day, though, my luck ran out. Heini and I had boarded the tram outside *Herr* Michael's grocery store. It seemed a perfect moment to hit. The driver was a one-legged veteran incapable of running after mischievous young boys. The ticket collector was a stout, middle-aged woman we had seen many times before. We didn't think her capable of scampering after us farther than a few yards.

The train gathered speed up *Kaiserin-Augusta-Straße* in an easterly direction—not high speed, mind you; I doubt it was able to go faster than fifteen miles per hour. We were alone on the rear control stand. Inside the passenger compartment, the ticket collector was walking away from us down the aisle, invalidating tickets with her clipper.

"Now!" shouted Heini, "Don't dawdle!"

I pulled the trolley pole down and immediately let it snap up again, past the overhead cable, while Heini turned the hand brake. Then we jumped.

Heini ran in one direction, I in another, diagonally across *Kaiserin-Augusta-Straße* toward *Omi*'s house. I could hear conflicting noises from the other passengers, some laughing and cheering us on, some taking the side of the ticket collector who, to my horror, had left her tram against her instructions and was now closing in on me with astonishing swiftness.

"I know you, you little horror!" she howled. "You have done this once too often!"

Seconds later, she grabbed my left earlobe and pulled me in the direction of *Omi*'s front door. She rang the bell. *Omi* opened it, wiping her hands on her apron.

"Your grandson here has committed an act of sabotage against my tram," she said in the most vulgar of Leipzig dialects.

"Don't be ridiculous," *Omi* answered. "He pulled a childish prank. That's not sabotage, which would be a capital crime. Surely you know the difference."

"So you are letting him get away with this?"

"Of course, I will discipline him," said *Omi*, "but not until you have kindly let go of my grandson's left earlobe."

I couldn't help giggling when I heard my grandmother address the ticket collector in her vulgar dialect; I never heard her speak like that before.

"Look at him! Look!" the woman shouted, beside herself. "Now your little lout finds this funny!"

"For that, I shall cuff his ears twice," retorted *Omi* coolly, boxing my ears twice.

"So now run back to your tram. You are already late, young lady," my grandmother went on, now in High German. As she shoved me into her apartment, I thought I saw the corners of her mouth twitch.

Ulrike laughs out loud as I rise to take my leave.

"Surely that was the end of your trolley pranks."

"Actually, it wasn't. Our most thrilling lark was yet to come: once Heini, I, Gerhard, and Karl, two of our urchin accomplices, stole an entire trolley train consisting of a power car and two carriages."

I had forgotten this hilarious incident because it was overshadowed by the most traumatic bombardment of Leipzig in World War II a day or two later, an event I shall describe in the next chapter. Still, my mother never forgot this caper. Though not endowed with an exaggerated sense of humor, *Mutti* was so bemused by it that she jotted it down in a notebook I found only recently in her Biedermeier desk, which, after her death in 1991, traveled with all its contents from Frankfurt via New York, Washington, and St. Louis to my current home in Orange County, California.

"Every true Leipzig urchin knew at least theoretically how to operate a trolley," I tell Ulrike. "We were barely tall enough to look over the motorman's console. But except for the very fancy, long-distance tramways, whose pilots sat isolated in their cockpits, there wasn't a streetcar in town without an urchin standing to the left of the driver watching him do his work."

One didn't have to be a genius to figure out how to operate a Leipzig tram. Its driver only had five devices to worry about, and they did not even include a speedometer. With his left hand, he operated the brass power handle, with his right hand the manual brake. There was a funnel through which sand could be dropped onto the right rail on icy days in the winter and an iron pole, which the motorman grabbed before jumping out of his cabin to throw a switch. Finally, there was, close to the driver's right foot, a round metal pedal to ring the warning bell.

We boys were mainly interested in the power handle. In the ten o'clock position, it was in neutral. If the driver moved it clockwise, the tram started to hum a tune in a deep alto. As it moved forward, it went into an ever-higher pitch while gathering tempo. By the time it reached its top speed of less than twenty-five mph, at the handle's six o'clock position, it emitted a shrill tune in a high soprano. As the train approached a stop, the driver threw the handle back to neutral, making the engine hum a soft breather for a second. Gradually, though, as he pulled the lever back toward the seven o'clock position, the trolley's voice darkened to a deep alto—*nawh, naawh, naaawh, naaaawh*—and then silence!

Ever musical, we Leipzig urchins, sons of the city of Johann Sebastian Bach, sang along with the trolley in perfect homophones, ignoring the driver's desperate plea with our rowdy chorus of louts to shut up.

I describe all this to Ulrike in minute detail to set the stage for my narrative of our biggest heist, of which even my mother was proud: the theft of a red-and-yellow tramway train consisting of the power car and two trainers.

"How old were you then?" Ulrike asks with a grin.

"Seven, all four of us: Heini, Gerhard, Karl, and I."

"I bet it required careful planning."

"It did. It took five urchin powwows to fine-tune this adventure."

We met three times at our favorite spot, a park bench in the southeastern corner of *Steinplatz*, our Leipzig Alps, and twice in the courtyard of our elementary school, the *Fünfte Volksschule*, a mere ten-minute walk from my grandmother's home.

There were several factors to ponder: First, when to strike. All four of us agreed that this should occur immediately after an air raid. Second, to plan a prank of this magnitude required intelligence work.

In front of *Omi*'s home, four tram lines crossed: the 14 and the 16 traveling from the northern to the southern outskirts of Leipzig, and the 1 and 22 chugging in a wide circle around the city, one clockwise, the other counterclockwise. Together they provided a rich selection of targets for scallywags like us.

When the sirens sounded the first alarm, all tram drivers were under orders to stop their trains immediately and send their passengers to the potato and coal cellars of nearby houses and then were to run for cover themselves before the second alarm told them what they could already hear and see anyway—namely, that the RAF bombers were directly overhead. The motormen were instructed to take their power handles with them, but this was often impossible, as we urchins had observed with great joy; on older trolleys, the power handles sometimes were hopelessly rusted to their consoles. This was, of course, the prerequisite for the execution of our scheme, for without a power handle, one could not hijack a trolley.

Standing at our front door one evening in late January of 1944, I noticed a woman tram driver entering our air-raid shelter empty-handed. I signaled this important news to Gerhard, Karl, and Heini, who had taken up scouting positions across the street. Then I rushed down to the basement into *Omi*'s arms. That night, the British Lancaster bombers spared our part of town. When the antiaircraft guns fell silent and the first "all clear" was sounded, I ran into the street, knowing that the tram driver and conductors were not allowed to leave the shelter before the second "all clear."

I met Gerhard, Karl, and Heini at a red-and-yellow trolley with two trailers on *Kaiserin-Augusta-Straße*, facing west. There was no rubble on the tracks. The overhead electric cables seemed to be intact. We jumped on board and found the power handle in its place. Immediately to the left of it was a smaller lever with three positions: forward, stop, and reverse.

"You drive, Uwe," Gerhard commanded. I flipped the small lever, and the trolley rumbled forward, causing the four of us to shriek with excitement. No sooner had I driven one block than the sirens wailed the second "all clear."

"Go faster!" Gerhard said. "We must reach *Adolf-Hitler-Straße*."

"Go faster!" Heini shouted now. He had positioned himself by the door, looking behind us. "The tram driver and the conductors are chasing us. They are catching up with us!"

At the intersection of *Kaiserin-Augusta-Straße* and *Adolf-Hitler-Straße* was a track switch, allowing us to turn either right, toward the city center, where this train was supposed to go, or left, in a southerly direction, toward the termini of three different trolley lines: the 10, the 11, and the 28.

"Stop!" commanded Gerhard, grabbing the iron rod to throw the switch.

That done, he screamed, "Go!" and jumped back on board. I gingerly maneuvered the tram into *Adolf-Hitler-Straße* when I heard the angry voice of a woman immediately behind me. Her left hand grabbed the power handle and pulled it to the "stop" position, while her right hand pulled my left ear and dragged me into the street.

Still holding onto my ear, she dragged me back to our house. *Omi* waited outside the door, grim-faced.

"This little lout stole my tram," the driver said.

"That wasn't funny, Uwe," said *Omi*. "That was an ugly, ungentlemanly thing to do!" She gave me a memorable slap and took me inside.

"Why was that not funny, *Omi*?" I asked her.

"Because it is hard enough for tram drivers to do their job in a bombing war. To make it even harder for them is just mindless cruelty," she answered and did not speak to me again for the rest of the day.

And never again did I try to steal a tram for the rest of World War II and beyond.

CHAPTER 6

Theology 101, under Bombs

"Time to leave. I have to see someone in Möckern," I tell Ulrike, getting up.

"Sorry to see you leave," she answers. "I was getting addicted to your stories. What's in Möckern? It is on the opposite side of town!"

"The Leipzig Tramway Museum. I have arranged to meet its chairman, Gerhard Wirthgen. We are contemporaries. When we talked on the telephone, we discovered that we pulled the same pranks in our childhood."

"For example?"

"Placing bombs under streetcars."

"Bombs? You wicked imps!"

"Actually, these were harmless bombs. They were tiny but made a lovely noise."

Placing miniature explosives on tram tracks became fashionable among Leipzig urchins in the waning months of the war when most streetcars no longer had glass windows in their passenger

Fellow imps: Uwe with Gerhard Wirthgen at the controls of an ancient streetcar. Wirthgen, too, pulled pranks on trolleys as a child. Now he is chairman of the Leipzig Tramway Museum.

compartments. They were replaced by cardboard with slits at eye level enabling people to see where they were.

Our urchin gang made these little bombs according to a recipe given to us by August, an older boy who at age fourteen had been drafted as an auxiliary antiaircraft gunner while still at school. We feared for August because we knew that flak emplacements were prime targets of RAF fighter-bombers accompanying the Lancaster squadrons on their raids.

August took us to a drugstore on *Adolf-Hitler-Straße* where, for two *groschen* (twenty pfennigs), we bought two chemicals: a weed-killer called *Unkraut-Ex* and an antibug powder by the name of *Wanzengas*. He showed us how to mix small portions of these substances together

THEOLOGY 101, UNDER BOMBS

and how to place this concoction with an aluminum one-pfennig coin in a gray envelope and double-fold it. Most envelopes sold in the war were made from recycled newspapers and were therefore gray, the ideal color for our purposes because the tram drivers would not see gray devices placed on gray rails, particularly at dusk.

"When our bombs detonated, they made such a racket that the tram's cardboard panels popped out of their window frames, baring the scared faces of the passengers. This was hilarious!"

"Monsters!" said Ulrike.

"I suppose we were! We stuck our tongues out and ran away! Bye now!"

I walk out of her front door, turn right, and go down a few steps to the basement, hoping vaguely that its door is open, allowing me to inspect the venue where I spent so many eerie nights in my childhood. But the door is locked. Still I linger on for a while, wistfully reminiscing about the space beyond, wondering, Why am I feeling so serene? Why am I smiling? Why don't I get goose pimples? Why am I not overwhelmed with dread? Why am I actually filled with a mysterious kind of gratitude Ulrike or anyone much younger than I could not possibly comprehend?

Of course, I shall never forget my foreboding when entering that dank, dark room night after night and often during daytime as well. We used to hurry down there knowing that we might not come up again alive and a slow death by fire or suffocation under tons of rubble could very well be our fate.

Of course, I remember the creepy atmosphere in that room lit by one candle on a wooden table. I remember the bunk beds lining the walls, the foul smell of their straw mattresses, and the frightened faces of neighbors curled up on them, their bodies jerking in anguish to the rhythm of the blockbuster bombs detonating nearby.

Of course, I recall seeing thick smoke and flames seeping into our basement through cracks in the outside walls. I remember how nauseating that smoke stank. It was a biting blend of chemicals, burning beams, and pulverized bricks wedded to the pong of rotting potatoes in the storage spaces behind the bunk beds.

Of course, I recollect worrying. Will I see my playmates again? Will Heini, Gerhard, Karl, and I be able to do mischief in the street as soon as the sirens wail the first "all clear" and then the second? Will we once more harass trolleys? Will we be fit to face up courageously to our rivals, the urchins of *Kantstraße*, one block north of us? Will we play cowboys and Indians or Bedouins at *Tauchscher*, the traditional Leipzig masquerading season at the end of August? Will *Herr* and *Frau* Michael, our greengrocers, be there to open their shop? Will I have a school to go to after the British bombers had finished their nighttime task of destruction and before American planes showed up overhead for their daytime raid?

And yet these are secondary reflections, a mere backdrop to the multilayered gratitude I feel: Naturally, I am thankful that I survived unharmed. But more importantly, I am cognizant of the powerful lessons for life I owe to those nights in the air-raid shelter. To begin with, I learned that in moments of extreme danger, I turn stone cold. I sense no fear, and I don't panic, but I don't turn inert either. I act emotionless and logical, like a robot.

I have no reason to take personal credit in this disposition that proved of great value later in life, for example, during the Vietnam War, which I covered over a period of five years as a combat correspondent. It is a gift I have not earned through any works of mine. Agnostics may call it a gift of nature; as a Christian, I know it to be a gift from God.

Most other lessons I learned by observing human beings while we were being bombed. I learned to act "like a Christian gentleman in calamitous circumstances," as my nineteenth-century grandmother phrased it: to show any signs of fear would have been ungentlemanly. I also learned what kind of a woman I would look for later in life; my wife Gillian has many of the qualities *Omi* possessed. I especially learned that humor, including salacious wit, has its proper place in moments of great danger, including during the prospect of death.

During one bombing episode, *Omi* started singing her favorite hymn, "Abide, O dearest Jesus, / Among us with Thy Grace" (LSB 919 / LBW 263).

Abruptly, she stopped in the middle of the first stanza. She nudged me in the side with her sharp left elbow. Nodding at a stranger whose huge, bald head shone like a halo in the light of our one and only candle, *Omi* whispered, "*Wer früh bürstet, braucht später nicht zu kämmen* (Those who brush early don't have to comb later)." Even urchins knew then that *bürsten* (to brush) was a Saxon synonym for sexual intercourse.

She chuckled and resumed singing her seventeenth-century hymn: "That Satan may not harm us / Nor we to sin give place."

In my wartime school of values, *Omi* was doubtless the principal, although my mother too was an inspiring teacher. As soon as the bombs fell, her least lovable trait—which later in life I identified as narcissism—evaporated, and she became downright selfless. No sooner had sirens sounded the "all clear" than she jumped on her bicycle and pedaled long distances through burning streets. When she returned hours later, she sometimes told us how she had to duck the machine-gun fire of American fighter-bombers trying to pick people off the streets when the US Flying Fortresses had completed their missions. This happened at daytime when the US Army Air Force attacked, not at night when the British bombed us.

"What were you doing cycling off after these air raids?" I asked *Mutti* later.

"Making sure that our friends, relatives, and acquaintances were alright. There was always someone who had lost his home and needed my help."

"Were you not afraid when American planes chased you down the streets?"

"No," she answered. "All I felt was numbness, which enabled me do what I had to do."

I understood what she meant.

My father, on the other hand, had a different priority: getting drunk. At the pre-alert, he opened the windows of his room, even on the coldest winter nights. Then he uncorked his first bottle of wine, finishing it rapidly in time for the full alarm, when he popped his second bottle.

Swaying gaily, he allowed his wife and mother-in-law to drag him to the basement where, for the rest of the evening, he sat smiling and making witty remarks as the bombs fell.

"Why did you get inebriated before most bombardments?" I questioned later in life.

"I put myself in a celebratory mood because I was hoping my life of misery would end that very night. I just hated being blind. I still do."

After *Vati*'s death in 1960, a big smile on his face reminded me of these scenes in my childhood.

The most significant education I owe to the air war was theological, and here *Omi* was my teacher. As soon as she heard the sirens, she slipped into one of her best dresses. In the winter, they were always black, in the summer occasionally dark blue accentuated by small polka dots, thus resembling the habit of some orders of Lutheran deaconesses in Germany. Usually, she wore a choker around her neck and lorgnette on her nose.

One night, we had a brief dialogue that I believe contributed to my decision to enroll in a Lutheran divinity school almost half a century later. There was a bombing lull after the first wave of Lancasters had unloaded their wares on us. We knew that a second wave was underway, but for now there was silence, except for the howls of the fire engines.

"You look very beautiful in your best dress, *Omi*," I complimented her.

"But, *mein Junge*, I dress festively every night. Haven't you noticed?"

"I know, *Omi*, but today you look particularly lovely! Why do you always change clothes for the air raids?"

"Because I might meet the Lord that night."

"But he won't see you in your wonderful dress when you meet him. It will have burned with your body."

"True, but Christ sees us coming before we die."

"Does this mean that dressing up for Jesus will get you into Heaven?"

"Of course not. We won't go to Heaven for what we do in life. We are saved by God's grace for believing that Christ died on the cross for our sins. You will learn this in catechism class soon," she said, stroking my head.

Not until I was a seminarian in Chicago twenty years after *Omi*'s death did I realize that between two waves of RAF attacks on Leipzig she had taught me the 101 of Lutheran theology: Pious deeds don't win you brownie points with God. Instead, you are saved by God's grace alone through faith alone in Christ's redeeming work for you on the cross.

Our discussion continued, however:

"So why do you put on your best dress before you die?" I asked *Omi*.

"To give Christ the honor. That's all, not to win any favors from him."

"But if Jesus sees us coming, why does He not stop us from getting killed?"

"Because his kingdom is not of this world. He said so to Pontius Pilate before his crucifixion."

This was the Lutheran two-kingdoms doctrine in a nutshell. It made sense to me then, when I was a seven-year-old urchin. It made sense when much later I covered the construction of the Berlin Wall, the assassination of President John F. Kennedy, and the Vietnam War as a journalist. It just made sense. I doubt that I would ever have come to believe in a gracious God in adult life had it not been for the recollection of this short discussion with my grandmother between two Lancaster attacks.

A further lesson *Omi* taught me then has not always proved helpful in my later career but enabled me to look at myself in the mirror: don't be afraid to speak your mind!

As four tramway lines crossed close to our front door, we never knew who would run to us for shelter when the first alarm was sounded. Once we had to host Nazi party bureaucrats known as *Goldfasane* (Gold Pheasants) because their brown uniforms were amply decorated with gold tinsel. Their other unattractive mark was that they were obese wimps.

The first bomb hit our neighborhood. Smoke seeped between two cracks in our outer walls and filled the basement. Everybody sat still, except for the Gold Pheasants. They began shivering. They cried out loud. Enormous black rings emerged on their brown shirts in the armpit region.

Omi lowered her lorgnettes, gave the Gold Pheasants a cold stare, and said, "*Meine Herren, meine Herren! Ach nein, Herren sind sie nicht!* (Gentlemen, gentlemen! Ah, no, gentlemen you are not!)

"*Männer also* (Men then)," she continued. "*Ach nein, Männer sind Sie wohl auch nicht!* (No, you don't seem to be men either!)

"Whatever you are, pray, pull yourselves together. You are setting a bad example for my grandson," she concluded. "This is *your* war, not ours! We have nothing against the English, the Americans, the French, the Russians, or the Jews. Kindly spoon out the soup you cooked yourselves!"

She placed her lorgnette back on her nose and resumed singing hymns and praying.

Early next morning, the doorbell rang. I opened the door. Two Gestapo officers in long leather coats walked in asking to see *Frau Netto*.

"She's here but is busy," I replied.

"We must speak to her now!" they said.

"Sorry, but she is saying her prayers."

Our bedroom door was ajar. The Gestapo men could see her sitting by her makeshift house altar. A candle flickered. Amazingly, they waited until *Omi* had finished her devotions. She came out, smiling.

"You are up early!" she said. "How may I help you?"

"You were overheard making seditious remarks last night, *Frau* Netto!"

"Seditious? You don't say!"

"You stand accused of saying that this wasn't your war."

"That's correct," *Omi* said. "I haven't voted for you. I am a monarchist."

Omi thrust her arms forward, wrists together, and said, "If you consider this seditious, so be it! Then you must arrest me. Go and arrest the widow of a major in the royal Saxon army!"

The Gestapo officers turned to go, presumably dreading the prospect of having this loudmouthed monarchist lady appear in a Nazi *Volksgericht* (peoples' court). But *Omi* calmly said, "Wait! I am not through with you!"

"What is it now, Mrs. Netto?" one of the plainclothes policemen asked.

"Explain to me why your Gold Pheasants are so obese. Why don't you send these fat wimps to the Eastern Front? I am told that's where you lose weight fast."

The Gestapo officers left quietly and never returned.

I thought of this wonderful scene with a smile while working on my theological MA thesis in my early fifties. In this thesis, I applied the Lutheran "Theology of Suffering" to the fate of Vietnam veterans based on the prologue of *Letters and Papers from Prison* by

THEOLOGY 101, UNDER BOMBS

Dietrich Bonhoeffer, the Lutheran theologian hanged by the Hitler regime.

"What lies behind the complaint about the dearth of civil courage?" asked Bonhoeffer, who went on to state, "In recent years we have seen a great deal of bravery and self-sacrifice, but civil courage hardly anywhere, even among ourselves."

I imagine how much comfort Bonhoeffer would have got from watching Clara Netto as she sent two Gestapo men packing with just a few intrepid words.

Edvard Munch's masterpiece *The Scream* evokes in Uwe memories of his screaming grandmother after she discovered that her sister had been killed in a blockbuster bomb attack.

CHAPTER 7

The Scream

IN THE EYES OF art aficionados, Edvard Munch's painting *The Scream* illustrates modern man's crisis of existence and the hopelessness of the self. Others see this expressionist masterpiece as a reflection of the diffuse nightmares plaguing Europeans at the beginning of the twentieth century, of those dark visions that soon enough became reality.

Whenever I look at this picture, I remember a cry from my grandmother going through marrow and leg. It was the desperate scream of an otherwise disciplined Christian lady who has never before and never since lost self-control in the presence of the child in her charge, of a woman who would never complain nor shed tears when I was around.

As I linger outside the locked door to our former air-raid shelter, *Omi*'s howl comes back to me as clearly as it did almost three-quarters of a century ago through the fog of war. In truth, it had never left me. It is the most spine-chilling noise I remember from that period.

The scream penetrated the horrific cacophony after the blockbuster attack of 20 February 1944, the most terrifying bombing I experienced. It left me, for more than twenty years, with a tick that, today, would be diagnosed as a symptom of PTSD; I shall return to this later.

At first, I did not even recognize *Omi* as the source of that cry piercing through the dissonance of collapsing buildings, the crackling sound of burning beams crashing down on sidewalks and tram tracks, the wails of fire engines and ambulances, the barking of German antiaircraft guns aiming their barrels futilely at British Lancasters heading home.

I stood in the front door of *Kaiserin-Augusta-Straße* 53 when I saw *Omi* emerging dimly through clouds of smoke, with flames from burning apartment houses and trees seemingly lashing out at her in a way that reminded me of pictures I had seen of the fires engulfing the damned in hell.

The figure staggering toward me hardly resembled the fastidious, dignified *Omi* I knew and loved. Her rich, graying hair looked disheveled, as if she had pulled big patches of it out of her scalp. Her best dress was in tatters. Her shoes were in shreds. One glass of her lorgnette was broken. Her firm little hands were dirty, her fingers bleeding. I embraced her, but she barely noticed me. She screamed and screamed.

I gently pulled *Omi* into the house. *Herr* Grüner, our landlord, happened to be at the front door, inspecting the bomb damage in his elegant art nouveau lobby. As I held *Omi*, he placed his huge butcher's hands warmly on her head, leaving them there until she calmed down enough to tell us what had happened.

Following an inexplicable urge, *Omi* had rushed out of the house immediately after the "all clear," paying only cursory attention to me.

Only the right hand of Martha Persing (left) was found under the rubble of her apartment building after it was bombed. All residents died. She was the sister of Clara Netto, Uwe's *Omi*.

"Martha needs me," she told me. "I must go. I must go! I must hurry. Make yourself a sandwich, Uwe. I won't be long. I must go!"

Martha Persing was the middle sibling of the three Stürtz sisters from Annaberg. Martha was not as zippy, classy, and quick-witted as *Omi*, the eldest of the three. Neither was she as introverted as Irene, her unmarried younger sister who managed the household and was the public companion, though probably not lover, of a former press magnate whose Social Democratic daily newspaper had been shut down by the Nazi regime. For the rest of the war, this courageous publisher lived under constant Gestapo surveillance after a series of arrests on political charges. Auntie Irene was under relentless Gestapo scrutiny as well, as was the publisher's pet parrot, a dangerously verbose bird with a vast vocabulary of slurs and insults.

Omi was very close to Martha, a friendly, plump woman, easy to be with, never prickly, always putting a copious meal in front of her husband Max, a middle-level company manager whom *Omi* found to be *etwas spießig* (a little philistine) while admitting that he was "actually a nice man."

The Persings lived in a comfortable belle epoque apartment building on *Scheffelstraße* 32, a ten-minute walk from *Omi*'s flat. In retrospect, it seems strange that, immediately after a harrowing night of blockbuster bombing, *Omi* ran to her sister's home without taking any interest in the drama that was unraveling in our house while the bombs still fell.

A dud bomb had hit our building and got stuck in the ceiling of the apartment above ours. It didn't detonate but caused an electrical short, triggering a fire, which then quickly spread throughout our neighbors' sitting room. The neighbors were away on vacation, but someone had noticed the flames and the smoke. Nobody had the key to their apartment. My mother foiled a disaster for all of us. With a steel pole, she pierced a hole into the ceiling of *Omi*'s living room. Through this hole she shoved a hose she had found in the cellar and then connected it to our kitchen tap. She proceeded to pump water into the empty flat above. With that, she extinguished the flames before they might have ignited the blockbuster dud, which threatened to bring down the whole building, burying all of us alive.

Omi was oblivious to this. When she arrived at *Scheffelstraße* 32, this four-story belle epoque structure was no longer there. A blockbuster bomb had reduced it to a steaming pile of rubble. Only one tenant survived this calamity by stepping outside the front door for a brief moment to smoke a cigarette. The detonation catapulted him toward the center of the street, saving his life.

All other tenants vanished without a trace, except for one woman's right hand with a wedding band, which rescue crews found a few days later. The ring had the name Max engraved inside, proving that this was Auntie Martha's hand. We later buried this hand in the *Südfriedhof*, Leipzig's largest cemetery, in lieu of Martha and Max Persing's bodies.

I turn my back on the basement door and leave the house where I lived during and after the war. Slowly, I walk to the stop of tram line number 10, which would take me to the streetcar museum in Möckern, but I still have time. I make a small detour to the place where Auntie Martha and Uncle Max were literally atomized by a blockbuster bomb on that twentieth day of February 1944.

At the junction of *Karl-Liebknecht-Straße* and *Scheffelstraße*, I cross the tracks and find myself standing at an empty, triangular area full of rubbish and weeds. Here the house *Scheffelstraße* 32 must have stood. Staring at the dirt and the wild growth in this area, I try to imagine what had happened when *Omi* arrived here and saw a gigantic heap of rubble from which flames were still flickering.

Did this resolute little lady sneak past rescue crews? Did she climb up this pile of debris in search of her sister and brother-in-law? Did she try to move red-hot stones with her bare hands before firemen stopped her? Does this explain the lamentable state of her clothing and the dirt and blood on her hands when I saw her later? We will never know. *Omi* never spoke of this traumatic incident again. She had more important things to do. She told us that she felt called to be, from now on, a substitute mother to Horst and Arndt, her late sister's two sons, both conscripts in the *Wehrmacht*, both serving as enlisted men, although they had graduated from the *Gymnasium*, the classical high school teaching Latin and Greek, which would have qualified them for officer training.

Horst was a corporal stationed in Rumania (now Romania), a pleasant and relatively peaceful assignment after months of heavy combat in North Africa. Arndt was a lance corporal serving at the Eastern Front. It took the military several days to notify them of their parents' deaths and grant them furlough. *Omi* billeted them in her living room.

As I stand at the desolate space where their parents had died, I remember the two young men sitting at our dining table—Horst to my right, Arndt opposite me next to my mother; Horst composed, Arndt in such despair that he could barely keep himself upright, blurting out, "I cannot continue to live without my mother! As soon as I have rejoined my unit I will put in for officer's training."

And so he did. The last thing we heard of Arndt was that he had indeed been commissioned. In that late phase of World War II, a freshly minted German lieutenant had a life expectancy of twelve hours. Arndt perished. His body was never found. He is still listed as missing in action.

Horst, by contrast, died in 2018 at the age of ninety-seven. When he first returned from the war, he trained to be a master druggist and then became a Lutheran pastor. When I last visited him, he told me how he had drawn an entirely different conclusion than his brother from the death of his parents: "It would have been wrong for me to die for Hitler after jumping off death's shovel at least two times in combat. Once, I almost drowned when the troop carrier I was on was sunk in the Mediterranean. Another time, I was in a foxhole near Bengasi when a British plane struck our position. I was buried under a pile of sandbags and almost suffocated but managed to dig myself out. I knew that God must have had a reason for keeping me alive."

Once ordained, Uncle Horst remained in Communist East Germany, insisting that a shepherd must never leave his flock at times of persecution. He and his wife, Ursula, raised three daughters who refused to join the Communist youth organization and attend *Jugendweihe*, a near-compulsory atheist substitute for Confirmation, which meant that they were ineligible for university studies. One of Horst's grandsons, Matthias Pankau, is my godson and a Lutheran pastor as well as the editor and CEO of a confessional, Protestant publishing house, the German equivalent of *Christianity Today*. As his mentor in journalism and in theology, I am thankful that his grandfather had heeded God's calling for him to stay alive rather than die for Hitler. Otherwise, Matthias would not be here.

The tram ride to Möckern is long, giving me time to reflect on that fateful day in 1944. We pass a truck on *Karl-Liebknecht-Straße*, once called *Adolf-Hitler-Straße*. In my warped mind, this vehicle converts into a horse-drawn cart I saw after a blockbuster attack. I shall never forget that cart's cargo: it looked like large, canvas-wrapped sausages, each one-meter long. Later, I overheard a fireman say that this is how victims of firebombs looked: shrunk to precisely one meter.

I recall going to bed and not being able to fall asleep. I heard *Omi* toss and turn and sob, "Martl, my Martl!" I tried to crawl under her duvet to comfort her, but she wouldn't let me. I wanted to say my prayers but at first could not find anything to thank God for after completing the Our Father. Then I remember *Mutti* coming home from her habitual bike ride across Leipzig after every bombing. She staggered through the door, spent.

"What happened, *Mutti*, what happened to your bicycle?"

"Shot to pieces by a low-flying American fighter pilot, but at least he didn't hit me!"

"That's something to be thankful for."

That night I began ripping the skin off the back of my heels. When I woke, my sheets were drenched with blood through and through. I continued to do this in irregular intervals for more than twenty years, sometimes so much so that blood came pouring out of my shoes as I walked through the streets of New York, where I worked as a young newspaper correspondent. Then, suddenly, after two years of married life, this tick was gone for good.

While the number 10 streetcar glides across central Leipzig on its way to Möckern, I recall almost word for word my conversation with *Vati* during a walk along the snowy bank of the Pleiße river two days after the Persings' deaths. I remember it so well because, unlike the usual conversations between a child and a parent, it had the character almost of a deep discussion between grownups tackling ethical questions about war and peace that would haunt me for the rest of my life, for instance, during my assignment as a combat correspondent in Vietnam—questions for which I never found a satisfying answer.

"*Vati*, why do you admire Churchill?" I remember asking him.

"Because he is the only great statesman of our time."

"But Auntie Martha and Uncle Max and all those people whose bodies I saw on horse-drawn carts after air raids were killed on Churchill's orders, weren't they?"

My father fell silent for a few seconds and then whispered, "Our *Luftwaffe* was first to bomb civilian targets in England."

"But *Vati*," I pressed him, "Auntie Martha and Uncle Max never did the English any harm. They didn't even have guns to defend themselves, as you did in World War I!"

"Have you ever heard the proverb '*mitgefangen, mitgehangen* (cling together, swing together)'?"

"Yes, I have heard it from *Omi*, but she called such thinking godless."

"Your *Omi* is right. However, this war has long degraded into godless barbarism. We experience this every night, and the English do too."

"*Vati*, did this blockbuster bomb hit the Persings' home randomly?"

"It might just as well have destroyed the house next door."

"Well then, in that case, some other defenseless people would have died. Does this not make Churchill a barbarian as well?"

For a long time, *Vati* did not utter a word before he said, almost inaudibly, "Oh, my boy, what questions! If only I could answer them!"

Thirteen years later we resumed this discussion. By then, I was a trainee journalist visiting him in his home on the shores of Lake Constance in southern Germany. We sat on his terrace drinking a glass of local wine when he suddenly said, "Do you remember our conversation the day after the Persings were killed?"

"I have never forgotten it."

"Recently I heard, in a radio broadcast, that the aerial bombardments we experienced were the brainchild of a man who was born not far from here, in Baden-Baden. His name was Frederick A. Lindemann. During the war, the British ennobled him, making him Viscount Cherwell. Last month, he died."

"A German, then?"

"Well, he was a British subject of German descent. But he studied in Darmstadt and received his PhD in physics in Berlin. Long before Hitler, he developed a deep hatred for the Germans; I don't know why."

"And what did he have to do with the air raids?"

"He was a professor at Oxford and one of Churchill's closest friends. As Churchill's chief scientific adviser, he developed a strategy designed to undermine the morale of German civilians."

"How was that supposed to work?"

"Lindemann presented Churchill with a memorandum, allegedly based on scientific calculations. Lindemann titled it 'The Dehousing Paper.' It proposed flattening 30 percent of the residential areas of fifty-eight German cities. In 1942, the British war cabinet integrated it into the strategy for its air war against Germany."

"Dehousing! What a grisly word! Sounds like delousing. It gives me goose creeps."

"Me too."

"What was the purpose of this strategy?"

"Lindemann figured that when a sufficient number of civilians, especially industrial workers, was rendered homeless, they would rise against the Nazi tyranny and topple Hitler."

"But that was delusionary. Lindemann clearly did not understand the nature of the totalitarian state we had experienced."

"Indeed!"

"This means that the RAF killed Auntie Martha and Uncle Max deliberately, fulfilling a strategic calculus!"

"Yes," said my father, "killed by a calculus that also leveled Dresden, our most beautiful city, and annihilated 635,000 German civilians, compared with 60,000 Britons killed in Luftwaffe bombardments on the United Kingdom."

"Have the British not committed a sin by doing that?"

"Ah, Uwe, sin is a theological term," my father answered. "As a jurist, I don't think in theological categories like your *Omi*. From the legal perspective, arbitrarily killing 635,000 German civilians, mainly women and children, would probably rank as a war crime because it violated the Geneva Convention protecting noncombatants. But then this war crime is negligible compared with the murder of millions committed by the Nazis in our name. That said, we do have a moral problem here: with their perverse dehousing strategy, the Allies followed us Germans into barbarity. This was humanly understandable but ethically untenable. They lowered themselves to the level of the Nazis."

As the number 10 tram approaches Möckern, my reflections move on to another awkward event that happened to my family the day after a blockbuster bomb had killed Auntie Martha and Uncle Max. *Mutti* was walking through the burning city to make sure that friends and relatives were unharmed. Suddenly, an enormously corpulent woman stopped her in her tracks.

"Ruth!" she said. "Don't you recognize me?"

"I can't say I do. Who are you?"

"I am Ursula, your high-school classmate. Don't you remember me?"

"Now I vaguely remember," *Mutti* answered. "You have changed a lot."

"I guess I have. That's because I am married to a country pastor and have four children. In the countryside, we aren't starving as you are here in the city. We are well fed."

"What brings you to Leipzig, especially after this horrible air raid?" *Mutti* wanted to know.

"I came here to offer you help."

Mutti became apprehensive when she spotted a suspicious pin on the woman's lapel identifying her as a member of the Free Sisterhood of the National Socialist People's Charity—in short, the NSV.

"NSV!" *Mutti* said. "Now I remember. Even before Hitler came to power, you were an ardent National Socialist, the only one in our class. Forgive me, but I don't need any assistance from the NSV. We are a Christian family."

"We too are Christians, Ruth, just German Christians! There is no divergence between us and the NSV. Why not accept my offer of help?"

"How can you help us?" my mother asked warily.

"You have a son. Uwe is his name, isn't it?"

"How did you know that?"

"There are ways to find such things out. How is Uwe? How is he coping with these air raids?"

"Very well until last night, when he lost his grandaunt and granduncle under grisly circumstances, so now he is quite disturbed."

"Send them to our rural parsonage, where he will have no bombs to fear. Where we live, there are no air raids. We have a big garden and plenty of food. You can visit him once a week. Give it a try!"

Thus, I wound up in the countryside. Later, *Omi* expressed deep remorse for having agreed to my evacuation.

"Where was my head?" she moaned. "I was too self-absorbed after Martha's death! I should have recognized the warning signs: the girth of that woman, her NSV lapel pin, and her commitment to the disgusting German Christian heresy. She belonged to the same bunch of *Lumiche* (scalawags) as the pastor of our local St. Andrew's parish, which I am boycotting."

Two days after my mother's encounter with her stout, former classmate, Dr. Beckmann pulled up outside *Omi*'s front door in his beige Adler Triumph cabriolet, a front wheel–driven automobile with elegant brown fenders. Dr. Beckmann was an enigma to *Omi* and me. He was a distinguished Roman Catholic gentleman with graying hair and the owner of H. Hollenkamp & Co., a famous firm of clothiers.

My mother, who has always had an affinity for fatherly friends, told me that this prominent squire had been her favorite, significantly more attractive than any of the others. As a businessman of note, he was also one of the few civilians in Leipzig allowed to own a car and buy gasoline.

Mutti and *Omi* stowed my favorite toys next to me in the Adler's back seat. The journey in this beautiful car was intended to console me a little about my separation from *Omi*, and I must confess that I found it an exhilarating experience; until now I had only traveled in horse-drawn carriages, trams, and railway trains.

I will not give the name of the village I was driven to, nor will I reveal the name of my foster parents, out of respect for their one surviving daughter. Suffice it to say that, in retrospect, this trip seemed to me an excursion from limbo to hell—from the arms of my funny, loving Christian grandmother in a Leipzig air-raid shelter to the brutal coldness of a violent National Socialist family, the likes of which I had never come across before and, thank God, since.

Dr. Beckmann's fancy convertible drove me into mendacious human shallows where only my ration coupons mattered, while I was considered a nuisance—worse still, a miniature relic of the cultured, urban, bourgeois class—whose values, comportment, and manner of speech the Nazis hated as much as the Communists that followed them. But we city-dwellers received better rations than our rural peers, who could live off their farms and gardens, and so I became a useful, albeit unwelcome, addition and contributor to the pastor's household. My ordeal lasted a mere five months, but it took years for me to trust a clergyman again.

The torment started immediately after Dr. Beckmann and my mother had dropped me off at the parsonage. The pastor's wife took all my toys away and gave them to her youngest daughter. I didn't see them again until well after the war, when my mother and Dr. Beckmann literally forced her to relinquish them.

Next, I discovered right away that she had lied when she told my mother, "Uwe will have no bombs to fear." No sooner had I gone to bed in my unheated room than the sirens wailed, just as in Leipzig. Instinctively, I opened the windows to guard against flying glass, just as *Omi* had taught me. From my window I observed a furious bombardment of a nearby airbase whose existence the pastor's wife had withheld from my mother.

It was supposed to be a secret installation where the "miracle weapons" of Luftwaffe chief Hermann Göring were tested—for example, the Messerschmitt ME 262, the world's first fighter jet. Of course, the British and Americans knew about this place and attacked it night after night before my very eyes.

That night, I again pulled the skin off my feet until my sheet was soaked, not only in blood, but also in urine; the blockbuster attack of 24 February 1944 had turned me into a bed-wetter.

When Ursula, the pastor's wife, discovered this mess, she pulled me roughly by the ear down two flights of stairs where her husband awaited me, his cane ready. Screaming like a drill sergeant, he threw me against the wall, thrashed my whole body, finally cuffing my ears with such a force that I feared going deaf.

I limped to school, past the village blacksmith's shop, where I would stop every day in the following months trying to regain my composure while watching the farrier shoe draft horses, a hugely calming scene.

"What do you look like?" asked my head teacher, whom I will call *Herr* Strand, which approximates his real name.

"I have been punished."

"What for? What have you done?"

"I soiled my bed with blood and pee after last night's air raid."

Herr Strand stared at me, aghast. He would have many more opportunities to give me such looks in the months that followed, for the pastor beat me up every day with the flimsiest excuses.

If I am today hugely allergic to the lunatic drivel of the postmodern word police, blame the German Christian pastor for that. Every time I hear gender-leveling gobbledygook on television, I feel jettisoned back to his dining room, which had become my torture chamber.

From the day after my arrival in the parsonage, I was made the whipping boy in a regional conflict within the larger framework of National Socialist terror. It was a class war fought by the philistine lower middle class, from which this pastor and so many of the most virulent National Socialists hailed, against the well-spoken Leipzig patriarchy that had mixed freely with Jews and foreigners for centuries and laced its speech with loanwords from French, the language of Germany's archenemy.

"May I have the sauce, please?" I asked at my first lunch in the parsonage, meaning gravy. The answer was an explosive slap, setting the whole left side of my face aflame.

"Speak German!" barked the pastor. "We call this *Tunke!*"

Another time I referred to my napkin as a *serviette* and was rewarded with a massive thump on the top of my head. "*Mundtuch*, please!" the pastor shrieked, using a revolting, fascist neologism that literally translates into "mouth cloth."

Once the pastor questioned me about the home we had lost in Leipzig on 4 December 1943 and about *Omi*'s apartment where we had found refuge.

"We lived on the third *étage*," I said, meaning third floor (fourth in American terms). "*Omi*'s flat is in the *parterre*," I continued, using the French word for *ground floor*.

Puce in his face, the pastor rose, yanked me out of my chair, and beat me black and blue.

"You were living in the third *Stockwerk*," he thundered, "and your grandmother's home is in the *Erdgeschoß*. Remember that!"

Early one morning, he caught me helping myself to a piece of fruit from the parsonage garden before going to school.

"Why are you doing that?" he asked before pummeling me.

"I am always starving, *Herr Pfarrer*,"[1] I said. "One slice of dry bread without anything on it and an apple cannot still my hunger during the morning break at school."

"Ursula!" he shouted to his wife. "For the rest of the week, you will give Uwe only a slice of bread and no apple to take to school. He is a thief! Who knows how many apples and pears he has already stolen from the garden!"

"Woe to you if you ever tell your mother about your punishments!" the pastor warned me another time. "If you do, I will make you suffer even more."

Once a week, *Mutti* visited me by train from Leipzig. The first time, she saw me sitting on a milestone. I was covered with bruises.

"What has happened to you, Uwe?" she asked. "How did you get all these black and blue spots?"

"I got into a fight in our schoolyard," I lied.

"And why are you so skinny?"

"I am very, very hungry, *Mutti*," I answered, breaking into tears.

She gave me a small stack of ham and liverwurst sandwiches she had brought for herself. I devoured one of the sandwiches and saved

---

1 Roman Catholics and Lutherans in Germany call their pastors *Pfarrer*, which derives from *Pfarr-Herr* (lord of a parish).

the rest for later. But Ursula found these provisions in my room, divided them up among her four children, and handed me over to her husband for a thrashing.

In the end it was *Herr* Strand, my school principal, who saved me. *Herr* Strand was a kindhearted teacher left over from the pre-Nazi era. He also served as organist in the village church that was flanked on its left side by the modest *Kantorenhaus* where *Herr* Strand lived.

The spacious parsonage stood on the right side of the ancient sanctuary behind which lay the graveyard, a busy place where, every other day or so, it seemed, a fallen trooper was laid to rest, and sometimes also a British or American airman shot down during a bombing raid.

There was a difference between the burials of German and enemy soldiers. The German was sent to his grave with a salvo fired off by an honor guard made of old *Volkssturm* warriors; the *Volkssturm* was the home army militia, made up of elderly men. Then a trumpeter played "Good Comrade," the traditional German military lament. There was no salvo or lament for the fallen enemy, but his coffin, too, had to be blessed by the pastor. I don't know how he felt about that.

Sunday services were my best moments during my evacuation because I didn't have to sit with the pastor's family. I always sat next to *Herr* Strand on the organ bench to turn pages and pull stops. When the pastor hailed Hitler from the pulpit as the "Redeemer of Germany," *Herr* Strand whispered into my ear, "He is lying, he is lying, he is betraying our Lord Jesus Christ!"

The first time I heard him say this was on the second Sunday after Easter 1944, three days after the *Führer*'s birthday, which the pastor had celebrated by flying the largest swastika flag in the village from his parsonage.

Although I was only seven-and-a-half years old then, I knew instinctively that I had to keep *Herr* Strand's remark to myself. I understood, even then, that by mentioning it to the pastor or his family, I might have dispatched my teacher to the guillotine.

One day, *Herr* Strand intercepted my mother at the train station, pulled her aside, and whispered, "I am worried about Uwe. He is constantly beaten in the parsonage and does not get enough to eat."

"I brought him some dextrose," my *Mutti* replied.

"Don't give it to Uwe," *Herr* Strand implored her. "He would have to hand it over to the pastor's wife, who will feed it to her own children, not to him. Give it to me. I'll administer it to Uwe every day."

And so I went to *Herr* Strand's house every day to be given three spoons of dextrose until Ursula found us out, just before the summer break. She burst into his kitchen, wrestled the dextrose from his hands, and threatened to report him to the *Gestapo*. That done, she grabbed me by my left ear and pulled me across the church square into the parsonage, where her husband gave me the most excruciating beating I have ever been subjected to in all my life.

But it also marked the finale of my martyrdom in the countryside. A few days later, my vacations began and I was allowed to go home to *Omi* in Leipzig. She stared at me in disbelief. "By God! What do you look like! You are bruised all over and as skinny as a soldier fighting on the eastern front! Now, tell me, what happened to you? Don't be afraid! I must know everything!"

And so I gave her a detailed report of my woes in a German Christian parsonage.

"The swine!" *Omi* said, seething. She immediately called my father and mother from their rooms for a colloquy.

"Tell your parents what happened to you during your evacuation, and don't leave anything out," she commanded, pulling my shirt out of my trousers to show my parents the bruises all over my upper body.

I did. When I had finished, *Omi* turned to my father. "What can we do, Karl-Heinz? A crime has been committed against Uwe. The evidence is overwhelming. Come on, now, Karl-Heinz, you are the prosecutor in the family. What can we do? This must not go unpunished."

"There's nothing we can do for now, Clara," my father answered. "These people are Nazis, we are not. Others suffer even worse under this regime than we." Turning to me, *Vati* said with unaccustomed softness, "In this house, you may say sauce, *serviette*, *étage*, and *parterre* again. I am so sorry that we put you through this."

"Yes, we can do something, Karl-Heinz!" *Omi* interrupted my father. "We can keep Uwe here and not send him back. *Einverstanden* (do you agree), Karl-Heinz, *einverstanden*, Ruth?"

"*Einverstanden*," my parents said in rare unison.

Following that, *Omi* proclaimed her mantra for the rest of the war: "We will either live together or die together. But Uwe stays with us."

This was my happiest moment in World War II.

"We will either live together or die together." I gave this quote to Gillian as we talked about our wartime experiences shortly after our engagement in London in 1962.

"Strange," she answered. "My father said the very same words, admittedly in a different kind of episode, which also began with a scream, though. Isn't it eerie?"

In Gillian's case, this happened four years before my parsonage tribulation, soon after the Luftwaffe had leveled her parents' home in Southampton early in the war. Gillian's father, Sidney Ackers, was a manager at Folland Aircraft Ltd. and a captain in the Home Guard; her mother, Ethel, was a classical musician like my mother, except that Ethel was a pianist.

After losing their house, they decided to evacuate Gillian to relatives in Pennsylvania. The steamer, *City of Benares*, was to bring her and some ninety other children to Canada, whence she would travel by train to her American kin.

"I stood in my blue school uniform on the platform of Southampton station, waiting for the boat train to take me to the ship," Gillian told me. "Suddenly I heard a piercing scream, 'Gillian!' I saw my father in his captain's uniform force himself through the thick crowds on the platform. Just as I was about to board the train, he grabbed me, slung me over his shoulders, and said, 'We will either live together or die together, but I won't let you go.'"

A few days later, on 17 September 1940, the German submarine U-48 sank the *City of Benares* as she was crossing the Atlantic. Of the ninety children on board, seventy-seven drowned. With his decision to either live or die together, this marvelous man had probably saved Gillian's life, just as my *Omi* saved my soul with the identical words four years later. For of this I am certain: another few weeks in that parsonage would have cost me my Lutheran Christian faith.

Only a few years shy of Gillian's and my diamond anniversary, not a day goes by that I don't give thanks for those brave decisions to which we owe our wonderful, long marriage.

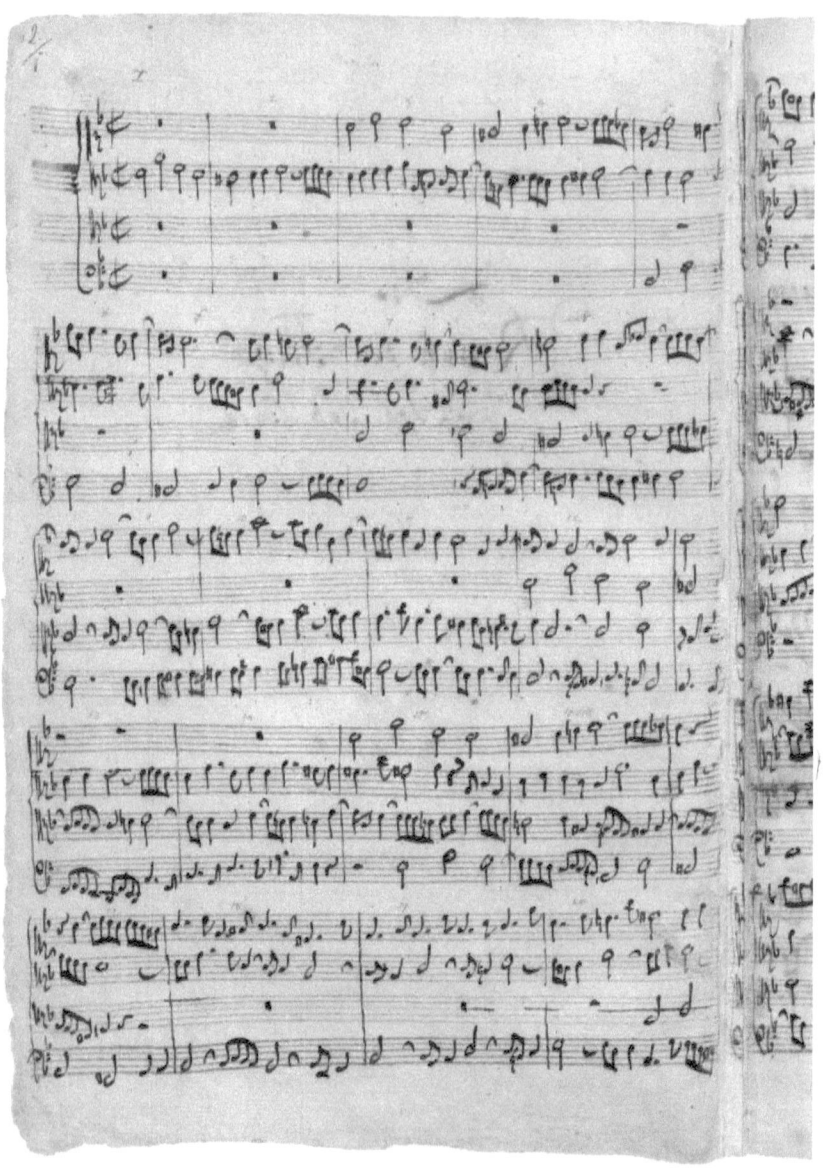

The *Art of the Fugue*, Bach's most abstract work, is Uwe's favorite piece of music. He says it orders his mind and ends writer's block. Our image shows the opening bars of this composition's first contrapunctus in Bach's own writing.

CHAPTER 8

Where Does the Urchin Belong?

I STOP THINKING ABOUT my Aunt Martha's death the minute I meet Gerhard Wirthgen, the chairman of the Leipzig Tramway Museum. We take one look at each other and burst out laughing, recognizing each other as fellow urchins emeriti. Wirthgen is a spritely old gentleman with a mischievous twinkle in his eyes and a wacky, Saxon sense of humor. Like the imps we used to be, we climb into the open-air cockpit of one of the trolleys built before World War I, the ones that waddled like ducks. We fiddle with its lever, pretending to drive it up *Kaiserin-Augusta-Straße*. Together, we hum *"nui-nui-nui-nui-nui,"* the song of these centenarian trams, sounding like my mother's vocal exercises. We vaunt our childhood pranks. We clamber around trams that had survived the war and are now being restored in this museum. For a fleeting moment, I imagine myself reunited with a long-lost member of the urchin gang, with whom I wreaked havoc during bombing lulls, costumed as Indian braves or Bedouins. I am happy.

In the tram back to the city center, I catch myself still smiling and wondering, Why? Whence my blissful mood after stumbling upon another old man? Why does this fill me with as much cheer as my hour with Ulrike in *Omi*'s former kitchen earlier this morning? And why do these feelings resemble the exhilaration I felt when inhaling the bear leek fragrance on my first morning back in Leipzig (chapter 1)? I resolve that I enjoy such moments of bliss because they satisfy my yen to belong somewhere, a need inherent to all human beings, according to the late British philosopher Roger Vernon Scruton. My peripatetic path of life has complicated this desire by never allowing me to affix my natural longing for *Heimat*, as we Germans say, to any specific locality. Up to a point, I concur with the German cultural theorist Peter Sloterdijk, who defined *Heimat* as one's "temporal existence in a nonexile."

My personal nonexile has several facets, starting on the humblest level with my delight of being in the presence of an authentic Leipziger ambling through life with the corners of his mouth turned upward. Gerhard Wirthgen fits this description. But my nonexile also consists of weightier elements. "Your home is where I am," Gillian had decreed early in our marriage. This surely counts as an enormous mansion in my nonexile, I tell myself happily, while brooding during my trolley ride, especially as it seems so palpable after fifty-seven years of marriage at the time of this writing.

Yet *Heimat*, as we Germans understand this word, is not something that begins in adult life. If due to biographical circumstances one's perception of *Heimat* cannot be tied to a specific location, it must be rooted in one's childhood. In 1964, Hannah Arendt told television interviewer Günter Gaus that the German language was her *Heimat*, though not the country of Germany, which under Nazi rule had driven this political philosopher into exile and murdered six million Jews like her.

This makes sense to me. For different reasons than Hannah Arendt, I have lived abroad for most of my life and spoken only in English with Gillian, the person I love most. Yet I count in German and say my daily prayers in my mother tongue. I get annoyed when some imbecile in the Anglo-Saxon media attacks present-day Germany unjustly, as if we were still ruled by Hitler. But I have reserved a special loathing for German television personalities doing injury to the beauty of the German grammar. Their relentless onslaught against the subjunctive 2 that expresses hypothetical situations and their inane substitution of the genitive case with the dative throw me into daily fits of fury.

Language is a mobile kind of *Heimat*. The same applies to classical and, most of all, sacral music, I resolve. I have music in my head all the time. Sometimes it's a hymn, sometimes a passage from a Bach cantata, or a Beethoven symphony, or an organ composition; sometimes it's a jazz tune. This begins when I wake up, continues when I walk and work, and lasts until I fall asleep.

As Leipzig's cityscape glides past my tram window, I remember an exotic experience in downtown Bandar Seri Begawan, the capital of the sultanate of Brunei. It was hot. I was thirsty and gasping for a beer, which of course was not to be found readily in this Islamic country. I fled into the coolness of an empty Chinese Taoist temple, where I stretched out on the marble floor, leaned against a column, and dozed off. When I awoke, I still could not see anybody in this sanctuary, but some kindly soul had arranged a five-course vegetarian meal around my feet during my sleep and placed a porcelain pot of tea by my right arm. At the same time, I heard Bach's organ prelude of *Now Thank We All Our God* in my head.

On the Leipzig trolley, I hum this tune softly, telling myself the following: I owe it to my mother's assiduous musical tuition that I did not feel out of place in a Chinese temple in the Islamic sultanate of Brunei. The same was, of course, true in much direr circumstances, such as house-to-house combat in the Vietnam War. The tunes in my head were more powerful than the *rat-a-tat-tat* of the Vietcong's AK-47 automatic rifles or the bang of a grenade detonating nearby.

Very early in my life, *Mutti* introduced me to this art form, which Luther considered to be the "second most beautiful thing in the world after theology." I was four when she began taking me to the weekly cantata services in the *Thomaskirche*, Bach's church. I was five when I first went with my parents on New Year's Eve to the *Gewandhaus*, Leipzig's famed concert hall, for the traditional general rehearsal of Beethoven's Ninth Symphony. Next, *Mutti* taught me the most abstract genre of music, the fugue, whose mind-ordering effect on me I have already explained in chapter two.

Lately, while working on manuscripts, I have begun listening on YouTube to the last movement of this glorious work, played by the late Canadian pianist Glenn Gould on his Steinway grand. In one arrangement, this movement is called Contrapunctus 19, in another Contrapunctus 14. It lasts twelve minutes and twenty-five seconds and culminates in one of the most dramatic moments of musical history: close to its end, Bach inserts the German notes B-A-C-H (B-A-C-B♭ in English), his signature, into this complex musical structure. He gently weaves his name through the multitude of themes. Then, abruptly, halfway into a bar, the music stops . . . because Bach died in the middle of writing it, leaving his most sophisticated composition unfinished. The silence that follows has a palliative impact on me. I am

Uwe kneels at Bach's tomb in the chancel of Leipzig's *Thomaskirche*, where the composer had been *Kantor*, or musical director, for twenty-seven years and wrote most of his music. People still bring flowers.

at peace. As Arthur Peacocke, an Anglican canon and biochemist, once said, "The Holy Spirit has dictated the *Art of the Fugue* into Bach's plume."

The trolley arrives at the *Hauptbahnhof*, where almost all thirteen Leipzig tramlines meet. I disembark and saunter west along a wide and busy street called *Tröndlinring*. My destination is the apartment of my godson, Matthias Pankau, and his Bulgarian wife, Svetlana. They have invited me for supper, but it is still only the middle of the afternoon, which gives me time to meander about and to resume my reflections about my venue-less *Heimat*.

I decide that, along with my love of language and music, my Lutheran faith is probably the most significant feature of what I consider my home. It was *Omi* who had planted the seeds of faith in me. In chapter 6, I described how she had taught me, in simple terms, the unique Lutheran doctrine of a Christian's dual citizenship in God's two distinct realms: on the one hand, Christ's eternal kingdom of grace, where I am a redeemed sinner, and on the other hand, the finite, sinful world where, like all Christians, I have a divine calling to serve my neighbor lovingly in all my assorted vocations, such as a son, a grandson, an elementary school pupil, or just, given the circumstances at the time, a little boy in an air-raid shelter back then and as a husband and journalist in adult life.

Walking on that sunny afternoon through the center of my pulsating hometown, I recollect a poignant scene in *Omi*'s basement during a break between two waves of Lancaster attacks.

"*Omi*," I asked her, "how do I serve my neighbor with bombs detonating all around us?"

"Let's begin with the most obvious: *I* am your neighbor," said *Omi*. "You serve me by giving me your love and allowing me to love you."

"Yes, *Omi*."

"Then there are all these other people in this basement. They too are your neighbors," *Omi* continued. "You serve them by being strong and fearless, by not flinching, and by smiling even when this house shakes and flames appear through cracks in the wall. You take their fear away by not showing any fear yourself."

Boom. A bomb exploded close by.

"How, *Omi*, how?"

"Make me laugh with your stories about your latest pranks on trams," she suggested.

I did. We laughed. I noticed our neighbors looking at us, the corners of their mouths slowly turning upward.

Boom, boom! More bombs detonated. Undaunted, *Omi* and I continued our banter about duck-like trolleys and laughed until our neighbors laughed with us.

My reflections about this unforgettable episode in our coal cellar must have put an infectious smile on my face, for as I walk from the *Hauptbahnhof* to Matthias's apartment, other pedestrians smile back at me. I remind myself that, during that air raid, *Omi* had taught me the rudiments of the Lutheran doctrine of vocation, which decades later would become so central to my theological thinking.

Two blocks from Matthias's home, I pause outside the Reformed Church. Ironically, this magnificent Renaissance Revival building, and not one of Leipzig's many Lutheran sanctuaries, was my spiritual home in my childhood. My home baptism—on New Year's Eve 1936 by Pastor Bachmann—is still listed in the register of this congregation, as are the home baptisms of many other infants, including the children of the composer Felix Mendelssohn-Batholdy.

I have glad memories of this church where I was catechized after my return from the odious pro-Nazi parsonage in the Leipzig countryside. I felt secure in the care of upright and kindly women of French, Swiss, Dutch, and northwest German descent. They weren't as funny and brash as my *Omi* but were rather more reserved, like *Omama*, my paternal grandmother, who worshipped here. Still, after five traumatic months in the home of a rural Lutheran pastor who beat me up for using French loan words and called Hitler our redeemer, I found their straightforward and honest ministrations a great relief.

I first went to classes at the Reformed Church in the autumn of 1944. Its sanctuary was a ruin then, its windows dead and black. The building had burned down in the same air raid of 4 December 1943 that had also destroyed our home. Classes and services were held in the parish hall next door, where congregants seemed traumatized by the death of their pastor Hugo Specht, his wife, their five children, and a female parish worker, all of whom had perished in that attack.

Pastor Specht was the successor of Rev. Bachmann who had christened me on New Year's Eve 1936. Staring at his beautifully rebuilt church, I ponder my father's perplexing character. To my knowledge, he never attended its services in my childhood. Yet he knew that the congregation, which had called Specht as its shepherd, was not infested by the pro-Nazi German Christian ideology. *Vati*'s explicit statement still rings in my ears: "Uwe will be safe in this church," and for once *Omi* agreed with her son-in-law, whom she otherwise did not like.

The Reformed Church exemplified the parallel universes that families belonging to the old German elites inhabited in the Third Reich; they created small oases surrounded by a desert of unspeakable evil,

The Reformed Church where Uwe was catechized: This neoclassicist [Renaissance Revival] building won the first prize at the Paris World Fair in 1889. Its congregation resisted the pro-Nazi doctrine.

of which I could not help being aware, even at the age of eight. While these oases might not have represented the brave forms of opposition, comparable to the bravery of those who went to the gallows for resisting Hitler, they did help keep our civilization alive. This does explain, in part, the emergence of Germany as a healthy democracy relatively soon after the war.

Hitler, his cohorts, and their politics were banned from many of these little fortresses. Only on one dramatic occasion, which I shall describe later, did my father let me into his political thinking during the war by discussing Nazi crimes in my presence. By the time I returned to Leipzig from my ordeal in the pro-Nazi parsonage in the summer of 1944, my parents' marriage had gravely deteriorated, but on one point they did concur, exemplified by a phrase from my mother: "Uwe must be raised in such a way that he will carry on our culture into the next generation—or die with it, if that is what God wants."

Hence *Vati*, *Mutti*, and *Omi* agreed on these key points: I was to be brought up as an informed Christian with a sense of history, a good understanding of music and language, and proper manners, particularly at the dinner table. As *Omi* said, "By all means be an urchin, speak dialect with your friends, if you must, but not at home; at home you will only speak *Hochdeutsch* and act like a gentleman."

My father was especially stern about my table manners, even though he could not see whether I held my knife properly and sat upright at the table. "We live in dreadful times," he said, "but this does not give us license to act dreadfully."

Trying to keep up bourgeois standards in the collapsing Third Reich was a surreal act of make-believe. We pretended it was peacetime and ignored the scarcity of food. We celebrated our meals even when we had little more to eat than swede stew or potatoes browned with a coffee substitute made from barley malt. We ate by candlelight, even at lunchtime, because our window frames were almost always filled with cardboard rather than glass and because the electricity was shut off following Allied attacks on power stations.

Vati insisted that I remain standing until *Omi*, *Mutti*, and female guests were seated and that I help the lady to my right into her chair. He told me to keep my wrists on the rim of the table but not the rest of my arms, and definitely not my elbows! It was at the rim of the table that I was to fold my hands at the beginning of the meal, while *Omi* said Luther's Common Table Prayer: "Come, Lord Jesus, be our guest, and let these gifts to us be blessed."

We ate in modest portions from *Omi*'s Meissen china, using her silverware. I had to keep quiet until my father asked me about my day, which he always did. I was allowed to regale my family with descriptions of my pranks but was never allowed to whine, least of all about the cold in *Omi*'s apartment in the winter when we lacked coal; after all, all of us suffered. And there was another taboo to be observed at our dining table: though Germany was at war, the regime's enemies were not ours. My father was an ardent Anglophile and my mother was a Francophile in addition to loving the Italians, the Spaniards, the Poles, and the Russians for their music. For her part, *Omi* loved all human beings as fellow children of God, regardless of their passports. To *Omi*, any kind of bigotry was un-Christian, ungentlemanly, and hence unacceptable.

Once the meal was over, *Vati* ordered me to help *Omi* carry the used chinaware and cutlery back into the kitchen and wash them up because we no longer had a maid.

I recall these meals, and my father's rigor, with gratitude as I stand outside the Reformed Church, his former parish. These might seem a bagatelle to cherish, yet I uphold them as touching attempts to maintain standards of civilization in profoundly uncivilized times. I decide that this, too, ranks alongside language, music, and faith as a significant element of my temporal existence in a nonexile—my ever-present awareness of belonging somewhere.

CHAPTER 9

Auschwitz and Superstition

I WALK ON. IT normally takes less than three minutes to get from the Reformed Church to Matthias's apartment, but this time I amble along very slowly, conjuring up in my head images spanning more than seven decades.

I cross the tram tracks on *Pfaffendorfer Straße*, a street about which I have a plethora of childhood reminiscences—some funny, some sweet, and some unbearable. The first building on this street has undergone a curious mutation. In my childhood, it was a hotel and restaurant called *Alte Burg* (Old Fortress). It was the venue of my most agreeable experiences during the brief American occupation of Leipzig immediately after the war. I shall return to that later in this volume.

Now the building, *Pfaffendorfer Straße* 1, houses an establishment with the arcane name *Dunkelrestaurant Mondschein* (Darkness Restaurant Moonshine—later I shall learn that in this place guests dine in darkness, and of course I wonder, Why would anyone want to pay a lot of money for eating something that cannot be seen?).

Staring at this odd eatery takes me back to a most hilarious gastronomic event in my professional life. On assignment by a German magazine, Gillian and I traveled by train from Boston's Back Bay Station to Oakland, California, in the fall of 1989. When the *Lakeshore Limited* pulled out of Boston, the headwaiter of the dining car walked through the carriages, asking passengers to place their orders. Gillian chose Dover sole, while I opted for a Cornish game hen.

We went to the restaurant car just shortly after we arrived in Springfield, Massachusetts. Suddenly, the lights went off because, we were told, a US mail wagon was being hitched to this long-distance train. The headwaiter said, "Ladies and gentlemen, tonight you will be dining in darkness, like in a fine restaurant. Unfortunately, we forgot the candles. But this is just as well. At least you won't see what's put in front of you."

Gillian's dish was easily identifiable. It stank of rotten fish. My plate, by contrast, featured a perplexing object. It was round and impenetrable. In the low-wattage light of the Springfield station lantern shining dimly through the window, it looked alarmingly like a roasted boxing glove.

When the ceiling lights of the train went on again, the steely-eyed Yank at the table across the aisle from me said reproachfully, "You didn't finish your plate!"

"I am not in the habit of eating boxing gloves," I explained.

"Let me see," he said, moving next to me on my banquette. He futilely stabbed the tough, round thing with both my knife and my fork and then concluded, "Not a boxing glove!"

"What then?"

"Calloused chicken."

Pfaffendorfer Straße 11: this beautiful belle epoque building was the Netto family homestead until Uwe's grandfather sold it after he lost his fortune in the 1929 Wall Street crash. The Nettos moved into an apartment, which they later ceded to their daughter. Uwe was born there.

"?"

"In this country, chickens are not usually raised in old-fashioned barnyards but tightly squeezed together in windowless batteries where they develop callouses all over their bodies. One of these poor birds ended up dead on your plate tonight."

Gillian and I left the dining car with empty stomachs but a marvelous yarn to tell for decades.

Again, my mind is wandering. I stare down *Pfaffendorfer Straße* looking for other familiar points of interest. A few steps up the street stands house number 11, the Netto family's homestead for three generations. Impoverished by the effects of the 1929 Wall Street crash, my grandfather sold this beautiful five-story structure and rented the apartment on *Sophienplatz 6*, where I came into the world seven years later.

When I was little, I sauntered often along *Pfaffendorfer Straße*. It runs from the city center north to Gohlis, Leipzig's smartest neighborhood, with elegant villas and apartment blocks that were, mysteriously, spared heavy bombing. "The Allies saved Gohlis to house occupation officers later," *Omi* mused.

And indeed, Gohlis became a ghetto of Soviet majors, colonels, and generals and their families in June of 1945. These were sturdy men with broad epaulets on their shoulders and clunky jackboots on their feet.

Most Leipzigers feared Red Army soldiers, and often for good reason. I, on the other hand, had a lovely encounter with one of them. He was a major who had a pretty black-haired daughter named Natasha. She became the first love of my life when we were both ten. She spoke perfect German and sent me amorous verses by the Bohemian lyricist Rainer Maria Rilke (1875–1926). In a later chapter, I shall return to our innocent romance, which ended tragically.

Farther up the street is the entrance to the Leipzig Zoo, one of the oldest and most celebrated in Europe, housing some eight thousand species. It was famous for breeding primates and great cats. More than 2,300 lions were born there in the twentieth century, including Jackie, the third in a succession of lions roaring at cinema audiences watching Metro-Goldwyn-Mayer films. The zoo shipped him to Hollywood in 1928.

Wandering through the zoo, hand in hand with Uncle Carl, was a most agreeable memory of my childhood. Dr. Carl Ballin, a noted chemist and pharmacologist, was not a relative. I can't even recall how our families had become such close friends; perhaps Carl Ballin and my father were fraternity brothers. At any rate, next to *Omi*, he was my favorite adult when I was a child, notably because of his screwy wit.

Uncle Carl hailed from a patrician Hamburg family. A stocky man with black hair and sharp features, his looks didn't match his Nordic personality. As we strolled through the zoo, he taught me *Plattdeutsch*, the earthy vernacular of northern Germany. Unlike my father, who loathed the Saxon dialect, Uncle Carl treasured it because it appealed to his sense of the farcical. Blending Saxon and *Plattdeutsch* terms, he coined absurdities that "lifted laughter up from the basement," as the saying went in the last months toward the end of the war.

The German word for the art of pointedly corny phrases that, though silly, were mirthful and solacing, is *kalauern* (its associated noun is *der Kalauer*). It would require pages to explain it to an English-speaking audience, killing its humor in the process. But I will try to give my readers at least one example.

One day, Uncle Carl and I happened past the hyena cage, where two of its residents trotted about in opposite corners of their residence.

"*Uwe, weisst Du, warum Hyänen Hyänen heißen?* (Do you know why hyenas are called hyenas?)" asked Uncle Carl.

"*Nein*, Uncle Carl."

"*Na, hie eene und da eene* (Well, one here and one there)," he replied, pointing at the two animals ignoring each other's presence (in German, a double *ee* or an *ä* is pronounced *aye*).

One such quip might seem wacky, but Uncle Carl's genius showed in creating such puns wholesale by the hundreds in our many visits to the zoo, sending me off with a welcome wealth of material with which to amuse *Omi* in our bomb shelter.

The high point of my walks with Carl was always a visit to the cage of *Affen-Eva*, a remarkably accomplished chimp, and her young daughter. Thanks to Uncle Carl's friendship with the director of this fifty-seven-acre wildlife park, we were allowed access to Eva's home in the presence of her keeper. She greeted us at her front door with a handshake and then guided us to her living room, where the coffee table was laid for five people. She gestured for us to sit down, gracefully placed a biscuit or piece of cake on our plates, and poured some dark liquid from her porcelain coffee pot into our cups as well as hers, her daughter's, and her keeper's.

Of course, this was no real coffee, a beverage strictly rationed for us humans and clearly not available to apes. But it was sweet and tasty; I suspect it was some kind of juice, most likely from sugar beets. We talked to her and she responded by caressing my arm or Uncle Carl's. When we rose to bid her farewell, Eva gave me a hairy hug and elegantly shook my uncle's right hand.

Later, Eva's name came up in an episode that could only have happened in Leipzig. To the right of the zoo's entrance stands the *Kongresshalle* (congress hall), a *Jugendstil* (art nouveau) structure with a large auditorium where the *Gewandhaus* Orchestra played for many decades after its original home, the *Gewandhaus*, had gone up in flames in the air raid of 4 December 1943.

Pausing at length outside *Dunkelrestaurant Mondschein*, I can't help thinking of that lovely building where, one evening in late 1944, I observed the weird airs and graces of a musical high-flyer. Like Uncle Carl and his wife, my parents held a subscription to *Kongresshalle* concerts. Most of the time, my father did not attend, preferring instead to be with his fraternity brothers or with the comely nurses of veterans' hospitals, as *Omi* surmised.

So on one of our concert-going days, it happened that Professor Wilhelm Furtwängler was the guest conductor. Furtwängler, the musical director of the Berlin Philharmonic, was reputed to be a supercilious performer whose haughty manner was particularly irksome at a time when the rest of Germany, and indeed the world, was vacillating between fears of hunger, bombs, and annihilation.

The program included Beethoven's Fourth and Fifth Symphonies. *Mutti*, the Ballins, and I sat in a row, each with the piano reduction of these two works on our laps, ready to be read during the performance, as was common among aficionados of classical music back then.

Furtwängler ascended the conductor's stand. His slender body bent forward, presenting his receding hairline to the admiring public, which applauded. With the slouchy zing of his extraordinarily long arms, he made the orchestra launch into the slow adagio at the beginning of the Fourth Symphony's first movement, which Leonard Bernstein would later describe as "a mysterious introduction, which hovers around minor nodes."

Then *boom, bang, thump!* After the first few bars, the audience was ripped out of its pensive torpor. What happened? Ah! The good professor had a hissy fit. Angrily, he slammed his baton to the ground and stomped off the stage, puce in the face. We looked at each other, puzzled. Then we waited, and waited, and waited. Would the maestro reappear, we wondered? More importantly, will the concert be over in time for Leipzig's music lovers to be home before the next bombardment?

Half an hour passed, maybe longer. Then a *Gewandhaus* officer, in a once-black suit that had seen better days, came out and explained that during rehearsals, Furtwängler had concluded that the acoustics in the *Kongresshalle* were flawed. He ordered a movable wall to be placed at the rear of the stage to improve the sound quality. But this contraption had gone missing on the day of the actual concert. Would the audience please be patient for this oversight to be rectified?

Ten minutes later, Furtwängler reappeared, conducted the orchestra with discernible listlessness, and did not waste much time taking applause. He was in too much of a hurry to catch the last train to Berlin, the unloved capital.

Leaving the building, Uncle Carl looked scandalized. He pointed wistfully to the closed gates of the zoo and said, "Agh, Uwe, how I wish we could say hello to our Eva now! This monkey has better manners than our musical star!"

The Ballins lived in a luxurious apartment in *Springerstraße*, a side street just a tad north of the zoo. My parents and I went there often for lunch—and to keep warm in the winter—because Uncle Carl's part of town had municipal heating that, mysteriously, was never hit in the air war; we, on the other hand, had to make do with coal and coke, which were tightly rationed.

At lunch at the Ballins one Sunday in late 1944, I became privy to the most gruesome news during the entire war, more gruesome than anything I had heard and seen thus far. Lowering his voice, Uncle Carl said to my father, "Karl-Heinz, two Gestapo officers have led away my new secretary."

"With what excuse?" *Vati* whispered.

"She is a quarter Jewish."

"Do you know where they have taken her to?" my father wanted to know.

"Theresienstadt, I believe," said Uncle Carl, referring to a concentration camp in the German Protectorate of Bohemia and Moravia set up by the SS for German, Austrian, Dutch, and Danish Jews. It looked like a comfortable showpiece camp designed to pass muster with International Red Cross inspectors, although its inmates were also murdered later.

"Thank God, at least not Auschwitz," *Vati* replied under his breath.

"What's Auschwitz, *Vati*?" I asked him softly.

He placed his right forefinger on his lips and then pointed to the four walls. I already knew this gesture. It meant "Careful! The walls have ears."

In the last six months of the war, I often guided my blind father during his excursions through the *Connewitzer Holz*, a wood not far from *Omi*'s flat. We wandered along the Pleiße, a river that was in a sad state due to the efflux from nearby chemical combines. Its water was dark purple and devoid of any life, with huge clouds of foam floating on top of it. This became, if anything, even worse under the Communist regime after the war but has been reversed since Germany's reunification in 1990; now the Pleiße is once again rich in fish and safe for swimming.

Back then, the river stank unbearably, which is why very few people chose it as a destination for their promenades. This was just fine for *Vati* and his fellow alumni of the Thuringia Leipzig student fraternity, for it allowed them to discuss politics without risk of being overheard. It was for this reason, too, that he asked me to take him there shortly after our hushed conversation in Uncle Carl's home.

I had realized for some time that my family, notably *Vati* and *Omi*, did not at all support the Hitler dictatorship, although, for my protection, they rarely hinted at this in my presence. This is not to claim that they were flaming members of the Resistance, like the theologian Dietrich Bonhoeffer, or Col. Count Claus von Stauffenberg (who tried to assassinate Hitler), or Leipzig's former mayor, Carl Goerdeler, who would have become German chancellor had the coup attempt by Stauffenberg and other senior officers succeeded.

Still, *Vati* participated in something called the "poor man's resistance" then. It involved hearing the broadcasts of *Feindsender* (enemy stations), such as the BBC. *Vati* did this several times per day throughout the war. While not exactly a display of martyrdom, it was nonetheless considered a felony punishable by death or long years in prison doing hard labor. My father also regularly tuned into *Radio Beromünster*, a Swiss station.

Since I am writing this chapter at the apex of the 2020 COVID-19 pandemic that, inexplicably, produced a worldwide run on toilet paper, I'm prompted to recount another form of "poor man's resistance" that, because it was almost unperilous, was relatively widespread. Like so many things German, it had a distinctly anal character.

I discovered this by happenstance during my evacuation to the pro-Nazi parsonage in the Leipzig hinterland. One Sunday after lunch in the early spring of 1944, I went to play in the garden while the pastor and his wife retired to their bedroom for a nap. When I went inside a couple of hours later, I found the reverend and his family assembled in their drawing room, doing what most Germans had to do back then, although not necessarily on Sunday afternoons: they cut up newspapers to aid in their lavatorial needs.

AUSCHWITZ AND SUPERSTITION

Yet, unlike in other households, including *Omi*'s, pages from the uniformly pro-Nazi press were, in this rectory, not simply divided into eighths; instead, the pastor, his wife, and his children meticulously snipped out all photographs showing Hitler and any other Nazi grandees in order to rescue them from having their faces soiled.

I couldn't wait to tell *Omi* my discovery when I was at last allowed to come home to Leipzig. *Omi* laughed and said, "These people did the opposite of what most people are doing."

"What do you mean, *Omi*?"

"Go to the bathroom and take a look."

I did. And there, hanging from a hook next to the toilet bowl, were scores of newspaper clippings, many of them showing prominently the *Führer* and his leading cohorts. This reminded me at once of the most popular of German invectives, which even Goethe used in his drama *Götz von Berlichingen*: "*Leck' mich am Arsch!*" I leave it to my readers to find an appropriate translation if they are so inclined.

To get back to my family's politics, I received the first clear hint at their views when the pro-Nazi newspaper, *Leipziger Neueste Nachrichten*, reported jubilantly that a month after the 20 July 1944 coup attempt, former mayor Goerdeler had been arrested in Marienwerder in West Prussia (now Kwidzyn, Poland). The gloom at our breakfast table that morning was so thick you could cut it with a knife.

"Who was Carl Goerdeler?" I asked.

"He was our mayor before you were born," said *Omi*. "He was a fine, fine Christian man."

"Did you ever meet him?"

"Yes," answered *Vati* curtly, and that was that, end of discussion.

It later turned out that while Goerdeler was on the run, the bookkeeper Helene Schwärzel recognized him in a café and denounced him to the Gestapo. He was hanged on 2 February 1945. Schwärzel pocketed a reward of one million marks for her betrayal. After the war, a West German court sentenced her to six years in prison and hard labor.

Eight members of Goerdeler's family were sent to concentration camps, including his daughter Dr. Marianne Meyer-Krahmer who, decades later, became a close friend of mine and a major source of information for my doctoral thesis, which dealt with the Lutheran roots of Goerdeler's specific form of resistance.

This dissertation, titled *The Fabricated Luther* in English, was published in four languages.[1] In it I show that, contrary to a widely held bias against him, Luther had developed a down-to-earth theology about resistance against tyrannical authority. Luther said, "It only makes sense that where prince, king, or lord goes mad, he must be deposed and arrested . . . because he is no longer rational." However, Luther also insisted that tyrants be toppled in an orderly, rational fashion and not by an insurrection, lest there be chaos leading to a rule of the rabble. "The mob possesses no reason," Luther insisted. Therefore, he considered it imperative that, before a despot is deposed, a worthy replacement must stand ready to assume his succession.

Poring over Luther's and Goerdeler's statements on this resistance, Marianne Meyer-Krahmer discovered that her father's and Luther's thoughts were identical. Thinking like Luther, Goerdeler tried to avoid an insurgence against Hitler, including a mutiny resulting from

---

1 For further reading on this subject, see Uwe Siemon-Netto, *The Fabricated Luther* (St. Louis: Concordia, 2007).

AUSCHWITZ AND SUPERSTITION

an assassination. Instead, he started scheming, well before World War II, to have Hitler arrested by the *Wehrmacht* and brought to trial before a German court. It was only after this had become impossible (following the *Wehrmacht*'s quick conquest of Poland and France) that Goerdeler agreed reluctantly—and against his better judgment—to participate in the plot to have the *Führer* killed.

May I be forgiven for this verbal detour! Where was I? Ah yes, of course, I was about to report on my walk with my father along the banks of the dirty Pleiße river a few days after I had heard about the Auschwitz concentration camp in Uncle Carl's apartment when I was eight.

"Look around—is there anybody?" my father asked me.

"No, *Vati*, we are alone."

"Will you promise not to tell anybody what I am about to tell you? This is a matter of life and death, Uwe! Promise!"

"I promise, *Vati*."

"At Uncle Carl's, you asked me about Auschwitz," *Vati* went on.

"Yes! What is Auschwitz, *Vati*?"

"It is a concentration camp where they kill the Jews by the hundreds of thousands."

"Kill the Jews?"

"Yes—men, women, and children."

"But why, *Vati*, why?"

"Because they are criminals," my father replied.

"Who? The Jews?"

"No, Uwe, the Jews are no criminals. Those who govern us are."

I often heard adults claim, after the war, that they hadn't known anything about the Holocaust during the war. Perhaps they spoke the truth. Perhaps they were too scared to ask questions about the fate of their Jewish neighbors and friends after they had been led away. Perhaps they closed their eyes and ears to it because any discussion of the genocide in the Third Reich carried a mandatory death sentence.

But I am here to say that I knew about this when I was eight years old.

Before my father died in 1960, I asked him about the source of his information.

"I had it from the husbands and sons of prominent Leipzig families who were officers at the eastern front. On home leave, they told us in secrecy that they had seen SS men murder Jews and that a mass slaughter happened in Auschwitz."

"So by telling you this they put their lives at risk? What brave young men!"

"Yes, they were! Perhaps they weren't supermartyrs, but brave they were, given they knew they would be tortured and beheaded or hanged if found out," *Vati* said.

After my long musings about what I had experienced on *Pfaffendorfer Straße* many decades ago, I finally turn my back to the "Restaurant of Darkness," electing instead to subject myself to the remarkable cooking skills of my godson, Matthias, although, even there, the past is catching up with me.

Matthias is a journalist specializing in religious affairs. He tells me that in our once solidly Lutheran hometown, only 14 percent of the five hundred thousand residents are still members of a Christian church. "At the same time," he adds, "esotericism is spreading like wildfire, especially the invocation of the souls of the deceased."

"That's not new, Matthias," I say. "It was worse when my *Omi* was born in 1888. She practiced her own kind of esotericism."

"Your *Omi*?"

"Yes, she acted as a medium during the war," I say, laughing.

"Ha-ha! Your ever-so-Lutheran *Omi* a medium? My grandfather's godmother a medium? The mother of my mother's godmother and grandmother of my godfather—she was a medium? You are making that up!"

"I am not making this up," I say, enjoying this immensely because it is one of my greatest *Omi* stories. To tell it, though, I must reach back into the nineteenth century, when Hippolyte Léon Denizard Rivail (1804–69) grew rich and famous after concocting a modern form of spiritism that has survived to this day.

A mathematics teacher, better known by his pen name of Allan Kardec, Rivail taught that the souls of the departed, while in transit from one body to the next, may be appealed to by the living for guidance. He memorialized this teaching in *Le Livre des Esprits* (*The Spirits Book*, 1857), which became a world bestseller and is still in print today. In France, he became such a celebrity that Emperor Napoleon III invited him to his court for philosophical discussions. But his beliefs spread to the comfortable classes throughout Western Europe, and North and South America, where it became chic to hire a medium and hold séances.

"One such medium was my *Omi*," I inform Matthias. Clara and Charlotte, his teenage daughters, became all ears.

Several times a month, *Omi* invited groups of society ladies from her neighborhood for a little hocus-pocus in her living room. It began in the afternoon when there was no bombing and ended before the air raids started after dark. The large, round sitting room table was moved to the tiled stove so that all might stay warm. Fresh, large lard cakes, called *Speckkuchen*, were served, a Leipzig specialty for which, I presume, *Omi* had collected ration coupons from her guests. Our family baker had delivered these salty delicacies hot for this occasion. They vaguely resembled pizzas but were a much heartier fare. The old ladies washed them down with *Allasch*, a liqueur made from caraway seeds.

Once they were fed and merry, I was ordered to take the porcelain and silverware to the kitchen; *Mutti*, whose sense of humor was restricted, found it beneath her dignity to participate in this charade, and my father wasn't home anyway, presumably killing bottles of Riesling with his fraternity brothers.

I, on the other hand, would not miss this for one moment. I knew my *Omi*: what was about to transpire would be fun. I lit incense left over from Christmas and placed candles around the room, including one on the table, before switching off the electric lights. *Omi* looked splendid, all dressed in black, her hair pinned on high, with a black fedora stuck on top of it, and a velvet choker around her neck. A lorgnette glittering merrily in the candlelight crowned her nose. *Omi*, my stern *Omi*, had even put on dark lipstick. What a foreboding sight she was!

In a deep voice, she began to mumble her self-composed mantra: "*Aumm, aummm, guam zä glaum, gaum zä glaum, aumm, aumm, aumm.*" Slowly the table began to vibrate.

Omi sat there stiffly, but I noticed that she moved the table from below with her knee. I pinched her gently on her thigh.

"*Omi*, that's you," I whispered and in return had my ears boxed so swiftly that the other ladies didn't even notice it.

"Shush. Don't chase away the spirit!" she whispered.

AUSCHWITZ AND SUPERSTITION

"Yes, *Omi*!"

Omi continued more forcefully now, "*Aumm, aumm,* ladies, we have a visitor from a higher world. Ask your questions!"

"Will the war be over soon?" one wanted to know.

The table wobbled vigorously in the affirmative.

"Will there be an air raid tonight?" asked another.

The table dithered, just shaking a little.

"Will my Florian come home from the front in one piece?"

The table remained still.

"Sorry, ladies, this ghost has moved on," said *Omi*, "but I sense another one is on his way. Be patient!"

And so the séance continued for two more hours until my grandmother announced, "Ladies, we have to stop it here. I want you to be home in time for the next alarm, in case there is one."

The ladies rose and praised *Omi* for her spiritual prowess and for her good contacts in the afterworld. I helped them into their overcoats and kissed their hands to bid them farewell. They had already reached the building's foyer when *Omi* called them back.

"*Gaum zä glaum, glaum zä glaum,*" she repeated, holding her hips, laughing and then repeating herself in High German: "*Kaum zu glauben!* (Hard to believe!)"

The other ladies stared at her, perplexed.

"You foolish geese!" *Omi* shouted. "Tonight we could all be dead. *Kaum zu glauben* (hard to believe) that in this situation you put more faith in a wooden piece of furniture than in our Lord and Savior Jesus Christ."

There was a moment's silence. Then all of them burst out laughing. After all, they were all good Leipzig Lutherans; they took this as a well-deserved practical joke.

CHAPTER 10

Of Bravery, Bach, and the Guillotine

IT IS STILL DAYLIGHT when I leave Matthias's apartment after dinner. I decide not to return to my hotel by tram but instead walk back, crossing the whole downtown area of Leipzig—one square kilometer, to be precise. At its very center is the *Markt*, which, a millennium ago, was the cradle of my hometown's international trade fair, the oldest in the world.

I crossed this square often when I was a child, either to visit Uncle Carl or *Omi*'s younger sister Irene who lived in Gohlis or to take my father's borrowed Braille books by handcart back to the library for the blind and get new ones. Occasionally I made a detour to a colony of allotment gardens, scrounging for some apples, pears, gooseberries, tomatoes, carrots, leeks, or cucumbers. I never had anything to offer the amateur gardeners in return, other than cheering them up with funny tales of my life as an urchin and his granny in times of war. Sometimes this worked, sometimes it didn't, but when it did, *Omi* applauded my entrepreneurship, regardless of what I brought home.

On this balmy evening, hundreds of people are milling about the *Markt* where, in one corner, an ensemble plays baroque music and, in another, a jazz band plays Dixieland. The square is filled with sausage and sandwich stands and lined with open-air restaurants, all of which are full.

I sit down at the last empty table on the terrace of the restaurant *Weinstock* and order a quarter liter of Pinot Noir from the *Schloß Proschwitz* winery in Meissen, which my father liked very much because its excellent wine was produced by the Princes zur Lippe, members of the ruling dynasty of the region in northwestern Germany where *Vati* was born.

Under Communist rule, this property on the banks of the Elbe river was collectivized and, not surprisingly, turned out an unpalatable hooch. But after the fall of Communism, *Schloß Proschwitz* was handed back to the current Prinz zur Lippe, who improved his wines to the precious and expensive tipple in my glass.

I let my gaze wander around the *Markt*. It was brutally damaged in the air war, but some of its most important baroque and renaissance buildings have been beautifully restored, notably the fifteenth-century former town hall (*Altes Rathaus*) that occupies the square's whole eastern flank.

A few yards from where I am sitting once stood, when I was little, the victory monument. It was erected in the memory of the Franco-German war of 1870 to 1871, which Saxony won on the coattails of Prussia. It was a statue of King Albert I in a hero's pose. Albert, our penultimate sovereign, signed Grandfather Netto's commission as second lieutenant, a document I still possess. The sculpture was

Saxons used to hate this monument to the 1813 Battle of the Nations because it glorifies Napoleon's defeat—and theirs, as they were allied with France against Prussia.

melted down after Germany's surrender in 1945, and nobody in my family or among our friends seemed to mourn it.

"Let's face it, King Albert, in the pose of a warlord, was too ridiculous for words," remarked Uncle Carl when we walked past the empty space where this edifice stood. "Granted, Saxons are cultured, musical, and often very funny, but military prowess is not one of their attributes. They have no appetite for a fight but rather talk themselves out of conflicts."

This statement resonated with me. I fit Uncle Carl's description of our tribe quite well. In my postwar years at boarding school, I baffled my classmates by my ability to escape every dorm brawl unscathed; they concluded that they and I fought with different weapons—they used their fists, and I let lethal verbiage pour from what they called my "ominous lower lip." So they nicknamed me Uwe Omsen.

Omi agreed with Uncle Carl that the notion of a Saxon hero was an oxymoron. "Your grandfather was a toy soldier," she once told me to the annoyance of her daughter, adding, "but he was *my* toy soldier." Her opinion on this subject was formed by observing her husband prancing around in his elegant uniforms and strutting off to do a little swaggering in his officer's club.

"The funny thing is," *Omi* continued, "that when he actually went into combat, after decades of peacetime bluster, he proved less than heroic. As soon as the French aimed their machine gun at his company, he fell off his horse and browned his underwear." My mother, the quintessential daddy's daughter, inevitably shed tears of wrath at *Omi*'s display of disrespect for the military intrepidness of her late husband. I, of course, enjoyed all this immensely.

To prove her point (and also to annoy her earnest daughter), *Omi* loved to tell the malicious story of her husband's usefulness to his sovereign at the inauguration of the clunky *Völkerschlachtdenkmal* in 1913, one century after the Battle of the Nations for which it was named. *Omi* called this 230-foot granite monstrosity, which was not far from her home, a Prussian cuckoo's egg imposed on our Saxon city.

Kaiser Wilhelm II traveled from Berlin to Leipzig to partake in this festive event, as did princes and other leaders from all European nations that had defeated Napoleon in this battle, which spelled the beginning of the end of Bonaparte's rule over most of Europe. On inauguration day, all stood there in their magnificent dress uniforms, waiting. And they waited, and waited, and waited, unable to do anything until Frederick Augustus III, our benign king of Saxony, showed up. He was, after all, the sovereign in Leipzig, this was his territory, and he was "very, very late!" as *Omi* related with a glee. "This was a deliberate slight."

"Why would the king slight the kaiser, *Omi*?" I asked her.

"Because we Saxons had nothing to celebrate. Like the French, we were the losers of this war, having sided with Napoleon. As a punishment, the Prussians took our king, Frederick Augustus I, prisoner and stole half of our kingdom, including such famous Saxon cities as Wittenberg, Halle, and Magdeburg."

I have to rely on *Omi* for the veracity of the subsequent part of this story, which might be apocryphal—who knows? But I'll tell it, nonetheless. It is just too funny to be excluded from this narrative.

According to *Omi*, Frederick Augustus III arrived one hour late in his convertible; I presume it was a Horch or an Audi, for these two luxury cars were built in his kingdom. If *Omi* is to be believed, the king stopped in front of my grandfather, who was sitting on his horse at the head of the infantrymen under his command.

"*Netto, wo kann ich denn hier mal scheißen?* (Where can I have a s—t around here?)" His Majesty loudly asked my grandfather, then a captain.

"Latrine over there, Your Majesty," my grandfather replied snappily, pointing the king in the proper direction, according to *Omi*.

"So to the latrine His Majesty went with measured steps, unfolding his copy of *Leipziger Neueste Nachrichten*. He sat down and studied his newspaper leisurely," *Omi* went on. "When finished, he came out and declared loudly in broad Saxon, while still buttoning his tunic, '*So, un' nu gann där Googlmoosch beginn'n!* (So, and now the tomfoolery may start!)'"

With that, military bands struck up "*Den König segne Gott*" (God Bless the King), the Saxon anthem that sounded exactly like "God Save the King." Next, they played "*Heil Dir im Siegerkranz*" (Hail to Thee in the Crown of Victory), the German national anthem in imperial days. Again, its melody was the same as the British anthem.

"What happened then?" I asked *Omi*.

"After speeches were given, marches played, and glasses clanked, your grandfather galloped home as fast as he could, stormed my parlor and howled, 'Clara, Clara.' He said, 'You won't believe what the king has done now!'"

As I said, this might or might not have been so—but at least I believe it was. Who would doubt the truthfulness of my Lutheran *Omi*? With this lovely anecdote in mind, I look over to the pretty baroque building at the southern end of the square. This is the *Königshaus*, or the house of the king, where the Saxon sovereign and members of his family stayed when they visited Leipzig.

Uwe with wine on the market square in front of the former town hall, a Renaissance building. For one thousand years, this plaza has been the venue of the world's oldest international trade fair.

On its balcony—this I know from Uncle Carl—stood Napoleon after losing the Battle of Leipzig, shouting to the large crowd of weeping Saxons on the square below him, *"Adieu mes braves Saxons!"* Then the French emperor rushed out of town, never to be seen again.

I order a second quarter liter of Prince zur Lippe's Pinot Noir and begin scanning the square clockwise. Over to the left of me, on the corner of *Katharinenstraße*, I notice a Communist-era apartment building, an eyesore that has replaced an enchanting renaissance house, which was bombed out in 1943. I remember passing its ruin with *Mutti* late one afternoon in the fall of 1944, when she suddenly started singing softly,

Ei! wie schmeckt der Coffee süße.

Ah! How sweet the coffee tastes.

"Frankly, *Mutti*, I prefer cocoa," I told her.

"*Dummkopf!* This was the first line of an aria of a secular cantata Bach had written for, and performed at, Gottfried Zimmermann's coffee house, which used to be in this building," she said.

"What? Was Bach a coffee house musician? How was it possible to perform a cantata in such a Saxon chatterbox, *Mutti*? The noise in such a place must have been deafening!"

"Bach played everywhere in Leipzig, including over there in front of the *Königshaus*, when members of the royal family were present. He had to make some extra money because his salary from the city paid him only one hundred *Thalers* (dollars) a year for his work as musical director at all three major Leipzig churches. As for the babble in this coffee house, it presumably stopped after the first line in the cantata's opening recitativo:

"*Schweigt stille, plaudert nicht!*

Be quiet, don't chatter!"

We both laughed, and then, staring at the black ruin of the place where Johann Sebastian Bach earned his pocket money, *Mutti* intoned softly the soprano aria of this secular masterpiece. She sang,

Ei! Wie schmeckt der Coffee süße,
Lieblicher als tausend Küsse,
Milder als Muskatenwein.
Coffee, coffee muß ich haben,
Und wenn jemand mich will laben,
Ach, so schenkt mir Coffee ein!

Ah, how sweet the coffee tastes,
Lovelier than a thousand kisses,
Smoother than muscatel wine.
Coffee, I must have coffee,
And if anyone wants to give me a treat,
Oh, just give me some coffee!

This is one of my most heartwarming childhood memories of my mother. On this eerily bomb-scarred square that was surrounded by black ruins, she sang just for me, smiling; there was nobody else around to hear her. The deep impression this scene left with me might be hard to appreciate for contemporary readers who are fortunate enough never to have experienced war on their own soil, but to me, hearing my mother sing smilingly a comical aria of a tongue-in-cheek cantata by Germany's greatest composer was a brief but powerful flash of light in the darkness surrounding us.

That night, the bombings resumed.

I pay my bill and set out crossing the square but stop at its very center, where a large mosaic is sunk into the cobblestone surface of the *Markt*. It shows the coat of arms of the city of Leipzig: a black lion standing upright in a gold field, seemingly trying to claw his way out; behind him are two blue vertical stripes. Leipzig had borrowed this image in the fifteenth century from the Wettin family, one of Europe's oldest dynasties, to which not only the ruling counts, dukes, electors, and kings of Saxony belonged, but also at various times the monarchs of Belgium, Bulgaria, Portugal, Poland, and Great Britain. Queen Elizabeth II, whose family name is now Windsor, is just as much a leaf on the Wettin genealogical tree as was our beloved Friedrich August III.

I am shocked that people are now traipsing mindlessly over this mosaic. No true Leipziger would have done so in my childhood. I once asked *Vati*, during one of our walks, about the origins of this tradition.

"The coat of arms on this square marks the spot where, in previous centuries, convicts were burned at the stake, quartered, or beheaded," he said.

"Yuck," I said.

"Well, they didn't think so in earlier centuries," my father continued. "School children were given the day off to watch these events. Before, during, and after an execution, the *Thomanerchor* sang Lutheran hymns, and two pastors prayed for the condemned man, provided he had confessed and repented."

"Yuck, yuck, yuck!"

"Thank God, Saxony abolished capital punishment in the middle of the nineteenth century—one of the first nations in Europe. Saxony had civilized rulers. But when Germany was unified in 1871, after the Franco-Prussian war, the death penalty was reinstated because the imperial government in Berlin imposed it on the entire country. But as long as Saxony had kings, they automatically commuted every death sentence to life in prison. Unfortunately, that happened in the Weimar Republic, when we had no more kings."

The topic of the death penalty came up again when *Vati* and I watched an elderly man cleaning the front yard of his house.

"*Herr Doktor, Herr Doktor!*" he exclaimed excitedly. "I am honored to see you outside my home. Why don't you come in for a glass of wine?"

"I'm *Herr* Gebhardt," he continued. "Come in, come in, meet my wife."

I felt my father stiffen. "Thank you for your kind invitation, but I must rush for an important appointment."

"Who was that, *Vati*?" I asked him as we walked on.

"A man of sinister fame in Leipzig. He is a descendant of the local dynasty of executioners."

"Did you know him personally?"

"No, but of course he knows me. I am the only blind prosecutor in Germany."

Ten years later, when I was a grown young man, I returned to this conversation.

"Have you ever been at an execution, *Vati*?"

"Yes, in the 1920s, when I was a young rookie in the prosecutor's office, my boss, the district attorney, deputized me to Dresden where a murderer was to be guillotined. I guess he thought that, as a blind man, I would not have to see this unpleasant event. So why not send me?"

"And?"

"This experience was so grisly that it turned me into an ardent opponent of capital punishment."

"But you didn't see anything, *Vati*!"

"No, but I have sensed the whole horror of an execution: the macabre ritual, the smell of sweat, and then of blood, the screams of the frightened felon when he first saw the guillotine, the hiss of the blade as it rushed down to his neck, the crunch as it chopped off the head, the thump as it fell into a basket, and the swoosh of his blood. I decided there and then: this is not how a civilized society should punish its criminals."

"But he was a murderer, *Vati*—has he not forfeited his right to life?"

"Human dignity can never be forfeited. Besides, I was thinking less of the condemned man's dignity; he was dead within a split second. I am referring to the dignity of the eyewitnesses: the prosecutor, the chaplain, the prison employees, ultimately even the executioner himself and his team. All of these men had their dignity violated by this. It has marked me for the rest of my life, and the lives of some of the others presumably too."

"Knowing this, what went through your mind when you heard about the Nazi crimes?"

"Shame, shame, shame, twelve years of shame. I voted for the Liberal Party, not for Hitler. I had forebodings that this would happen when Hitler was elected. I was ashamed that I did not do much to oppose his rule. Perhaps I should have done more, even as a blind man. This would, of course, have endangered you and your mother, your *Omi*, and my own parents. But I suppose that's how all too many Germans talk today."

With my father's words resonating in my head, I quietly continue my walk back to my hotel. Tomorrow I will retrace my last steps in Nazi Germany and my first steps of my life in occupied Leipzig.

CHAPTER 11

Urchin's Defeats

THE NEXT MORNING, I decide to pay *Omi*'s former home one more visit because I want to refresh my memory of the last days of the war, Germany's surrender and the occupation of Leipzig. By this time in my narrative, we are a little more than half a year away from the occupation of Leipzig, first by American troops, and then by Soviet troops.

First, I make a detour along *Kronprinzenstraße*, a leafy street not far from *Omi*'s apartment. This broad boulevard is now named *Kurt-Eisner-Straße*, after an extreme leftwing revolutionary who briefly became premier of the short-lived People's Republic of Bavaria in November 1918 and was assassinated three months later. *Kronprinzenstraße* was the site of some embarrassing personal defeats in my childhood.

The most annoying object of defeat for our shrinking gang of rascals was a trolley bus line, the only one in all of Leipzig. It defied our attempts to pull pranks on it. We could not yank down its pantographs, much less steal them after an air raid, because they were impossible to enter when stationary and, besides, required driving skills.

Our urchin powwow on how to resolve this issue proved futile, in part because we were only three, the others having moved out of town, including Heini, the most resourceful member of the gang. The older ones—those between the ages of ten and fourteen—were no longer available because they had been drafted into the *Jungvolk*, the junior branch of the Hitler Youth. They were busy learning Nazi doctrine and being given premilitary training, such as target shooting with small-bore rifles. *Vati* once warned me that they were also taught to inform the authorities on their parents, relatives, and neighbors.

So the three of us urchins felt that if we could not steal a trolley bus, or deprive it of power, it might at least make itself useful as a traction engine pulling us on our roller skates, much as speedboats pull water skiers.

The eastern terminal of the trolley line was at the intersection of *Kronprinzenstraße* and *Bayerische Straße*, where the driver and the ticket collector took a cigarette break before heading west again. We observed them while they smoked; they did not seem to pay any attention to the rear of their vehicle. Feeling undetected, each of us hooked a rope to its bumper. The driver and the ticket collector went inside the bus and closed its door. The three of us stood upright like toy soldiers in our skates, expecting to be whisked at least to *Adolf-Hitler-Straße*, the next stop.

We didn't reckon with the electric bus's power of acceleration, nor with the deplorable condition of the boulevard's surface consisting of cobblestones and potholes. The bus made a swift start, and *bang*, we three urchins landed simultaneously on our bottoms, leaving each of us with ripped shorts at a time when textiles were almost unavailable. Moreover, we lost our ropes; they flopped merrily from the tail end of the bus as it gathered distance.

The loss of the rope and the gash in my shorts earned me a fast clip from *Omi*'s right hand, although she could not suppress a grin when I told her what had happened. I found her smile most gratifying.

The municipal pool at the western end of *Kronprinzenstraße* was the venue of further defeats. Three times, in August 1944, I went there for swimming lessons. Three times, the kindly woman instructor held me on something resembling a fishing rod while I was in the water. Three times, I had to come out minutes later because the sirens sounded a preliminary alarm. I never learned to swim in Leipzig but made up for this five years later when I spent my summer holiday at my godfather's home in northern Germany.

Once, as I ran home from the pool, I was forced to duck for low-flying fighters—*Tiefflieger*, as we called them in German. Unlike the bomber crews, the *Tiefflieger* were loathed by civilians because their pilots were mostly young men who seemed to have fun picking off people from the street and/or workers from the field, as I had seen during my evacuation to the countryside outside Leipzig.

I had witnessed *Tiefflieger* mischief repeatedly in the village where, in 1944, I spent those few miserable months in the pro-Nazi parsonage. Only a few kilometers separated us from Brandis airbase. This was a top-secret installation where the *Luftwaffe* tested all kinds of new planes, including the famed ME-262 "Schwalbe," the world's first jet fighter, and the Sack AS-6, an experimental fighter-bomber that looked like a flying saucer because of its circular wings.

German civilians could see and hear what was going on there, yet they were not allowed to discuss it, especially not in the fanatically German Christian parsonage where I had been deposited. But the Allies knew it was there and logically bombed Brandis nearly as often as Leipzig; I watched all these attacks from my bedroom window.

The British came at night, the Americans during the day. Their bomber formations were accompanied by *Tiefflieger*, which sometimes flew low over the fields after the raids, machine-gunning farmworkers, mainly women and prisoners of war from France, Poland, and the Netherlands. These foreigners were particularly infuriated by the attacks.

This posed a dilemma for German military police. When a plane was shot down and the pilot died, he was given a Christian burial in the military section behind the churchyard—ironically, with the pro-Nazi pastor presiding. But if the pilot ejected and came down alive in his parachute, German MPs were at pains to get to him ahead of the irate farmworkers, for they were ready to kill him.

When my profoundly prowestern father heard these stories, he became very angry.

"What immature punks!" he fumed. "When officers hunt civilians down like rabbits, they give the professional soldiers a bad name, regardless of which side of a war this happens," he said. This was an unusual comment from a World War I veteran who otherwise never uttered a word against the western Allies, not even against the Anglo-American bomber crews who had killed more than six hundred thousand German civilians in World War II.

"Why did you show such understanding for the actions of these Anglo-American bomber crews, *Vati*?" I asked him when I visited him shortly before his death in 1960.

"Because they only did what we Germans had done before in Warsaw and Rotterdam. We started this. They retaliated."

"Did the Allies, then, not lower themselves to Nazi standards by killing civilians?"

"They did, they did! But let us not hold this against the airmen who risked their lives to win a war. Later historians and ethicists might blame the politicians. But this is not something our generation of Germans should do. After all, Hitler was elected democratically, a despicable error by the people of a cultured nation. All of us should, instead, feel collective shame, as President Theodor Heuss (West Germany's first chief of state) advised us to."

My thoughts return to *Kronprinzenstraße* because I am eager to tell the story of my most memorable wartime defeat near the end of 1944. *Mutti* took me to her dentist, whose practice was on this street. Fearless at first, I sat down in his operating chair. I opened my mouth and let the doctor insert his drill. But right then, the sirens sounded the first alarm. They had not stopped howling when, for some reason, we had a blackout.

Eeerrrhhh, the drill ground to a halt in my lower right jaw. I screamed. The dentist managed to separate his drill from its tip, but the tip refused to let go of my tooth. (In those days, German dentists did not anesthetize their patients before treating a cavity.) I had to get out of there!

"It would be best for you to go seek shelter in our basement. We'll fix this when the air raid is over and the lights come on again," said the dentist. *Mutti* agreed. I didn't!

"I want to be with *Omi*," I cried, running out of the good man's surgery, down the steps to his front door, and out into the street.

With American bombers and low-flying fighters overhead, with green-colored fire engines racing through the streets, with air-raid wardens and their teenage auxiliaries in Hitler Youth uniforms futilely trying to stop me, with my mother chasing me dementedly, and with my jaw hanging sideways to accommodate the tip of the dentist's drill, I hurried home to my grandmother; I swear I had never run that fast before. I made it.

Omi sat in her coal and potato cellar, giving me a mocking look. "You do look funny with that screwed-up face, Uwe," she observed. Minutes later, *Mutti* came in and told her what happened. *Omi* hugged me and softly stroked my head, saying, "We'll have that fixed soon. I want to get my good-looking boy back."

On that latter point I begged to differ with my beloved *Omi*. I did not give a hoot how I looked. I wasn't going back to that dentist ever! Not ever! That was my firm decision. What ensued was a weeks-long tug-of-war between the rest of my family and me about the metal bit in my mouth, with which I fully intended to spend the rest of my life, the pain and my funny looks notwithstanding.

All this happened shortly before 25 October 1944, my eighth birthday. When the sirens sounded the "all clear," *Omi*, my grinning father, my irate mother, and I sat down for lunch, which I found difficult to chew. They tried to persuade me to return to the dentist. I refused. They told me I would not get any birthday presents. I didn't care. When my birthday came, there were no gifts. I still refused to go to the dentist.

A month went by. I stubbornly lived through November, always with my chin in an odd position. Then Advent loomed.

"On Christmas Eve, you will get both your birthday and your Christmas presents, Uwe, but not if you don't go to the dentist soon," *Omi* said.

I weighed these prospects and decided it was to my advantage to relent. And so, in late November, just before the first Sunday in Advent, I went back to the dental practice at *Kronprinzenstraße*, but by myself, not with *Mutti*. This time my visit turned out to be almost painless. The dentist repossessed the tip of his drill and filled my cavity, and a few weeks later I received the first small installment of my rewards.

Before going to sleep on the night of 5 December, I hung a stocking on the outside door handle of my room, as is the custom in Germany. The next morning, St. Nicholas Day, I found it filled with *Omi*'s advent cookies, with marzipan from my paternal grandfather's storage facility in the countryside, and with a round, red-and-white tin marked *Scho-Ka-Kola*. It contained a dark, bittersweet chocolate normally reserved for *Luftwaffe* pilots, Panzer, and U-boat crews because it was enriched with caffeine to enhance the alertness of airmen, soldiers, and sailors. As a gravely wounded veteran, *Vati* was allowed a monthly ration of this delicacy.

On Christmas Eve, I found an abundance of gifts under the tree, including a three-volume set of *Winnetou* by the roguish Saxon writer Karl May (1842–1912), whose adventure novels, set in the American Old West and in the Middle East, reached a worldwide circulation of two hundred million. *Winnetou* was the story of a benevolent Indian brave, which triggered, in German-speaking countries, a wave of tawdry sympathy for Native Americans.

Another memorable present on that last Christmas in World War II is still with me. It is a pretty, beige descant (a soprano recorder in C^2), which would accompany me for the rest of my childhood and now rests in a drawer of my Biedermeier *secretaire en portefeuille* in California.

As usual, there were no bombardments over Christmas and New Year's. Perhaps my many gifts explain why I didn't sense the gloom that had beset the grownups. Half a million bombs had already been dropped on Leipzig, and more would be on their way before this nightmare was all over.

On New Year's Eve, we went to the *Kongresshalle* to hear the Gewandhaus Orchestra play Beethoven's Ninth Symphony, as was, and still is, the tradition. After the concert, in the tram, *Mutti* hummed the first stanza of this work's choral finale, the *Ode to Joy*.

It might be worth reading the English translation of Friedrich Schiller's poem "*An die Freude*" (Ode to Joy) because it was so ironic, given the grim conditions under which all of us lived:

> Joy, beautiful sparkle of the gods
> Daughter of Elysium!
> We enter fire-drunk,
> Heavenly one, your shrine.
> Your magic again binds
> What custom has firmly parted:
> All men become brothers
> Where your tender wing lingers.

I arrive outside the apartment building where I had shared a bedroom with *Omi*. This time, I don't ring Ulrike's doorbell. I simply want to pause outside the locked door to her basement trying to remember what happened to us in this place in the less than four months between that New Year's Eve and the end of Nazi rule in Leipzig on 20 April 1945, Hitler's birthday.

CHAPTER 12

White Flags and Black Friends

ONCE AGAIN, I STAND before the locked door of *Omi*'s former cellar, remembering the beginning of 1945 when all of us realized that, while the year would certainly bring us the end of the war, it would be a bitter end. Of the 539,000 bombs that fell on Leipzig during that conflict, many had not yet fallen, and those were going to be nasty ones; this much we knew.

We all felt dark gloom. "Germany will soon get its just desserts," *Omi* said after table prayers at our New Year's Day luncheon, which consisted of dumplings with an onion gravy containing no meat—because there was no meat to be had.

This was *Omi*'s only comment ever hinting at the misdeeds of the Hitler regime in my presence. She said more when she sat with my parents in the parlor next to our bedroom. As usual, I had my ear pressed to the door separating the two. I heard them whisper but caught only snippets such as "Jews," "Auschwitz," and *"Flüchtlingswelle,"* meaning the wave of refugees from East and West Prussia, Pomerania, and Silesia fleeing from a vengeful and marauding Red Army.

Omi and my parents whispered not just to withhold upsetting news from me but even more so to avoid being overheard by strangers at the tram stop on *Bayerische Straße* just below our window. That window no longer had double-glass panes but consisted of cardboard, through which one can hear everything. To be heard by strangers could mean death by hanging or beheading; "defeatism" had been elevated to a capital offense. Still, that Germany's defeat was imminent all of us understood, children included.

What I missed audibly, I could fill in easily, for my schoolyard had become an open forum. Already, as an eight-year-old, I was familiar with the entreaty by Russian poet Ilya Ehrenburg (1891–1967) to Soviet troops: "Kill the Germans, wherever you find them. Every German is our mortal enemy. Have no mercy on women, children, or the aged. Kill every German—wipe them out!"

"*Die Russen kommen!* (The Russians are coming!)" Every child had, by now, been told this fearsome cry, and understood what it implied. Nazi propaganda had made good use of Ehrenburg's diatribe and its appalling results. For example, in the East Prussian village of Nemmersdorf on 22 October 1944, troops of the second battalion of the Soviet Twenty-Fifth Guards tortured, raped, and killed seventy-two girls and women, from tiny little girls to octogenarians, and nailed several of them, naked, to barn doors. This wasn't just one of the many exaggerations spread by Joseph Goebbels's press office but a factual occurrence verified by an international commission and duly noted, after Germany's collapse, by US military authorities. For good measure, the Russians also shot and killed fifty French and Belgian prisoners of war. Having replicated Nemmersdorf many times over in their rapid progress toward the heart of Germany, they would soon arrive at the Saxon border.

My new best friend, Josef, and his mother had barely escaped this fate by fleeing ahead of the advancing Soviet divisions from the Prussian province of Upper Silesia to Leipzig, where they now shared one room with his aunt a block away from us. Josef was a brooding, earnest lad with a strange Silesian accent, which at first I found difficult to understand. It was impossible to elicit much personal information from him: How did he get here? What has he been through?

"It's like trying to get bogeymen out of Josef's nose," I remember telling *Omi*.

"*Du Ferkel!* (You piglet!)" *Omi* said. "What a revolting image! Have patience with Josef! Not all Germans are like Leipzigers." But all my patience did not do me any good. Josef would remain an enigma for the two-and-a-half years we were together, before we were forced to flee into two different regions of western Germany.

Josef and I met on our way to school the very day classes resumed after the Christmas break in early January 1945, a walk that normally took me twenty minutes. It was such a memorable encounter that I am quitting *Omi*'s cellar door for a few moments to retrace my steps to the southwest corner of *Kaiserin-Augusta-Straße* and *Elisenstraße*, just outside the *Schreibwarengeschäft*, or stationery store, that used to be there, where I bought my pens and school books.

Classes started at eight in the morning. It was pitch-black dark, and the sidewalk was covered with snow. And it was very cold. The streetlights had been turned off for fear of attracting the attention of enemy aircraft. I did not even see Josef at first; suddenly he was by my side.

"Are you also going to the *Fünfte Volksschule* (Fifth Elementary School)?" he asked me.

"Yes, I am," I answered, trying to look up at the shadowy figure next to me; he seemed at least a head taller than I.

"Which grade are you in?"

"Fourth grade."

"Fourth? So am I! You seem older."

"I am eight. My name is Josef. What's yours?"

"I am also eight. My name is Uwe."

"Uwe—this is not a Christian name, is it?"

"I don't know. It is a north-German name. My father is from northern Germany. But I believe my mother chose my name. I have no idea why, and I never liked it. I would much rather be called Sebastian, after Johann Sebastian Bach. Uwe is nice and short, though. Perhaps it is not Christian, but I am a Christian. My *Omi* has taught me the Small Catechism and that Jesus died for my sins on the cross. My *Omi* is a good teacher and very funny. You must meet her."

"What's the Small Catechism?"

"Martin Luther wrote it."

"That's why I didn't know it. I am Catholic. But I believe in Jesus and pray to Him."

"I never met a Catholic before. It's a funny thing to be."

"I am from Upper Silesia, where everybody is Catholic. May I sit with you in school? I don't know anybody here."

"Of course. There's a free place by my side. My best friend Heini used to sit next to me. But he has left Leipzig with his mother just before Christmas. You'll be the new Heini now," I answered and laughed. He didn't laugh. In fact, I never heard him laugh. He just wasn't a Leipzig urchin, but I liked him. I instantly knew I could trust him.

WHITE FLAGS AND BLACK FRIENDS

That Josef was a Roman Catholic intrigued me. To us Leipzigers, the Catholics were an exotic species. "What are Catholics?" I asked *Omi*.

"Christians like us," *Omi* said. "I do admire their faithfulness. When I was a child in Annaberg, in the Erzgebirge Mountains, my mother often took me across the border to Bohemia. Bohemians spoke German then because Bohemia was part of the Austro-Hungarian Empire. They were all Catholics, and they treated us like brothers and sisters. Why not go to Mass with Joseph? You will like it!"

And so I did. Leipzig's tiny Catholic minority no longer had its own sanctuary. It burned down in the air raid of 4 December 1943. Since then, they worshiped in the *Paulinerkirche*, the Lutheran University church, a gracile, late-Gothic gem. It was uncanny going there. We took the number 10, 11, or 28 streetcar, which rambled down *Adolf-Hitler-Straße*, crossed *Königsplatz* (King's Square), proceeded to *Augustusplatz*, where we got off, and then continued its journey to the central railway station.

The elegant ruins of the university and the Café Felsche (formerly Café Français) flanked the church, which the British bombs had spared (but was blown up in 1968 on the orders of East Germany's boneheaded Communist Walter Ulbricht, a fierce atheist).

There were two services every Sunday morning in the *Paulinerkirche*: first the Latin Mass and then the Lutheran *Gottesdienst* for students and faculty. We attended both. One Sunday, *Mutti*, the consummate Latinist in my family, accompanied us and translated the Latin text into German, explaining that our liturgies had an almost identical content of entirely biblical origin.

Josef often sat with *Omi* and me in her basement during daytime bombardments, either because we had run home from school together or because we had been playing in our courtyard or in *Omi*'s apartment.

Although Josef never laughed, I sometimes did make him smile with my tales of Heini's and my pranks. It was a lovely, grateful, but very strange smile, and it made me proud.

"His is an adult smile trapped in an eight-year-old boy's face," as *Omi* observed. "I wonder what this poor boy has been through," she said, adding once again: "Pray for him, and pray with him."

"I do pray with him, *Omi*," I answered. "But when we say the Lord's Prayer together, he never ends it with 'For Thine is the Kingdom . . .'"

"Never mind, just keep on praying."

I have rarely thought about Josef in the more than seventy years that have passed since our separation. But now, back at that basement door, I can't get his face out of my mind. It was a long, thin face with a long, thin nose, thin lips, and deep-sunken blue eyes. He actually didn't look much different than the *Wehrmacht* soldiers I had seen in the streets, home on furlough from the eastern front. In fact, this became a problem for him, for he was repeatedly stopped by the *Kettenhunde* (chain dogs, as we called military policemen because of the metal breastplates with the inscription *Feldgendarmerie* [field police] dangling from their necks). They suspected this eight-year-old child of being an army deserter.

When these battle-scarred soldiers, usually sergeants, realized their mistake, they showed great compassion for him, sensing what horrific experiences might have aged this child's face, experiences not dissimilar from their own. Sometimes they rewarded him with sweets from their own meager rations.

Hitler Youth (HJ) patrols were a different matter. They were, by that point of the war, thoroughly fanaticized and nasty.

WHITE FLAGS AND BLACK FRIENDS

Nasty, just as *Vati* had warned me. Once, I was with Josef when three older boys in snazzy HJ uniforms confronted us. Their leader was a *Scharführer* (squad leader or staff sergeant) who might have been fifteen or sixteen years old, though not much younger than the average age of *Wehrmacht* troopers at that time, which was seventeen years.

"Why are you not in uniform?" the *Scharführer* snarled at Josef.

"What uniform?" Josef asked.

"The HJ uniform," said the *Scharführer*, boxing Josef's ears. Josef didn't flinch.

"I am only eight, not even old enough for the *Jungvolk*," Josef replied, giving the *Scharführer* a piercing stare.

"You look old enough to man a flak position," the *Scharführer* responded inanely. Then, without a word of apology, he and his fellow Hitler Youth boys turned heel and marched away.

This happened just after we participated in a haunting ceremony at our elementary school. A fifteen-year-old eighth-grade student, most likely a repeater, had been drafted into the *Luftwaffe* auxiliary and assigned to an antiaircraft gunnery position, where he was killed by an American fighter plane. At the 10:00 a.m. lunch break, all pupils were commanded into the schoolyard for a fifteen-minute remembrance.

A *Luftwaffe* truck unloaded a wreath draped with the swastika flag. A one-legged air-force trumpeter, with the rank of a sergeant, intoned the "Good Comrade," the traditional lament played and sung at the funeral of fallen German soldiers since the early nineteenth century. Our principal had instructed us students beforehand to take our caps off, bow our heads, and sing along softly.

Most of us knew this song by heart. I certainly did because I had heard this tune so often at the frequent military burials in the churchyard beyond the garden of the village parsonage, where I lived a year earlier. Josef sang with me. He, too, must have heard this beautiful song many times when fallen warriors were buried in his village in Upper Silesia before the Russians came. Its lyrics read,

Ich hatt' einen Kameraden,	I once had a comrade,
Einen bessern findst du nit.	You will find no better.
Die Trommel schlug zum Streite,	The drum called us to battle,
Er ging an meiner Seite	He walked by my side,
In gleichem Schritt und Tritt.	In the same pace and step.
Eine Kugel kam geflogen:	A bullet came a-flying,
Gilt's mir oder gilt es dir?	Is it my turn or yours?
Ihn hat es weggerissen,	He was swept away,
Er liegt zu meinen Füßen	He lies at my feet,
Als wär's ein Stück von mir.	As though he were a part of me.
Will mir die Hand noch reichen,	He still reaches out his hand to me,
Derweil ich eben lad'.	When I am about to reload.
Kann dir die Hand nicht geben,	I cannot hold onto your hand,
Bleib du im ew'gen Leben	You stay in eternal life
Mein guter Kamerad!	My good comrade!

At least this was not a Nazi anthem like the *Horst Wessel-Lied*, which rejoices over "millions looking to the swastika, full of hope," a song we also knew verse-by-verse, if only because we heard it sung every day in radio broadcasts, at the beginning of convocations in the school's auditorium, and preceding newsreels in movie theaters.

The beautiful verses of the "Good Comrade" were written in the early nineteenth century by Johann Ludwig Uhland (1787–1862), one of Germany's foremost poets at the time of the *Befreiungskriege*, the wars of Germany's liberation from Napoleonic rule.

Strangely, while I recall many details of my previous elementary school (the one that burned down before my very eyes in 1943), I have little recollection of this one, *Fünfte Volksschule*, perhaps because I spent so little time there. In the second half of 1944, and in 1945, the number of daytime attacks by US bombers increased, forcing us children to try to run home after the first alarm late in the morning. There was a constant departure and arrival of faculty members. Most were wounded veterans missing an arm, a leg, and an eye or, as in one case, nearly half his head. But even those were called up again, if only for military desk jobs in the rear, relieving healthy soldiers for frontline duties.

Many teachers were old men, older than sixty, which was the upper limit of the draft age. Perhaps because of this, we weren't exposed to too much Nazi fanaticism as the war entered its final phase. Of course, all of us were expected to give the "German salute"—*Heil Hitler!*—when classes began or when we met each other (especially when we met grownups, because this was the law).

Josef refused to do this, and as I sat next to him, I did too. No teacher chided us for this, but the janitor did.

"*Guten Morgen* (Good morning)," we greeted him.

"*Heil Hitler*," he snarled back. "Why did you not give the German salute?" he angrily asked Josef.

"Because I am Catholic," Josef answered. "We Catholics only hail Jesus Christ."

The janitor was not a very bright man. He just gave us an uncomprehending stare and moved on. The incident had no consequences.

"You do have guts, Josef," I said when we were alone.

"I don't know about guts. But we must remain faithful to Jesus," Josef replied. "Hailing anybody else would be *Götzendienst* (idolatry)."

"This is more or less what *Herr* Strand, our principal and organist in the village to which I was evacuated, whispered into my ear when the pastor proclaimed Hitler as the redeemer of Germany."

"He was a good Christian, your organist."

"Who taught you all this, Josef?"

"Our village priest in Upper Silesia."

"In my case, my *Omi* teaches me the Christian faith every day."

"We are both very fortunate."

"Yes, we are."

"I like your *Omi*. I feel safe in her presence."

"So do I."

From that day on, Josef spent most of his time with my family, and even homeschooled with us, much to the relief of his mother. We rarely saw her because she worked for a Catholic relief service looking after the ever-growing number of refugees from Silesia, East and West Prussia, and Pomerania pouring into our badly wounded city.

Omi taught us basic arithmetic and religion. *Mutti* instructed us in history, music, literature, and writing. This last one became problematic, though. She used the Latin script, but Nazi education flip-flopped back and forth between the Latin and the beautiful old German style, which *Omi* mastered.

In my first year at school, the regime was still über-nationalistic and insisted that all children use the German system. Then, when Germany was the master of most of Europe, Hitler became more cosmopolitan and ordered that we switch to the Latin script used by all Europeans (except for the Russians, Bulgarians, and Serbians, who use Cyrillic script). But in late 1944, when the western Allies and the Red Army approached, it became patriotic again to write in German script.

Hence, Josef and I were taught both systems at home—the German script by *Omi*, and the Latin by *Mutti*. We actually enjoyed this, but many of our classmates found the ideologically motivated flip-flop the government imposed on us schoolboys annoying.

When *Vati* was around, he gave us a very rudimentary course in ecclesial and secular law, the two fields in which he held doctorates. Based on the constitution of the Weimar Republic (which Hitler abolished), he specifically explained to us fourth-graders the basics of western democracy—for example, that in a free society, all are equal.

"Does this apply to Catholics too, Dr. Siemon?" asked Josef.

"All are equal, Josef, all!"

"And Jews?"

"I said that in a democracy, all are equal before the law. I repeat: all."

I feel privileged having learned this so early in my life, and I doubt that other members of our class at Fifth Elementary School received such instruction on what it means to be a citizen of a free society. If the fathers of any of the other boys were still alive, they would have been in uniform, serving at Germany's eastern, western, northern, or southern fronts. In that sense, it was my good fortune that my father, so severely wounded in the First World War, could not serve in the Second.

After the war, I asked my father why he had been so blunt in front of Josef.

"Because he had almost become part of the family and was a devout Catholic," *Vati* answered. "Neither he nor his mother would have run to the Gestapo to report me."

"But the top Nazis were also Catholics, *Vati*. Hitler was a Catholic. So were Himmler and Goebbels, for example."

"Lapsed Catholics," my father said. "At any rate, Josef asked me whether a key principle of democracy pertained to his faith, and I told him the truth. Period."

While the grownups were circumspect in voicing their political opinions in our presence, Josef and I discussed it freely between us.

"This war is *verrückt* (crazy)," he said one day on our way back from school.

"It is, but what makes you say this now?"

"The old man on the fourth floor of your building has been drafted into the *Volkssturm*."

The *Volkssturm* (literally, people's storm) was a national militia established on Hitler's orders in 1944. All males between the ages of sixteen and sixty, who were not already serving in the armed forces, were conscripted into this new force, about which blasphemers joked, "Why is the *Volkssturm* the most precious resource of the Fatherland? Because its men have silver in their hair, gold in their teeth, and lead in their bones."

The "old man" Josef referred to did have lead in his bones. He was severely shot up in the First World War and therefore not drafted in

WHITE FLAGS AND BLACK FRIENDS

the Second. He was a widower, in his late fifties, whose name I have forgotten. He was a pleasant, midlevel bureaucrat always ready to help *Omi* when she needed it and always eager to sit next to us in the air-raid shelter.

Shortly after being called up, he invited Josef and me to his barracks. Forever practical, *Omi* urged us to go with him: "At least they will feed you there."

In the *Kaserne* (barracks), young boys and mature men were milling about, all in civilian clothes but with SS-like black armbands showing the German eagle with the swastika and the inscription "*Deutscher Volkssurm Wehrmacht.*" They had steel helmets and an assortment of guns, which our friend called "dogs from every village," meaning captured from the Belgian, British, French, American, and Soviet.

"Why are you not in uniform?" I asked him.

"Because we are not part of the *Wehrmacht*, even though you can see the word '*Wehrmacht*' on our armbands. We are under the direct command of the NSDAP [the Nazi party], which does not have special uniforms for hundreds of thousands of us militiamen."

Omi was right: Josef and I were fed well at the barracks. We were handed bowls of a thick and delicious pea soup with bits of meat and sausage.

"These poor bastards," *Vati* said when I described to him our venture into the paramilitary world. "They will be wiped out."

And so they were. Three months later, when the Americans laid siege to Leipzig, our friend's unit was made to participate in a foolish last stand. We never saw him again.

In this twilight period between war and peace, between a Nazi tyranny and a Communist despotism (with the sunny respite of the brief

American occupation in between), *Mutti* doggedly pursued her passion for music, and I still bless her for it. She organized house concerts every Friday afternoon featuring, as a new adjunct to our family, the enormously gifted pianist Käthe Pohl, a Baltic-German refugee from Riga in Latvia.

I was only eight when Auntie Käthe first set foot in *Omi*'s apartment, but I fell hopelessly in love with her. In retrospect, I can only describe my reaction to this beautiful young musician, with her pitch-black hair and the enthralling Baltic lilt in her speech, as a pre-pubescent erotic attraction.

I tried to sit next to her, inhaling her intoxicating scent whenever I could, turning pages for her when she played at *Mutti*'s Friday concerts, and I finagled to sit between her and *Omi* in the shelter. To this day, I have her interpretation of Bach's Italian Concertos in my ears. Never before (and never since) have I heard anybody interpret with such passion—a passion fitting her exciting persona.

It wasn't until long after the war that *Mutti* told me about Auntie Käthe's horrific experiences during her flight from Latvia through East and West Prussia to Leipzig. She saw how Red Army soldiers raped and killed German peasant women and was only spared the "Ilya Ehrenburg treatment" (see the earlier explanation) because she and her sister Gisela, also a gifted concert pianist, spoke perfect Russian and gave concerts for Soviet officers on the grand pianos in the stately homes they had confiscated from Prussian noble families.

Käthe and Josef were with us on the day when I saw *Omi* cry for the second and last time in our life together. It was the night of 13 February 1945. As usual, there was an alarm, and, as so often, it was a false alarm because we weren't the target of the huge fleet of British bombers. Dresden was. We never thought that this would happen because the capital of Saxony was of no strategic value.

A man shouted, "They have hit Dresden! I have heard it on the radio."

We rushed outside and stared at the night sky. Dresden lies a little farther than one hundred miles east of Leipzig. We saw the horizon turn red. We did not know, at that point, that 722 RAF bombers had caused a firestorm that destroyed 1,800 acres of the center of Germany's most beautiful city and killed at least twenty-five thousand people. But *Omi* already understood that, by annihilating Dresden, the British and (later that day) the Americans had set a torch to the very essence of German culture that she, the nineteenth-century monarchist, cherished so much. "They have burned my heart out," she said. Käthe, Josef, and I took her to her parlor.

Auntie Käthe sat down at *Omi*'s Feurich piano and played—this time not with passion but with calm care and thoughtfulness—the *Art of the Fugue*, thus ordering, as Bach's masterpiece always does, the thoughts and emotions of everybody in the room. I didn't have to turn pages for Käthe. She knew it by heart. Instead, I held *Omi*'s right hand. *Mutti* held the other. When Käthe had finished, *Omi* got up, wiped her eyes dry, said, "God bless you, Käthe," and retired to her bedroom. I knew she wanted to be alone to say her prayers. I stayed with Käthe, *Mutti*, and Josef in the parlor. Käthe played and *Mutti*, Josef, and I sang the hymn that had become my life's keynote: "*Ach, bleib mit Deiner Gnade bei uns, Herr Jesu Christ*" (Abide, O Dearest Jesus, among Us with Thy Grace).

From that day on, *Omi* began what can only be described as a marathon of prayer, sometimes spoken, but mostly silent. All of us knew that the war would soon be over. Yet the bombing continued, often as double-whammies, British at night and American during the day. Two weeks after the destruction of Dresden, there was another attack on Leipzig, with 1,044 dead and more to come. The last air raid killed seven hundred civilians, just five days before Leipzig surrendered, and its mayor, SS *Gruppenführer* (major general) Alfred Freyberg, its treasurer, as well as both their wives and daughters committed suicide in city hall.

I knew that *Omi* wasn't praying for us to be spared by the bombs and somebody else to be killed instead. But what was she praying for? I asked her this question shortly before her death at age eighty-seven in 1976. Her answer showed how much she saw the Nazi era and the war as a particularly heinous manifestation of Original Sin, which the Augsburg Confession, the Lutheran Church's central statement of faith, describes as a disease that can "only be overcome by the cleansing, healing, and forgiving blood of God's own Son."

"In my prayers, I thanked Christ for His sacrifice and asked for forgiveness of the immense suffering we as a nation had inflicted upon the world," *Omi* said. "I begged God to give Germany another chance."

Omi, being *Omi*, did not cast away her zany sense of humor while in prayer. One morning in the shelter, she suddenly looked to her left, saw me literally snuggled up in Auntie Käthe's armpit, gave me a mocking stare, and said, "*Friss die arme Käthe nicht mit Haut und Haaren auf. Lass uns noch etwas von ihr uns übrig* (Don't eat poor Käthe, skin, hair, and all. Leave some of her for the rest of us)." That said, she lowered her head to pray some more.

I am still standing outside the locked door to *Omi*'s former basement, thinking of the morning of 19 April 1945 when everything

WHITE FLAGS AND BLACK FRIENDS

changed. It was the day before Hitler's birthday when, by law, everybody was expected to exhibit his swastika flag, an event we children found entertaining because it betrayed the level of our neighbors' commitment to the *Führer*. Some exhibited huge banners, others midsized ones, still others small bits of textile, and some brave souls none at all. *Omi* belonged to the latter species. She only owned and flew the white-and-green ensign of Saxony with the royal coat of arms in the center.

I remember all of us, including Käthe and Josef, sitting between our coals and potatoes where the sirens had sent us. We heard snarly announcements from loudspeakers mounted on vehicles driving up and down the streets. They ordered us—by whose authority we did not know—to remain in our cellars until further notice.

We heard detonations, but they did not seem as menacing as the sound of the blockbuster bombs with which we were familiar. Neither

The sixty-ninth US Infantry Division conquered Leipzig on 19 April 1945, one day before Hitler's last birthday. A welcome sign greeted American units and imposed a fifteen mph speed limit on them.

did we hear the engine noises of bombers overhead, nor the bark of the German flak, nor the wail of fire engines and ambulances.

"Heavy howitzers!" my father said. "I only hear outgoing, not incoming, fire."

"Still, it's loud, *Vati*." I said. "This seems to be just around the corner."

"Well, it could be a few kilometers away. Howitzers are noisy."

Hour after hour went by. The loudspeakers left. "Some imbecile seems to have forgotten to sound the 'all clear,'" *Omi* said.

"Let's just take a look, Josef," I said, and before anybody could stop us, we were out in the courtyard, peeking through its cast-iron gate at a sheer endless convoy of military vehicles.

"Are they ours or theirs?" asked Josef.

"Can't tell," I answered, but quickly corrected myself: "It's them, Josef!"

"How do you know?"

"Look, there's a truck full of black soldiers."

We waved at them. Unlike their white comrades before them, they waved back.

"We don't have black soldiers, do we, Josef?"

"I don't know."

"Why do black men have white palms?"

"I don't know, Uwe, I have never seen a black man in Upper Silesia. Have you seen one in Leipzig?"

"No."

"Look, look, these black men are driving through a white forest," I shouted, pointing at a huge assortment of white textiles that were popping out of one apartment after another in our building and all the houses next to it. Some were just handkerchiefs, some were towels or rags, others entire bed sheets.

We rushed back to our basement.

I asked, "*Vati*, do we have black soldiers in our army?"

"Not since General von Lettow-Vorbeck roamed German East Africa with his Askaris," *Vati* answered with a grin.

I gave *Omi* an uncomprehending look.

"Last war," she said with a smile.

It must have been the following day that Auntie Irene, *Omi's* youngest sister, walked in, beaming uncharacteristically all over her otherwise always most serious face. She had just taken the number 24 tram from Gohlis, eager to tell us what she saw outside the *Alte Burg* hotel.

"*Lachende Mohrenköpfe in jedem Fenster* (Laughing Moors' heads in every window)," she said.

Before the ridiculous onset of political correctness, *Mohrenköpfe* (plural) was the German name for chocolate-covered marshmallows, a popular pastry, and certainly not meant to be a pejorative term for the many friendly black faces smiling at Irene.

"You know, what?" Irene went on. "They all waved at me, and their palms are white!"

Now I must leave my post outside *Omi's* cellar door for good. It is time to return to the *Dunkelrestaurant Mondschein* and once again reminisce about the *Alte Burg* it used to be.

CHAPTER 13

The Sunny American Interlude

ON MY WAY BACK across downtown Leipzig to the Restaurant of Darkness, I keep racking my brain: How soon after Leipzig's surrender did Josef and I walk to this spot in pursuit of new friends—black American friends? Was it two or three days later? Was it perhaps a week? At any rate, we connected with them before the rest of Germany surrendered on the eighth of May.

My mind returns to the day of Leipzig's surrender. Surfacing from our air-raid shelter for the last time, we celebrated this welcome caesura in our lives with a meal in *Omi*'s dining room. As the American convoys rumbled down *Bayerische Straße*, she asked me to bring out her

Black GIs were often more welcome in occupied Germany than white soldiers because they were friendlier and did not give a hoot about Gen. Eisenhower's nonfraternization edict.

best Meissen porcelain. There wasn't much for her to cook: two halves of a hard-boiled egg in a mustard sauce and a potato for each of us was the one and only course because that was all we had. My father contributed a bottle of his Elbe wines.

Omi said the Lutheran table prayer, "Come, Lord Jesus, be our guest . . . ," but then switched quickly to her pert mode, announcing that she was not going to expose her beautiful white linens to the dirty air outside, which was rich in diesel fumes and battle dust.

"This was not my war," she declared. "Therefore I have no reason to capitulate."

"There's still a lot of shooting going on outside," *Vati* observed. "It seems that the Americans are targeting their howitzers at the *Völkerschlachtdenkmal*," he said, referring to the nearby monument to the Battle of the Nations in 1813.

"Excellent! That's the perfect target!" rejoiced *Omi*, forever the royal Saxon patriot. "Let's hope they blast this hideous Prussian thing from the face of the earth!"

"Clara!" my father reproached her; as a native of north-western Germany, he felt closer to the Prussians than to us Saxons.

"Am I not right? This monster deserves to be blasted away!" *Omi* shot back, smiling sheepishly.

That afternoon, we discovered that, after the city of Leipzig had capitulated, a Colonel von Poncet had entrenched himself with three hundred *Wehrmacht* soldiers, *Volkssturm* militiamen, and Hitler Youths in the monument's crypt as an act of last resistance. The US howitzers fired off one round after another against this massive structure but barely dented it.

THE SUNNY AMERICAN INTERLUDE

At 2:00 the next morning, Colonel von Poncet and his men gave up, even though they had enough provisions to survive in the crypt for many months. When they came out, arms raised, the US forces found vast amounts of food and gourmet items, such as butter, ham, a huge variety of sausages, canned vegetables, fruit and rye bread, bottled duck and goose meat, sacks upon sacks of rice and flour, honey, canned fruit, mineral water, French wine, champagne, and brandy and tobacco. The Americans invited Germans living closest to the monument to help themselves to some of these goods but then took the bulk away to feed victims of the Third Reich.

The Americans stayed in Leipzig for just three months. For my family, this was a sunny interlude between the twin tyrannies of National Socialism and Communism. No longer did bombs drop on our heads. No longer did walls have ears. In other words, no longer did we have to fear informers. No longer did an SS general reign in the *Neues Rathaus*, the new city hall that stands on the site of the former *Pleißenburg*, where, in 1519, Martin Luther debated his Ninety-Five Theses in the historic Leipzig Disputation with the Catholic theologian Johannes Eck. As interim mayor, the Americans appointed Dr. Wilhelm Johannes Vierling, a resolute anti-Nazi who was my father's fraternity brother and friend from law school.

The only inconvenience we incurred, apart from hunger, was negligible. When the Allies disarmed all German civilians, we, too, were made to surrender our one and only weapon in the form of my maternal grandfather's officer's épée, which *Omi* kept in her attic; his *Pickelhaube* (spiked helmet) and epaulets had already burned with the rest of my toys in my parents' apartment during the bombardment of 1943.

To my mother's chagrin, *Omi* also made me take her husband's World War I medals to the collection point in the abattoir, where everybody in our neighborhood had to drop off our martial souvenirs. The American duty sergeant took just one look at grandfather's decorations, realized that they preceded the Nazi era, grinned, and told me in broken German to take them back to my granny. For once, *Mutti* was the stage winner in her ongoing war of words with *Omi* over Curt Netto's heroism. His medals are now on exhibit in my office in California, and every time I look at them, I have to chuckle.

Josef and I had much time to kill during the American interlude. Our school was closed while our teachers were being investigated for their Nazi loyalties. *Mutti* sent me to her former Latin professor for private, one-hour lessons every morning. But otherwise, we were free to embark on our search for the black soldiers, knowing that that they would not adhere to Gen. Dwight D. Eisenhower's edict forbidding GIs to fraternize with the defeated Germans. They had waved at us German children when they arrived, hadn't they? Their white comrades-in-arms didn't do that at first, although that changed soon enough, and in our case for an amusing reason.

Ever since the Americans had taken over Leipzig, a US Army jeep with a radioman was parked across the sidewalk outside *Kaiserin-Augusta-Straße* 53. The residents of our building greeted him politely, but obeying Eisenhower's nonfraternization order, he ignored them (though he smiled at us children).

One balmy afternoon in late May, I sat in *Omi*'s and my bedroom by the open window, memorizing Latin vocables, declensions, and conjugations. *Omi* was out on a stockpiling trip to the Reiches' farm in Dölkau but in the end was not allowed to cross the Prussian state line. In the parlor, *Mutti* sat at the piano bellowing out her vocal exercises: *nui-nui-nui-nui-nui-nui-nuiiiii* and *wa-wa-wa-wa-wa-waaaa*. The parlor window was also open.

Suddenly, the doorbell rang furiously. I opened the door. Outside stood the boyish American radioman with a contorted face. "What the hell is this awful noise?" he shouted, more in distress than in anger. I led him to the parlor, where he saw a beautiful, dark-haired woman at the keyboard of a piano and was immediately entranced.

"How may I help you?" *Mutti* asked him in English.

"Um," stuttered the GI, puce in the face. "Would you kindly close your window? You see, your voice is drowning out my radio."

My mother apologized and closed the window, which by now had glass panes again. In return, the soldier brought a box of K-rations, including small packs of four Chesterfield cigarettes for my father. When we urchins resumed frolicking through the streets again, costumed as Apache or Sioux braves, he showed us how to stick feathers into our hair properly, Indian-style. Before long, Josef and I set off on an expedition through canyons of Leipzig's ruins in search of food and smiling black men.

We loaded my handcart with children's clothes I had outgrown since moving in with *Omi* and some of her china, hoping in vain that we might barter these goods against spring vegetables and berries from somebody's private garden. We were more successful in finding the black GIs. As my Aunt Irene had said, their smiling faces filled out virtually every window of the *Alte Burg* hotel. They spotted us. They waved at us. They bombarded us with cinnamon-flavored chewing gum and Hershey bars. We became instant friends.

Communicating with these strangers was a problem at first.

"*Sprecht ihr Deutsch?*" we asked. No, none of them did.

"Speak English?" they asked. We didn't.

Standing outside this former hotel, I recall my minute of glory.

"*Français?*" I asked.

"*Oui, je parle Français!* (Yes, I speak French!)" one of them yelled cheerfully, and the next thing I knew, he and a couple of other soldiers were with us on the sidewalk. It turned out that he was from Louisiana. He was enormously tall.

"What's your name?" I asked him.

"Louis."

"Like Louis Armstrong?" I said.

"How old are you?" he wanted to know.

"Eight."

"What? You are only eight, and you know Louis Armstrong? Here in Germany? How come?"

I explained to him that I hailed from a musical family and that, while my mother loved Bach, my father preferred Johann Strauss's Vienna waltzes and Louis Armstrong's jazz. I told Louis that *Vati* had hidden his collection of Hot Five and Hot Seven records in his parents' apartment at *Beethoven-Straße*, where he kept a room as his marriage rapidly deteriorated. Once, when I visited him there, he played a couple of these tunes for me, which was dangerous. In the Third Reich, listening to "jungle music," as the Nazis called jazz, was a crime.

"Can you bring us some of your daddy's records?" Louis asked me.

"Tomorrow."

On our walk home, Josef and I stopped at my paternal grandparents' apartment where, in recent weeks, my father spent more

THE SUNNY AMERICAN INTERLUDE

time than with us, a sure sign that his marriage was falling apart. As expected, *Vati* was there. He gave me two of his records. I still remember the funny names of tunes that have remained in my head ever since, even though I would not hear them played again until eleven years later when I lived in Paris and frequented the *Caveau de la Huchette*, a jazz club and favorite haunt of students and artists. One of these pieces was called "Heebie Jeebies," the other "Muskrat Ramble," and then there was the "Basin Street Blues," probably my favorite of all Louis Armstrong's recordings.

We took them to Louis and his friends the following day. They brought down a gramophone, and next they were jiving on the sidewalk outside their hotel. They also taught Josef and me to jive.

"May I have these records? I will pay you for them," Louis asked. *Vati* had prepared me for that.

"A carton of Lucky Strikes or Chesterfields," I answered.

Louis agreed. A few more deals of this kind followed. I brought more records, and Louis brought more cartons of cigarettes, which I divided up with my grumbling father, who claimed that he was entitled to all of them.

Cigarettes were the only hard currency in Germany in those days. One pack was worth two kilos of ham on the black market. I am proud to say that, with my transactions, I helped keep *Omi*'s household fed for the rest of the summer, even after the US had ceded western Saxony and neighboring Thuringia to the Soviet Union in exchange for the Western sectors of Berlin.

I never found out what my father did with his share of Lucky Strikes and Chesterfields; as a blind man and senior civil servant, he couldn't very well go to any of the black markets that had sprung up around town, but I suspect that as a good-looking, well-dressed *Herr Doktor* and a war hero, he suffered from no shortage of sweethearts prepared to do this for him.

This was the last time I saw my father in Leipzig. He left town. Through channels still obscure to me, he was taken to Kirchberg an der Jagst near Stuttgart in the US zone of occupation. There, the American military authorities maintained a rest and training center for Germans they (and the British) intended to appoint to senior positions in the emerging democratic Germany. *Vati* and I did not meet again until an ill-fated Christmas together in a Bavarian inn two years later.

For now, though, I was left alone with *Omi* and *Mutti* and Josef. I gave Josef a few packs of Chesterfields to help feed his mother and his aunt. Louis and his friends soon left Leipzig, thus ending the briefest and most benign phase of my short childhood. But before they did, Josef said to me, "Here is your chance! Ask Louis why the hands of black men have white palms."

I did.

"*Aucune idée* (No idea)," Louis answered, shrugging his shoulders and laughing uproariously.

A little later, Martl stood agitated in our front door. Martl used to be *Omi*'s cleaning woman. Her real name was Martha, but *Omi* didn't call her that so as not to confuse her with her sister, whose right hand we had buried after her death in an air raid a year earlier.

"The Americans are gone, including the jeep with a radioman outside this house," Martl reported. "Ivan [the Red Army] is here. The Russians are just down the road on *Andreasplatz*." Martl pulled *Omi* and me outside to show us a new forest of flags flying from almost every window. This time the flags were not white but red in two distinct shades: they were mostly faded red, almost pink, but featured a big, dark red, round blob in the center.

When *Omi* and I saw this, we burst out laughing because this scene was so grotesque to a boy and his grandmother who had just lived through years of war and oppression—we had seen these same rags hanging there so many times before, for they were the old Nazi flags with a white round field and the black swastika stitched to the center of a red cloth. All that was needed to adapt the banner of one tyranny to the symbol of another was to remove the white field and the swastika. What, until recently, had been Nazi had now become Bolshevik in two tones.

"Disgusting!" *Omi* exclaimed. "No hole in the world is too stinky for some Germans not to crawl into."

Within days, *Omi* was given reason for more nausea. No sooner had Soviet *muzhiks*[1] entered town in a weird assortment of horse-drawn wagons and US-built trucks than a vulgar character, known to us for past chicaneries, barged into our apartment, informing us that he was the new street warden of the Communist Party.

"Wait a moment!" *Omi* said. "Were you not the Nazi block warden only a few days ago?"

"I was, but that was just a cover," he conceded. "Secretly, I was always a Communist."

"Secretly!" huffed *Omi*. "Congratulations, you really have found an original way to prolong your political career."

---

1 Russian peasants, generally; but more specifically, the nickname for basic infantrymen, the lowest rank in the Red Army. When such a Soviet soldier was assigned to an officer as a personal servant, like a batman in the British military or a *Bursche* in the German, the officer would refer to him as "my Mushik."

Stomping furiously up and down our corridor, he spotted *Omi*'s telephone, and he screamed, "Why do you still have a phone?" He ripped it out of the wall.

When he was gone, *Omi* said to me, "You will be surprised how many old Nazis will show up soon presenting themselves as Communists. They are the same riff-raff."

Thus ended for me a short period of enchantment. What followed in the next two years were a famine, class warfare, tuberculosis, and my bowels full of worms, all made worse by my parents' divorce, my unavoidable flight from Communism, and, consequently, my separation from my greatest treasure on earth: my *Omi*.

CHAPTER 14

The Hungry Urchin's Russian Love

EIGHT-YEAR-OLD BOYS SHOULD EAT at least 1,745 calories per day, according to the British National Health Service. The victorious Soviets allowed Germans in their zone of occupation seven hundred calories. The torment this inflicted on us children was made worse by the thousands upon thousands of pinworms feeding on the sparse contents of our innards. We felt as if we were being gradually devoured from within because, for months, there were no drugs available to kill off these beasts. Dr. Firnhaber suggested carrots as a reasonable remedy against maggots, but carrots, too, were severely rationed.

"Why are the Russians starving us, *Omi?*" I asked.

"Because the poor devils are themselves starving," she said.

I can't remember any of us disliking ordinary Soviet soldiers. By the time the Red Army arrived in Leipzig its men had long acted out Ilya Ehrenburg's invocation to kill and rape German civilians. The worst I ever saw *muzhiks* do was drive drunk on sidewalks injuring civilians, an offense for which their sergeants or military police mistreated enlisted men so cruelly on the spot that Germans began to feel sorry for them.

No sooner did the Soviets arrive in Leipzig, though, than their German gofers made life even more miserable for the civilian population than it already was. I already mentioned the former Nazi block warden who mutated into a Communist party warden and ripped *Omi*'s telephone off the wall. His female counterparts were even harder to look at and to listen to. They wore clunky, broad-shouldered suits, never smiled, and made threatening pronouncements that were, in *Omi*'s words, "sheer ideological twaddle." I can't spare my readers this aside: these women looked—and were—as charmless as certain feminist-inspired midlevel American executives in the 1990s and beyond.

In Dölzig, a German red rabble tore down Uncle Alfred Seltmann's lovely rococo manor house, claiming that he was a *Junker*, or rich landowner, although his farm had long shrunk to 120 acres due to decades of mismanagement. Uncle Alfred, a sweet, mentally disabled man who had never harmed anybody, and was much beloved by his employees, was deliberately starved to death. Communist thugs divided up his land and livestock among his farmworkers, locked him and his female cousin into two rooms of his former gardener's house, and posted sentries outside its door to prevent his former workmen from bringing him something to eat. Reduced to seven hundred calories per day like the rest of us, Uncle Alfred died two months later in the hospital of the Leipzig suburb of Schkeuditz.

For us, this meant not just the loss of a faithful family friend but also the loss of a source of food. This was made worse by the fact

THE HUNGRY URCHIN'S RUSSIAN LOVE

that the smallholding of the Reiches in Dölkau, the next village over, was temporarily beyond our reach because the new Communist administrators closed the border between the state of Saxony and the former Prussian province of the same name.

Suddenly, though, there came in those days of misery an unexpected moment of reprieve as a reward for *Omi*'s ladylike behavior in happier times.

One Saturday morning, the doorbell rang. *Omi* opened the door and saw an elderly man with a Communist party badge in his left lapel. Seeing this symbol, she instinctively wanted to slam the door in his face, but the man pleaded with her in broad Saxon: "*Frau* Netto, *Frau* Netto, don't you recognize me?"

"No, who are you?"

"I am Baake, your coachman in the 1920s!"

"O Baake, Baake!" *Omi* cried, incredulous. "No, I didn't recognize you at first. I am so sorry."

"The war has changed so many of us, *Frau* Netto," Baake replied.

"It has," *Omi* agreed. "But not all of us wear Communist party badges."

"Don't take my badge seriously, *Frau* Netto. Please let me in to explain to you why I've come. I mean no harm."

Omi beckoned Baake in. He said, "*Frau* Netto, I have never been a Communist. I was a Social Democrat before the war, which is why the Communists have given me a job as a driver—but on condition that I become a party member. So now I am the chauffeur of the Communist district chairman. His BMW is parked right outside this house, ready to take you wherever you want to go."

"Why are you doing this, Baake?" *Omi* asked.

• 231 •

"*Frau* Netto, I have never forgotten how kind and generous you were to me when I worked for you and Major Netto before the war. Now that I am living around the corner, I often see you standing in line outside the grocery store for a pound of potatoes or some carrots. This is not right! You should not have to do this! So I decided to return your kindness. I figured that perhaps you would like to be driven to the countryside to visit a farm you know."

"Are you allowed to cross the border to the province of Saxony, Baake?"

"Anywhere, *Frau* Netto."

"Give me ten minutes, Baake," said *Omi* joyfully.

She rushed into our bedroom and put on a good dress. Then she rustled up shopping bags and milk cans from the kitchen larder and, accompanied by Baake, walked upright to the party chief's dark-blue BMW. Baake opened the right back door. She took her seat, waved at me proudly, and allowed herself to be chauffeured to the Reiches' farm in Dölkau.

When they returned, the BMW's trunk was filled with vegetables, fruit, poultry, homemade sausages, milk, eggs, and other victuals. *Omi* offered Baake a generous share, but he wouldn't take any of it. "No, no, *Frau* Netto, this is all yours," he told her. "As a party functionary, I have better rations than you." Baake never returned. "I fear that he was found out and punished," said *Omi*. One month later, when everything was eaten, we were as hungry as before.

I can't recall when, exactly, school started again. But when it did, it was with new teachers and subjects, Russian being one of them. "There is nothing wrong with learning Russian, a beautiful, musical language," said *Mutti*, after reading in a handout about my new post-Nazi curriculum that included the idiom of our conquerors: "Speaking Russian does not make you a Bolshevik." In return for studying their idiom, the "victorious brethren"—as the Soviets were now called in their zone of occupation—rewarded us with a daily bread roll per pupil during the ten o'clock break in the schoolyard. The bread roll was big and gray—like a *Wehrmacht* soldier's uniform—and had nothing on it, not even margarine or jam. I took one bite and immediately purged my mouth of this evil-tasting matter by spitting it far from me.

"Yuck! What is this?" I asked Josef.

"Chaff," he said, spitting it out as well. "Any idea what we could do with this?"

For once, my urchin spirit returned: "Let's turn it into a water bomb."

We scooped out the dough from inside our buns, replaced it with water, rushed to our classroom on the second floor, opened a window, and lay in wait for a moving target. Soon enough, the target appeared in the shape of a tall, gawky man tiptoeing awkwardly along the sidewalk. He looked so goofy that we simply had to hit him. Together we took aim and scored. Water dripping from his hair, the guy looked up and spotted two laughing boys in the classroom window. He also laughed, exposing a very incomplete set of teeth. Waving at us, he entered the school.

Minutes later he was in our classroom, his head and shoulders still drenched from our chaff bombs. From close up, he looked like a ghoul. The skin on his gaunt face was as white as cottage cheese. Still smiling, he introduced himself as *Herr* Ziegenbalg, our Russian teacher. We immediately liked him because he made us laugh with his funny looks and his sense of humor.

Was Ziegenbalg a German? He did not look it. We never found out what he was or how and where he had spent the war. I now suspect he was a Sorab belonging to a western Slavic minority living in Eastern Saxony. The Sorabs play bagpipes made from goatskin called *Ziegenbalg* in German, which would explain this teacher's name. Their language is related to Russian, and the Nazis had persecuted them. Hence it was quite likely that our *Herr* Ziegenbalg was a Sorab who suffered in a concentration camp. But all this is conjecture. He didn't tell us anything. Neither did he spout Marxist-Leninist drivel. The only part of his Russian courses that reminded us of Bolshevism was the textbook printed in Moscow featuring a "Товарищ Петров" (Comrade Petrov).

Josef and I quickly became his pals and best pupils, earning the German equivalent of an A with every test or paper. After a few months, he asked us to stay behind after class.

"You boys look hungry," he said. "Come visit me tomorrow. I'll get us some cake and cocoa. I only have a small attic room on *Elisenstraße*, but it is well heated. You'll be fine."

"Shall we go?" I asked *Omi* after telling her about the invitation.

"Yes, but always go with Josef, never alone, and don't allow him to touch you. He probably won't. I suspect that he is a very lonely man, happy to have new friends who were not Nazis. Be careful, but be nice to him."

"We *are* nice to him. We like him, *Omi*, although we are the only ones in our class who do. The others probably don't care for him because they hate the Russian language."

It was already getting dark when we knocked at *Herr* Ziegelbalg's attic door on the fifth floor at four o'clock in the afternoon. His room was cozy, heated by a round-iron stove. But it was also spooky. Skulls were staring at us with hollow eyes from all around the room. There were skulls on the top of his bookcase, skulls separating Russian and German books, skulls on top of the kitchen cabinet, skulls decorating his bedside table and his windowsill, and skulls gawking at us from all four corners of the room. Forty-eight skulls we counted. Some were genuine human skulls, *Herr* Ziegenbalg informed us, while others were gypsum copies, though they looked very real.

There was even a skull on the coffee table next to the platter of cheesecake, streusel cake, and poppy seed cake to which *Herr* Ziegenbalg beckoned us. This sight didn't spoil our appetite in the least. We were hungry!

"Why do you have all those skulls, *Herr* Ziegenbalg?" I asked him.

"I am just fascinated by them. Knowing that they once contained thinking brains made me a skull collector."

"And where did you find them?" Josef wanted to know.

"There's no shortage of skulls in Germany, my boys."

"True," Josef answered cryptically.

"And I stumbled across gypsum skulls in the cellar of a bombed-out school," added Ziegenbalg.

"Are you married, *Herr* Ziegenbalg?" I wanted to know. "Are your parents alive? Do you have brothers or sisters? I don't see any family photographs in this room."

"All dead," he said. "But let's not dwell on this. Let's talk about the Russian language. It is lovely, especially when written by a genius like Anton Chekhov. He wrote beautiful short stories. Let me read one to you. It's called *Difficult People*. I will read it in German. Perhaps later you will be able to read it in Russian. Help yourselves to some more cocoa."

With that, he grabbed a slim volume sitting next to a skull on the bookcase. I still remember the first paragraph of that wonderful tale:

> Yevgraf Ivanovich Shiryaev, a small farmer, whose father, a parish priest, now deceased, had received a gift of three hundred acres of land from Madame Kuvshinnikov, a general's widow, was standing in a corner before a copper washing-stand, washing his hands. As usual, his face looked anxious and ill-humored, and his beard was uncombed.

Josef and I leaned back, enjoying the warmth emanating from the round-iron stove. We soaked in this wonderful tale of nineteenth-century Russia, forgetting bombed-out Leipzig, shattered Germany, and the forty-eight skulls around us. It was a memorable experience.

"How was it?" *Omi* asked when I got home.

"Forty-eight skulls, three kinds of cake, cocoa, and a short story by Chekhov."

"Explain!"

I did.

"God knows how many oddballs this war has produced," *Omi* said with an understanding smile. "But I am so glad he fed you well and read Chekhov to you; Chekhov is my favorite Russian author."

We returned to *Herr* Ziegenbalg's attic room often, at least once a week. Eventually, he began reading Chekhov to us in Russian. We didn't understand much of it, but it sounded so beautiful that we could not hear enough of it. Had I remained in *Herr* Ziegenbalg's class for a few more years, I most certainly would speak perfect Russian by now, which would not be bad at all. Most important,

Josef and I noticed how happy we made him by sharing his love for the Russian language, and that, in turn, made us happy. He was such a good guy!

However, Ziegenbalg's praise and good grades soon caused me great humiliation, at a point when I could least afford it—namely, when I encountered the Russian girl Natasha and fell in love with her. We were both nine when we first saw each other in a magnificent villa managed by my aunt, Irene Stürtz, *Omi*'s youngest sister, and decided then and there that we should get married as soon as legally possible. Our friendship confirmed the adage that "opposites attract." Natasha had shiny, pitch-black hair and alabaster-colored skin; I was blond and had inherited from my father a disposition to get a tan at the first hint of sun.

I tried to impress her with my broken Russian. She smiled sweetly, put her soft right hand on mine, and answered in such superb German that forthwith I no longer dared to address her in her mother tongue; instead, we confessed our love in mine and continued to do so whenever we saw each other. She was a mere child, yet she knew German poetry. One morning, when I came to see her, she gave me a piece of paper with her slight adaptation of a verse by the Bohemian lyricist Rainer Maria Rilke:

Ich möchte dir ein Liebes schenken,
das dich mir zum Vertrauten macht:
aus meinem Tag ein Deingedenken
und einen Traum aus meiner Nacht.

I am no lyricist and must therefore beg my readers to forgive me for my wooden translation of these romantic lines:

I want to give you a love
that makes you my confidant:
a memory of my day
and a dream of my night.

Natasha had discovered this poem in the library of the villa in Gohlis where her family was billeted. Her father was a Soviet major and, like his wife, had a flawless command of the German language, which they must have studied at university or perhaps even on their parents' laps. I never found out what they were in civilian life but learned that they belonged to the minority of Christian noblemen and patricians who had been persecuted for decades until Stalin concluded a brief tactical peace with them toward the end of the war, "allowing" them to serve in the Red Army, even as commissioned officers.

Natasha's parents and their *muzhik* (batman) lived their Christian faith openly. Like good Christians, they shared their rations with Aunt Irene and invited her to continue living in the villa. Like good Christians, they extended their generosity to me as well, and to Josef when he was with me. Like a good Christian, their *muzhik* literally commanded us to eat his food when he saw us enter the house through the kitchen door. Once we arrived just as he was spooning his noodle soup. He rose, pointed at his plate, and said in broken German, "*Du essen* (You eat)."

Sometimes the major asked *Omi* and me to lunch in the villa's elegant dining room, where he and his family followed the same protocol I had been taught at home. As master of the household, he had his place at the head of the table, but before he sat down, he helped *Omi* into the chair on his right. Aunt Irene sat at his left. My chair was between *Omi* and the major's wife, whose place was at the bottom of the table, opposite her husband. This meant that I was her dinner partner. I took her to her chair, earning praise from the major for my knowledge of table etiquette. I must confess that her perfect figure and heady perfume caused me a level of unease my twenty-first-century readers might not find virtuous. Natasha sat opposite me. Torn between adoring her large black eyes and inhaling her mother's inebriating scent, I found it almost impossible to concentrate when the major invited *Omi* to speak Luther's Common Table Prayer before he chanted a lengthy Orthodox supplication. My libidinous awakening at that lunch did not escape *Omi*, of course. In the tram home, she pulled my right ear and said, "*Du kleiner Lustmolch!* (You little lecher!)" She laughed, and when she saw that I turned red in the face, she laughed even more.

As for the meal the *muzhik* brought in from the kitchen on a large Meissen china platter, *Omi* and I found it exotic. It consisted of thick slices of white bread covered thickly with sweet butter and even more thickly with sugar. Following the major's example, we ate the bread with knives and forks. We found it delicious and ate several slices; we were so hungry!

On Sunday mornings, the major and his family stopped by *Omi*'s apartment to take me to Mass at the Orthodox Alexi church that had been built in memory of the twenty-two thousand Russian soldiers who had given their lives in the Leipzig Battle of the Nations in 1813. The major's staff car looked like a carbon copy of the two-tone Adler convertible in which Dr. Beckmann, *Mutti*'s friend, chauffeured her about, except that Dr. Beckmann's was beige with brown wings, while the major's was white with black fenders. The *muzhik* sat at the steering wheel, the major next to him, and I luxuriated on the back seat between his delicious wife and Natasha, whose hands I held.

The Mass in the Alexi church was challenging. It lasted three hours, during all of which I had to stand, for there were no pews. As an organ aficionado, I missed the "Queen of the Instruments." On the other hand, the singing was stirring, and the liturgy was exotic and dramatic. The best part of the service came at the end, when bread rolls, blessed by the priest, were distributed to the worshippers at the exit. They were not to be confused with the altar sacrament to which I, as a Lutheran, was not admitted; they were just bread rolls, but worth standing three hours for.

I told Josef about that, and we decided to extend our ecumenist ventures to Eastern Orthodoxy forthwith. Thereafter we eschewed the Catholic and Lutheran services at the university church and went every Sunday to the Russians, with or without the major and his family.

One Sunday morning, though, the Alexi was empty. All the Soviet officers, their wives, children, and *muzhiks* were gone, including our major, his beautiful wife, and my beloved Natasha. The only worshippers left were a few old codgers in tattered civilian clothes. Panic-stricken, I forewent the roll at the end of Mass. I ran out of the church with Josef in tow. We jumped on the next tram to the central railway station, ran to the nearest stop of the number 24 line, and got off at *Kickerlingsberg-Straße*, where Aunt Irene lived and where I had experienced a romance of unforgettable beauty.

We ran to the villa. Its gate was open. The white-and-black Adler convertible was gone. We stormed into the kitchen. At its table sat Aunt Irene, holding her head and shaking wildly.

"Where is the *muzhik*, Aunt Irene?" I asked her, full of foreboding. "Where is the major? Where is the major? Where is his wife? WHERE IS MY NATASHA?!"

"All gone! All arrested!" Aunt Irene cried.

"Who arrested them? When? Why?"

"The GRU [Soviet military intelligence]. They came in the middle of the night. They stormed their bedrooms and ordered the major, his wife, and Natasha to dress. They handcuffed them, shoved them into a box wagon—even little Natasha—and drove off with them."

"And why is this kitchen in such a mess? Why are pots, pans, and chinaware on the floor?"

"This is nothing compared to what the rest of the house looks like, Uwe. Go take a look."

Josef, Aunt Irene, and I inspected the villa with increasing horror over the chaos the GRU goons had left behind after rummaging through every room, every chest of drawers, every closet cupboard, and every bookshelf. Books, clothes, and other personal belongings were strewn all over the floor. I went into Natasha's little chamber. In contrast to the diabolical chaos in the rest of the house, there were her Sunday clothes, neatly laid out on a chair next to her bed: a white blouse, a dark-blue pleated skirt, white stockings, and a pair of dark-blue patent-leather shoes.

I stood there staring at this image that would remain in my head for the rest of my life. I was never "built close to the waterworks," but now I screamed. My whole body shook.

"Take these clothes with you to remember Natasha by," Josef said inanely.

I couldn't. Had I followed Josef's suggestion, I would have felt like a pilferer, no better than the GRU swine who had taken my beloved Natasha from me in handcuffs in the dark of the night. Even as I am writing this, I feel tears welling up in my eyes when I turn to the next scene of this tragedy, which resembled a black-and-white Hollywood horror film yet was dire reality.

Josef and I took the number 24 tram back to *Kaiserin-Augusta-Straße*. We arrived almost simultaneously with Aunt Käthe at *Omi*'s flat. She, too, was weeping. Filled with dark misgivings, I asked her, "You have so many Christian friends among the Russians, Auntie Käthe. Have they also been arrested last night?"

"Every one of them."

"Where have they been taken?"

"I fear they are already on their way to Siberia."

At that point, I did something *Omi* would have never allowed me to do in the air-raid shelter: I wept. *Omi* took me into her arms and gently stroked my head. We both knew that we would not see Natasha, her beautiful mother, and her noble father again. Soon, our darkest fears were confirmed. We learned that, in one fell swoop, Stalin had purged the Red Army of all its Christian officers.

Aunt Käthe sat down at *Omi*'s piano to cheer us up by playing the allegro of the first movement of Bach's Italian concerto, as she had done so often when we were grieving during the war.

CHAPTER 15

Urchin's Farewell to Childhood

WHEN STALIN STOLE NATASHA from me and sent her to the Gulag, he inflicted on me the most painful of a series of losses I suffered in 1946, making it my annus horribilis, my year of horror. Natasha gave me an unwavering sweetness I had not known before, not even with *Omi*, who was lovable but by necessity tough and stern—the only genuine figure of authority in my young life.

In the few months Natasha and I were together, I never doubted that she would one day be my bride and that the major and his wife would become my in-laws; that they would be to me the warmhearted, selfless parents for whom I had yearned.

Natasha's disappearance was sudden and brutal, but other losses sneaked up on me, such as the gradual decline of my health. No longer the sturdy urchin I used to be during the war, I was now too weak even to load my father's Braille books on my handcart before taking it to the library for the blind. *Omi* gave me a hand.

Why didn't *Vati* do it, I wondered? If he wasn't with his parents, he sat aloofly by the open window of his room, his fingers gliding over the tactile knobs of his Braille pages. He seemed in no mood to speak with any of us; then he was gone from one day to the next without bidding me farewell.

"He will not come back!" said *Mutti*.

Boom! Another loss!

Mutti and I were walking in the Connewitzer Holz, the forest through which I had led my father so often and where he had told me about Auschwitz.

"You must be strong now," *Mutti* said.

"?"

"*Vati* and I have divorced."

"What about the sixth commandment?"

"The sixth commandment is not about divorce. It's about something you are too young to understand."

"Aha," I answered and fell silent, remembering the assortment of "uncles" she had brought home and of *Vati*'s "juicy nurses," as *Omi* called them.

"I initiated this divorce and took exclusive responsibility for it," *Mutti* went on.

"Why?"

"You are too young to understand," she said.

"Try."

"He was so cold, so unloving, such a penny-pincher. We were incompatible. We had drifted apart."

"Aha."

"Come to think of it, perhaps this wasn't even his fault either, nor mine. It was the two World Wars, Uwe. You must understand: the wars! He must have had a screw loose since being wounded in France,

In the Leipzig city archives, Uwe discovered a poster announcing his mother's first concert after the war. Titled "Songs of Europe," it featured lieder from all parts of the continent.

and besides, had we not lost our home in the last war, our marriage would never have broken up."

"Really?"

I thought of my classmates, most of whom had lost their fathers in combat. Many had told me how much they envied me for having a family. A real family: father, mother, and child. Why did *Mutti* rip it apart?

"Don't worry, my Uwe. The court awarded me full custody of you. I will always be with you," she tried to reassure me, but couldn't. I knew what was going to happen: *Mutti* fulfilling herself. *Mutti* spending endless hours at the piano, singing *wa-wa-wa-wa-waaa* and *nui-nui-nui-nui-nuiii*. *Mutti* rehearsing for a concert series titled *Europa im Lied*, or Songs of Europe.

Now, seven decades later, I often think back to this conversation. Remembering how little I trusted her then, I have her voice in my head when I read that, in the United States, the country where I now live, between 70 and 80 percent of all divorces are initiated by women.

Of course, I loved *Mutti*'s passion for music and shared it. But already, as a child, I wondered about her strength of character, which was no match for *Omi*'s. My instincts told me that she would drop me one day, just as she had dumped my father, because her career as a singer took priority. As it turned out, my instincts were right.

"Where is *Vati* now?" I asked.

"With the Americans in Kirchberg an der Jagst."

"Where is that?"

"Near Stuttgart. The Americans are grooming him for a senior civil service position in western Germany."

"Should we not be with him?"

"I am meant to be here in Leipzig, Uwe. This is the city of music; music is my calling."

"What are your plans for me?"

"*Kommt Zeit, kommt Rat* (Time will tell)."

"Hmm."

Lost in gloomy thoughts, I walked with her back to *Omi*'s flat. Obviously, I could not blame *Mutti* for my loss of Natasha; that was Stalin's fault. But now she had deprived me of my erudite father who took me seriously enough to discuss with me the state of the world; who told me about Churchill and how free countries work; who told me about the Holocaust, who called the Nazis criminals, and who knew that I would keep my mouth shut so as not to endanger the whole family by chatting about it at school or on the street.

Of course, I still had *Omi*, but a dark premonition told me I would soon be separated from her as well. Never before in my nine years had I been so afraid, not even when bombs dropped on Leipzig. Suddenly I was scared. Why? Why was I crying silently in my bed at night, hoping that *Omi* would not notice? Why had I lost my sense of mischief? In retrospect, I believe this was, at least in part, because I felt sicker by the day.

Thank God I still had Josef as an ally and *Herr* Ziegenbalg as an important mentor. And suddenly Dr. Ernst-Theodor Eichelbaum,[1] a friend of my mother's from pre-Nazi days, assumed a brief but powerful role at a pivotal point of my life.

I had heard his name whispered often in the war but never met him. Like my "uncle" Felix von Bressensdorf, he couldn't socialize freely during the Hitler dictatorship for two reasons: he was partly of Jewish descent, and he was very active in the anti-Nazi Confessing Church. Now, however, Eichelbaum had become a political heavyweight as cofounder of the Christian Democrat Union in Soviet-occupied Saxony and first deputy mayor of Leipzig.

One day in 1946, he sent *Mutti* a note announcing his forthcoming visit.

"What does he want to see you about?" I asked her.

"Perhaps because he is the brother of Agathe Eichelbaum, my favorite teacher at prep school. We were very close."

"Where has he been all these years?"

"Probably hiding on a farm in Mecklenburg."

"Why Mecklenburg?"

Omi chortled.

"Perhaps a witticism by Prince Bismarck will explain it," *Omi* said. "Bismarck was once asked what he would do if he knew the world would come to an end tomorrow. 'I would move to Mecklenburg,'

---

1 Dr. Ernst-Theodor Eichelbaum, born 1893 in Berlin, escaped to West Germany in October 1948. He became headmaster of a *Gymnasium* in Wuppertal-Elberfeld, where I paid him a visit and thanked him in 1952, the year he cofounded the Association of Refugees from the Soviet Zone, becoming its chairman in 1963. From 1957 to 1965 he served as a Christian Democrat member of the *Bundestag* (German parliament). Eichelbaum died at the age of ninety-seven in 1991, seven months after the reunification of Germany. In 2000, Leipzig named a street after him.

he answered. 'Why Mecklenburg?' the questioner wanted to know. 'Because in Mecklenburg, everything happens fifty years later.'"

"In other words, Nazism hadn't had time to catch on in Mecklenburg."

"Yes," said *Omi*.

Dr. Eichelbaum was the kind of ancien régime German gentleman *Omi* liked: a product of the monarchy and a highly decorated veteran of World War I, where he had served as a lieutenant, earning both an Iron Cross and a Knight's Cross. He was also a *Gymnasium* professor of German, religion, and history and a steadfast Protestant; in other words, a man worth being served cakes on *Omi*'s best Meissen china.

Eichelbaum came with a dire message: eastern Germany was on its way to becoming a Communist dictatorship, no different from the Nazi nightmare we had just experienced. The Christian Democrats, still a free party then, would soon become a pawn of the Bolsheviks.

"Why are you still here? Why have you and Uwe not gone with your husband to western Germany?" he asked *Mutti*. She tried to explain. He looked at her, unconvinced.

"What about Uwe?"

"*Kommt Zeit, kommt Rat* (Time will tell)," *Mutti* answered meekly.

"He will soon be of high-school age. The Communists have already closed all traditional *Gymnasiums* in Leipzig, calling them bastions of bourgeois reaction, and have replaced them with socialist comprehensive schools where children will be thoroughly indoctrinated. You don't want that for Uwe, do you?"

"No," *Mutti* said.

"There might be a way around this," Eichelbaum proposed. "The *Thomasschule*, where I used to teach, will be allowed special Latin classes, not just for members of the *Thomanerchor*[2] but also for talented external pupils. Only the two best pupils in the fourth and fifth grades of each elementary school in Leipzig will be allowed to sit for its entrance exams. How are Uwe's grades?"

Mutti showed him my midterm report card. He read it quickly, patted me on the back, and said, "All ones [very good] and twos [good]. That's excellent. I especially like his one in Russian, which is unique in Leipzig. What worries me is the three [satisfactory] in arithmetic. Work on it, Uwe!"

"I will, Dr. Eichelbaum."

Shortly after his visit, I received an official request to present myself for tests lasting two days. With *Omi*'s help, I crammed in arithmetic. With *Herr* Ziegenbalg's assistance, I studied German grammar. *Mutti* taught me composition, geography, music, and history. *Mutti* and *Omi* sacrificed much of their meager rations to strengthen me physically for the test. *Herr* Ziegenbalg kept sending Josef over with cakes.

Just before the summer break, Leipzig's two hundred best elementary students assembled in four classrooms for the written examination, which lasted almost the entire first day. It started with an essay on one of three topics. I chose the life and music of Johann Sebastian Bach. The more I wrote, the more I relaxed, reaching a state of elation that stayed with me even when we were given arithmetic problems, which I solved easily, as if in a haze.

The orals on the following day went even better, thanks to my experience as a fast-talking Leipzig street urchin. It was a balmy, early-summer day. I remember walking home in near ecstasy.

---

2 One of the most revered boys' choirs in the world.

"I am sure you have passed," *Mutti* said and rewarded me with a precious gift, a fountain pen made of glass. A few days later, a nice letter arrived from Dr. Helmuth Heinze, headmaster of the *Thomasschule*, congratulating me on doing so well in the exams and telling me that he was looking forward to seeing me in class in September.

I can't remember much about my summer break apart from my new abode. *Omi* assigned me the sunny room formerly occupied by my father. I read more books about cowboys and Indians and walked a little every day with Josef. A new life as a *Gymnasiast*, a student at a classical high school, was looming, which made me feel rather grand.

Then, less than one week before I was to report to the *Thomasschule*, *Mutti* received a letter from the school board informing her, in one dry paragraph, that since there were still too many candidates for the Latin classes, some boys had to be dropped from the list, and I was one of them. I was to report instead to the 10th Socialist Comprehensive School, which was none other than my previous elementary school.

Boom! Another loss!

What went wrong? Had not Ernst Eichelbaum told me that I was among the eighteen candidates who had passed the entrance exam with the highest grades? Faithful Dr. Eichelbaum came over immediately to tell us about the extraordinary scene when the list of successful candidates for the Latin classes reached City Hall.

"Helmut Holzhauer, the fourth deputy mayor responsible for education, flew into a rage when he read all the names of prominent Leipzig families on this list, for he is a fanatical Communist," Eichelbaum said.

Evidently, Holzhauer summoned Headmaster Heinze to City Hall, threw the list of names at him, and roared, "*Warum ließen Sie alle diese Bürger- und Akademikersöhne bestehen?* (Why did you allow all these sons of bourgeois families and university graduates to pass?)"

"*Ich habe sie nicht bestehen lassen, Herr Holzhauer. Sie haben ganz einfach bestanden* (I haven't 'allowed' them to pass, Herr Holzhauer. They have passed. Period)," Heinze replied.

Thereupon Holzhauer deleted eighteen names from this list. All were names of the pupils with the best grades but of a provenance unwelcome in the class struggle that was about to unfold in East Germany. *Omi* and *Mutti* knew most of these boys. They were the children from our circle of friends—of doctors, lawyers, dentists, engineers, and university professors.

"I have an idea," Ernst Eichelbaum tried to console us. "Perhaps we can get Uwe into the *Thomanerchor*, which would guarantee him a place in one of the Latin classes. The choir does not come under Holzhauer's jurisdiction."

The *Thomanerchor* was founded in 1212 to sing at Sunday services and funerals, but also (in the Middle Ages) at executions on the market square, provided the delinquents had confessed and been communed before being burned at the stake, beheaded, hung, or quartered. Johann Sebastian Bach was its *Kantor* and musical director from 1723 until his death in 1750.

In 1946, the *Thomaskantor* was Günther Ramin, Bach's twelfth successor. Dr. Eichelbaum arranged for me to have an interview with him almost immediately so that I could move into the *Alumnat*, the choir's boarding school, right away, if I passed muster. Though academically linked to the *Thomasschule*, the *Alumnat* is an autonomous entity. City Hall has no say over who may or may not be admitted to it. That is the *Kantor*'s prerogative.

Ramin tested my knowledge in musical theory. I passed. He made me read a score. I passed. He made me play a few bars on the piano and told *Mutti*, "This boy has two left hands." Then he made me sing. I sang. I coughed. I sang, and I coughed even harder. Ramin rose from his piano stool and said, "Madame, your son has a fine voice, but he is ill. This is no common cough! You must take him to a doctor now. This is serious."

Mutti took me straight to Dr. Firnhaber, who referred me to a pulmonologist. The lung doctor diagnosed me with tuberculosis. No clinic in Soviet-occupied Saxony had any bed to spare for a child with TB because all the hospitals were filled up with *Wehrmacht* soldiers wounded, and civilians injured, in the bombing war. I was confined to my home. I remember little of the months that followed, other than that *Omi* and *Mutti* took turns in taking care of me, that they prayed with me every morning and evening, and that Josef brought cakes from *Herr* Ziegenbalg but was not allowed to enter my room. To enable me to talk to him for a few minutes, *Omi* or *Mutti* had to take me to the open window. Josef stood outside and told me about all the changes at school, but I couldn't take it in.

In the spring of 1947, I was beginning to feel better. The lung doctor found that my tubercles had encapsulated, which meant that I was no longer a danger to other children, and so, after the Easter break, I entered the brave new world of the 10th Socialist Comprehensive School, where I was assigned to a class of eighty students, some sitting on the floor and others standing during lessons.

I recognized none of the faculty members. *Herr* Ziegenbalg was nowhere in sight. My class teacher was a *Neulehrer* (new teacher) with proletarian—but no academic—credentials. He belonged to a species of instructors mass-produced by Communist academies in six-month courses.

I can't remember his name. He was a little man with sharp features and a high-pitched voice who told the class every morning, "*Unter Euch sind noch vier Christenschweine. Gebt ihnen Prügel, bis sie zur Vernunft kommen* (Among you there are still four Christian pigs. Beat them up until they come to their senses)."

Josef and I were two of those "Christian pigs." The other two were Lutherans we had never met before. As soon as school was over, we ran. In fairness, most of our classmates showed no inclination to beat us up; they just went home—but that also means they did not come to our defense. Some allies would have been nice, however, because ten or twelve classmates *did* chase after us, hooting and jeering. Thankfully, they didn't succeed this time, but we knew that it would get worse and that we had to organize our defenses.

Mutti, always a brilliant organizer, called a powwow of us "Christian pigs" and our mothers. Together, we hammered out a scheme that would prove hugely successful: every day after school, we "pigs" would separate, each running in a different direction to the nearest tram stop. This would split up the horde of our pursuers and thus weaken it. Each of us would be given a monthly ticket for the public transport system, which allowed us to change trains as often as necessary to shake off those who chased us.

It worked. We were never beaten up, although our fanaticized classmates often managed to hop on the same trains as we did (though usually on a different car). Following a strategy developed by *Mutti*, we threw them off guard by transferring to other lines at unexpected stops and not only at the central station, where most Leipzig trams met. Still, it usually took several hours of streetcar travel around town to save our hides. Rarely did I come home before four o'clock in the afternoon. I was always exhausted, hungry, and too tired to do much homework.

"This cannot go on," *Mutti* decreed. "You won't have to do this after the summer break. I promise."

"Where will I go?"

"*Kommt Zeit, kommt Rat* (Time will tell)," Mutti answered, repeating her favorite slogan.

Weeks of silence followed, but I wasn't worried. I had learned that while *Mutti* was ditsy on an emotional level to the point that her teacher, the eminent professor Edith Laux-Heydenreich, always addressed her as "my pudding," she was a crafty and courageous schemer in bypassing the bureaucratic constraints of a dictatorship.

In mid-July 1947, I noticed that *Mutti* and *Omi* were sending several parcels with my clothes and other things to an obscure address in Ulm, a city south of Stuttgart (in West Germany). Mysteriously, they collected Montblanc fountain pens and similar portable valuables from Aunt Irene and Aunt Käthe Pohl. Dr. Eichelbaum came to our apartment a couple of times for meetings, from which I was excluded. *Mutti* went off to secretive meetings with people unknown.

On the eighth of August, *Mutti* filled two rucksacks with travel necessities; on the ninth, *Omi* prepared a luxurious lunch that turned out to be my farewell meal from Leipzig.

"We'll leave tomorrow morning," said *Mutti*.

"Where?"

"To the mountains of Harz. I have managed to get a room for you in a spa to heal your lungs. But that's not where the journey will end."

"Where will the journey end?"

"In Ulm. You will be staying with Hans and Lily Eckart. He owns a tannery, and she is Swiss, which is good because she has access to lots of food."

"Who is she?"

"One of *Vati*'s old girlfriends."

"Will you also stay with the Eckarts?"

"No. I'll take you there and then return immediately to Leipzig. My work is here, and I have to look after *Omi*."

"You do not have to look after me," *Omi* protested. "I can look after myself."

Uwe's father in-between two female eye patients in the Thuringian Forest in 1928. The lady holding his left arm is Lily from Switzerland who briefly became Uwe's foster mother after his escape from the Soviet zone in 1947.

"Do we have exit permits?" I asked.

"Of course not. We will cross the border illegally. I have hired the best guide in the business. Trust me. I have been busy in the last few weeks."

"Was this what you have collected all those fountain pens for?"

"Among other things."

"What time is our train?"

"We won't go by train. The trains are overcrowded with people traveling on the roof, on running boards, and in the restrooms. Also, you never know when they will arrive, with locomotives fired by lignite, which does not produce enough heat. No, we travel luxuriously by bus," *Mutti* said, beaming.

"By bus?"

"Yes, I have obtained two seats for us on a special transport of the VVN."

This was the German acronym for the "Union of Persecutees of the Nazi Regime," which was heavily dominated by the Communist party.

"Did Dr. Eichelbaum finagle that? He was persecuted by the Nazis."

"I am not saying anything. The less you know, the better."

Early the next morning, *Omi*, *Mutti*, and I boarded the tram to the *Hauptbahnhof*, where a shiny yellow-and-brown bus was waiting for us. The other passengers gave us curious looks—we were the only young people on this trip, whereas they looked haggard and prematurely old. Most were former concentration camp or prison inmates: mainly Jews, Communists, and Social Democrats, as *Mutti* told me much later—she had this information from Dr. Eichelbaum.

Dr. Ernst Eichelbaum, a friend of Uwe's family, was deputy mayor of Leipzig but also leader of a network helping people to flee from the Soviet zone. He also helped Uwe escape.

The bus had two triangular back windows, through which I watched *Omi* wave me goodbye. Smaller and smaller she grew as the bus rumbled through canyons of ruins. Then I lost sight of her. *Mutti* stared at me, worried, but I didn't cry. *Omi* had taught me that crying in such a situation is un-Christian and ungentlemanly. Shedding tears now would be an offense to the person I loved so much.

Yet I knew then that on that tenth of August 1947, I was suffering my most profound loss in my ten years of life thus far. I was being separated from my pillar of stability; from the woman who was a stronger, wiser, and more loving parent to me than *Mutti* and *Vati* put together; from my source of joy and my teacher of Lutheran *Gottvertrauen* (trust in God).

What I did not know at the time became evident to me when, exactly forty years after this unforgettable August day, I enrolled as a student at a Lutheran seminary in Chicago. It was *Omi* who had triggered my passion for theology by teaching me two Lutheran treasures in the air-raid shelter. She taught me, in her unique, hands-on way Luther's two kingdoms doctrine, which assigns me the role of God's mask in his finite realm where the hidden God reigns through masks like me; and she taught me how I am to serve God in this world—by serving my neighbors in all my worldly endeavors.

When *Omi* and I embraced before I boarded the bus to the Harz, I essentially bade farewell to my childhood—and a real childhood this had been, bombs, hunger, and TB notwithstanding. *Omi* made it so. I had had a home with her, and from now on it was no more. I could not know then that two decades later, I would finally have a home again when my English wife, Gillian, told me, "Your home is wherever I am."

URCHIN'S FAREWELL TO CHILDHOOD

The bus hobbled west on war-damaged roads toward the Soviet-occupied part of the Harz mountains. I counted the potholes and thought of them as an allegory for the potholes on the road of my life ahead. I decided then and there to make the best of my caesura by thanking God for placing me in *Omi*'s arms while He protected us from the bombs that rained on us for so many nights. With *Omi*'s help, He imparted to me, the Leipzig urchin, a survival instinct that equipped me to handle whatever lay ahead while always remaining an urchin at heart.

CHAPTER 16

Urchin's Journey into Exile

"GENTLEMEN DON'T STARE, THEY just sneak a peek," *Omi* had taught me. Therefore, I attempted to act gentlemanly on our bus ride to the Harz while trying to figure out, inconspicuously, my fellow passengers. They seemed so unlike any other group of people I had encountered before; they looked like skeletons covered in gray skin.

None showed emotion. There was no indication that they were looking forward to their rest in one of the most beautiful regions in Germany. None spoke to *Mutti* or to me throughout the journey; in fact, they did not seem to talk to each other much. Occasionally, some gave me a dead look, glancing at me without hostility but also without the warmth grown-ups usually display when they see a child. When I smiled at them, they didn't smile back.

The next day, when nobody could hear us, *Mutti* and I discussed this encounter.

"They must have suffered very much," *Mutti* said. "Their traumatized facial expressions reminded me of how people looked after a heavy bombing."

"Were they Jews?"

"Some of them must have been Jews. Others were probably Communists. Did you notice their badges?"

"Yes, I saw their emblem featuring an upside-down red triangle over four vertical blue stripes on a white field."

"This is the badge of the VVN, an organization that was founded just a few months ago," *Mutti* explained. "The VVN is said to be an offshoot of the Communist party. Still, it is shameful what the Nazis have done to these people."

"But Dr. Eichelbaum is not a Communist, is he?"

"No, No! Quite the contrary! He is a faithful Christian. It's only a matter of time before the Communists drive him out of Leipzig. They are already giving him a hard time in City Hall. But he has contacts with the VVN, which is why he was able to arrange this trip for you. We must be grateful to him."

Late in the afternoon, the bus dropped us off in the center of Ellrich, a little mountain town in Thuringia, before delivering the other passengers to a VVN sanatorium nearby. A young man in a threadbare *Wehrmacht* tunic picked us up and led us to a farmhouse, where a dozen other people with suitcases and rucksacks were already waiting. He introduced himself as our guide. *Mutti* handed him his fee—in the form of a carton of Lucky Strike cigarettes—but she kept a second carton in reserve, presumably for her return trip. She later told me she had obtained the cigarettes on the black market in exchange for a Montblanc fountain pen.

A kindly woman, presumably the man's mother, made us sandwiches with *Harzer Käse*, a local cheese that stank atrociously but tasted delicious. Then our guide advised us, "Now lie down wherever you can and try to get some sleep! We must leave in the early hours of the morning."

Mutti and I shared a sofa; this was the first time I remember sleeping in my mother's arms, though it wasn't for long. After a few hours, the guide shook us gently.

"Let's go! Let's go! We have no time to lose," the guide said.

"Why so early?" *Mutti* asked him.

"The Russians will change guards soon. Thank God they are sloppy. They don't mind leaving their section of the border unattended for half an hour before their replacements arrive. This is good for us. It allows us to walk through the tunnel safely."

"A tunnel? What sort of a tunnel?" I asked.

"We will have to walk through the railway tunnel to Walkenried in the western part of the Harz. There are no trains at the moment. The tunnel is only 268 meters (880 feet) long. You will find this excursion interesting, though. This tunnel runs through the largest gypsum cave in Europe. It is thirty-five meters (115 feet) high and seventy meters (230 feet) wide and feels like a cathedral. The gypsum is extracted from the western side of the tunnel."

Our group of refugees was remarkably disciplined. Nobody spoke a word. Noiselessly, we crept behind our guide to an embankment, behind which he made us duck while observing the Red Army soldiers from a distance of one hundred yards. We heard their boots crunch on a footpath alongside the tracks. Crunch, crunch, crunch, and they were gone.

"Now!" whispered the guide.

Quietly we slipped into the tunnel and began walking on the railway tracks.

"Look up—how beautiful this is!" said the guide, briefly directing a torch toward the ceiling of the gypsum cave.

"Thank you!" we whispered. The minute he switched off his torch, we saw early daylight at the end of the tunnel.

"A few more steps, and you are in the west," he said.

Just at this point, the most hilarious machine backed into the tunnel's western exit. I couldn't wait to clamber on top of this funny truck that looked like a Heath Robinson contraption.[1]

It was a lopsided, rust-covered Büssing NAG lorry, tilting alarmingly to the left. The vehicle seemed overloaded with gypsum bags. On its left side, directly behind the driver's cabin, I made out a huge gadget resembling the boiler in *Omi*'s bathroom. This was a wood gasifier, from which a concertina tube ran like a huge, fat snake over the cabin to the engine.

"There is your freedom express," our guide informed us, grinning.

"Is it roadworthy?" asked one of the refugees.

"It only looks unsafe, but it has already transported countless tons of gypsum and many hundreds of refugees," said a well-built man in a *Wehrmacht* officer's jacket who suddenly descended from the passenger side of the truck's cabin. He had lost one arm in the war, which is why his right sleeve was affixed to his left shoulder with safety pins.

"Meet the *Hauptmann* (captain)," our guide introduced. "He'll take care of you from now on. I am leaving you here."

---

1 W. Heath Robinson (1872–1944) was an English cartoonist, illustrator, and artist, best known for drawings of whimsically elaborate machines to achieve simple objectives. He became my favorite cartoonist when I developed a fascination for caricatures in my late teens.

"All aboard now!" the *Hauptmann* said. He grabbed me around the waist with his strong left arm and slung me on top of the gypsum bags.

"Were you really a captain?" *Mutti* chirped flirtatiously as he gallantly helped her climb on top of the truck.

"Yes, I fought with the Twelfth Panzer Division at the eastern front where I was wounded," he answered. "This was a blessing; at least I was not killed or taken prisoner of war by the Russians."

I sat down next to the gasifier to warm up because this early in the morning, it was still rather cool.

"Be careful! Don't sit there," the *Hauptmann* warned us. "As soon as the sun is up, it will get very hot today, and the gasifier and gypsum will make the heat unbearable. Move toward the back. You'll find it more comfortable there."

Once we had settled down, I complimented *Mutti* on her crafty organization of our escape.

"*Das lief wie am Schnürchen* (That went like clockwork)," I said. "How did you engineer it?"

"Our friend in City Hall [meaning Dr. Eichelbaum] put me in touch with an extensive network for smuggling refugees out of the Soviet Zone," she whispered. "This network operates out of West Berlin but has its tentacles everywhere. Our guide, and the *Hauptmann*, are part of it."

Belching and snarling, the truck began its crawl westward. The *Hauptmann* sat down next to us; I noticed sparks flying between this young ex-officer and *Mutti*.

"How far will this truck take us, *Hauptmann*?" I asked.

"Almost to the border of the American zone. We are now in Lower Saxony, which is British-occupied. There are rarely guards posted at the border to US-occupied Hesse. In case there are any controls, I'll show you a safe bypass."

August 1947 was one of the hottest months in twentieth-century Europe. By eleven o'clock, the heat was almost unbearable.

"Anyone hungry?" the *Hauptmann* asked. "We have sandwiches, eggs, and fruit on board."

"Water, just water," the refugees groaned.

"Water it will be," the *Hauptmann* said. He retrieved a *Wehrmacht* jerrican of fresh water from behind the driver's cabin. *Mutti* helped him pour it into *Wehrmacht*-issue aluminum cups. I drank more than seemed wise.

"If you must relieve yourselves, please remember that we cannot stop this truck until our final destination, lest we lose power. It takes hours to fire up the wood gasifier again."

Well, I did have to relieve myself and announced it in Saxon jargon: "*Mutti, ich muss äma seech'n!*"

Ashamed of her son's vulgarity, *Mutti* chided me: "*Pfui, Uwe, sprich Hochdeutsch!* (Speak High German!)"

But the captain laughed and said, "*Seech'n* is such a funny word! It makes me feel homesick. I am also from Leipzig."

Cheerfully, we started a human chain, allowing me to do what I had to do without falling off the truck. The *Hauptmann* made me stand at the very back of the vehicle, facing the street. He sat down behind me and slung his left arm around my middle to make sure I didn't fall off as I unbuttoned my fly. *Mutti* crawled behind the *Hauptmann* to sling both her arms around him, ostensibly to give him support. Another passenger felt that this was a good opportunity to embrace an attractive young woman, and so he did.

All on board laughed, as did farmworkers in the fields we passed. The scene of a lopsided, groaning gypsum transport topped by a cockspur of refugees securing a urinating child must have been a hysterical sight. Some wise guy on board coined the word *Pinkelkette* (pee chain). The more water we drank, the more *Pinkelketten* were formed, sometimes including more than half our party of refugees. Again and again the *Hauptmann* shouted commands, and when a woman had to lower herself over the back of the truck, he snarled like a drill sergeant: "*Die Herren alle Augen schließen!* (All gentlemen, close your eyes!)" All men followed his orders, while women forged a *Pinkelkette* for the lady in need. I, of course, ogled and thanked God for equipping males and females differently.

A few hundred yards before the Lower Saxon-Hessian state borderline, the Büssing NAG turned into a warehouse to discharge its passengers and unload the gypsum bags. The *Hauptmann* helped my mother and me down and led us to a homestead across the road, where he introduced us to the farmer's wife. She invited us to clean up in her bathroom. *Mutti* put on a fresh blouse, and I donned a fresh shirt and a fresh pair of socks.

"We will have to hitchhike from here. Looking neat helps secure us a lift," *Mutti* said. I never forgot her advice about looking proper because it made travel around Europe so much easier for me later in my teenage years, especially when I enhanced the practice with a new hitchhiking technique for which I claim a worldwide patent.

I had noticed that, almost always, only single men stopped for hitchhikers, but never single women, and very rarely couples. To render women more hiker-friendly, I bought flowers before each journey, stuck their stems into a potato to keep them fresh, and wrapped the potato with aluminum foil. When a car with a woman driver (or a female passenger) approached, I stepped forward, bowed courteously while holding the flowers in my outstretched left hand, smiled, and indicated with my right thumb that I needed a lift.

It nearly always worked. Women stopped or made their husbands stop. If they took me a long distance, I gave the lady the whole bunch—usually yellow roses. If she gave me a lift for only a short distance, I rewarded her with only one flower.

"You slimy bugger!" said my wife, Gillian, when I told her about this tactic.

"What was slimy about it?" I asked. "The women loved it, and I, a penniless young man, was able to see the world. Sometimes my flower trick even resulted in romantic episodes."

At the homestead near the British-American border in Germany, the farmer's wife prepared us liverwurst and ham sandwiches, gave us apples from her garden, and dispatched us to the main road to Kassel.

"Safe travels!" she said. "There is not much traffic out there except for tractors, horse carts, some lorries, and very few cars. Beware of British military vehicles! The English often arrest refugees from the Soviet zone. They don't send them back east but sometimes intern them in camps. You don't want that, do you?"

"No," *Mutti* answered.

"God bless you!"

No sooner were we on the main road to Kassel than an olive-drab street cruiser stopped. It was a Packard Clipper, as I later discovered, with a big, five-pointed white star on each of the rear doors.

"Let's run!" *Mutti* said, and we started running into the field.

"Don't be afraid—come back!" a pleasant female voice called after us. "We are Americans and are not going to harm you."

A smartly uniformed woman sitting in the back waved at us through the open car window.

"Do you speak English?"

"Yes," said *Mutti*.

"Please, do get in! I would like to talk to you. Where are you going?"

"Kassel."

"So are we. You are refugees, aren't you? Where are you from?"

Mutti described our escape from Leipzig and regaled the American woman with the funny story of the lopsided gypsum truck that brought us here.

"Considering you have just fled from the Soviet zone, you look amazingly neat, as if you had just stepped out of the shower."

"We washed in the farmhouse back there and put on fresh clothes."

"How very German! I like that."

We sat next to the American woman in the back of the car.

"Are you thirsty?" she asked me.

I nodded.

She handed me a Coca-Cola bottle, the first in my life. I had seen rusty old Coke ads from prewar days at a snack bar in Leipzig but had never tasted one.

"Do you like it?" the American woman asked.

"*Ja, danke* (Yes, thank you)," I answered. In truth, I didn't like it and never got used to the taste. But it would have been impolite to tell this nice lady that.

"We are crossing the border to the American zone," she said. "There are no guards here anymore."

She pulled a notebook out of her breast jacket along with a writing utensil I had never seen before: a ballpoint pen. Then she queried *Mutti* about the reasons and details of our escape: about the discrimination of bourgeois children by the Leipzig education department, about our Communist teacher inciting a class of eighty boys to beat up the four practicing Christians among them, about our well-organized flight, and about the ranking official of Jewish descent who had helped us flee. Who was he? Could *Mutti* give her his name? *Mutti* hesitated.

"You need not worry," the woman said. "We definitely won't pass his name on to the Russians. There's a new war now, this time between the Soviet Union and the West. It is a 'cold war.' This is why I find your report about this man so interesting. We need men of his caliber for leadership positions in the new democratic Germany we are trying to build over here."

I didn't fully understand what she was saying at the time, but *Mutti* told me later when we were alone.

Mutti eventually relented and gave Dr. Eichelbaum's name to this pleasant lady she suspected of being a military intelligence officer.

We arrived in Kassel. The American insisted that we cross the city center on our way to the central station.

"*Herr, erbarme dich!* (Lord, have mercy!)" Mutti exclaimed as she surveyed the field of rubble that was once an unspoiled medieval downtown area.

"It looks worse than Leipzig," I said.

"I cannot tell you how ashamed I am," replied the woman. "When we occupied Kassel, we found that 97 percent of the city center was wiped out in one night in October 1943. More than seven thousand people died that day, mainly women and children. To me, this makes no sense!"

Kassel's *Hauptbahnhof* (main railway station) looked nearly as awful, although trains did arrive and leave the station, all packed with passengers on roofs, running boards, and even coal tenders. Long queues of lethargic people in tattered clothes had formed in front of the ticket counters.

Our benefactor walked with us through the station. "You won't get anywhere here because you don't have the necessary papers," she said. "You could try to hitchhike again, but it will take you days to get to Ulm that way, and where would you and your child sleep? I wouldn't risk it."

Scanning the pandemonium in the station, she spotted a glistening train on an almost empty platform. "Wait! I have an idea," she said, "Come with me." We squeezed our way through the crowds to that train.

"This is a DUS—a US military train," she explained. "It will travel to Munich via Stuttgart and Ulm. Only Allied personnel and Germans with special permits are allowed. But don't worry, I'll get you past our military policemen, who only patrol the platform. They respect my uniform. Let's get on board and find you seats."

"What shall I do when the conductor comes into the compartment and asks for our tickets?" asked *Mutti*.

"He won't kick you out. He will be a German. Give him a pack of cigarettes and pay him twice the fare. That will make him happy. Trust me, I have done this before."

She found us a third-class compartment with wooden seats. It was almost empty except for one other passenger, a young sergeant. He jumped up and saluted our uniformed friend.

"Look after these people, Sergeant," she said, "They are in need of good care."

"Yes, ma'am," he answered.

Before the American woman left the train, *Mutti* asked her for her notebook and ballpoint pen and wrote "J. M. Eckart, Gerberei und Lederfabrik, Ulm" on it with a telephone number.

"Please call them and tell them the time of our arrival."

"I'll do that as soon as I get to a phone," the woman promised with a lovely smile. "Goodbye, and God bless!" She got off the train seconds before it rolled out of the station.

"What did you write? What was that about?" I asked *Mutti*.

"That was the name and number of the tannery where you are going to stay. I hope they will send somebody to pick us up at the station in Ulm."

"A tannery?"

"Yes, a tannery turns hides into leather. Hans Eckart owns it. The Americans have commandeered his villa temporarily, which is why he has had an apartment built in his factory compound. This is where you are going to live. You'll be fine."

"How did you meet them?"

"I didn't. *Vati* befriended Lily Eckart in an eye clinic in Thuringia long before he and I met."

"He seems to run into many women at clinics, if *Omi* is to be believed."

"I wish you good luck with Lily!" said *Mutti*.

"What's she like?"

"I am told she is very stern."

"Like *Omi*, with a fast right hand?"

"No! *Omi* is funny, even when she is stern in her Lutheran way. She cuffs you and kisses you and makes you laugh. Not Lily. *Vati* told me that she is very Swiss Reformed: grim, strict, and a little self-righteous. With her, nothing is a laughing matter."

"Kind of like the women in the Reformed church in Leipzig," I said. "Actually, I liked them."

"Well, you will find out."

The train picked up speed. The conductor entered our compartment and was happy with the double fare and the cigarettes, just as the American woman had predicted.

It was starting to get dark, and *Mutti* unpacked the sandwiches the farmer's wife had given her. She offered the sergeant one.

"This tastes fantastic!" he said. "Shall I get us drinks from the dining car?"

Mutti offered him some *Reichsmarks*.

"Keep your money," the sergeant said. "They don't accept German currency on this train, only MPCs [Military Payment Certificates]."

He returned with bottles of orange juice for *Mutti* and me and a beer for himself. After dinner, *Mutti* sent me to the lavatory to clean up.

Now it was really getting dark. *Mutti* and I stretched out on the banquette of wooden slats on our side of the compartment, and the sergeant laid out on his. I immediately fell asleep; it had been a strenuous day.

We awoke in the early hours. The sergeant brought coffee for *Mutti* and himself, cocoa for me, and some biscuits. When the train reached Stuttgart, the sergeant got out. For the rest of the journey, *Mutti* and I were alone.

"How long will you stay with me in Ulm?" I asked her.

"I am going back to Leipzig tonight."

"How?"

"The same way we came. The conductor just told me that he is going to be on the night train to Kassel and will allow me to travel with him. Somehow I'll find my way back to the farm in the British Zone..."

"... where you will connect with the *Hauptmann* and travel with him in his funny truck to the tunnel and the guide," I interrupted her.

"Smart kid."

"Why the rush?"

"I have to prepare for a concert in Leipzig next month, and, at any rate, there is no room for me at the Eckarts' apartment above their factory."

"Will *Vati* visit me there?"

"I have no idea. We haven't been in touch lately."

"I see."

I left the compartment and opened a window in the corridor to catch some fresh air. The train had entered an extremely steep and sharp right curve, allowing me to see its front and its back. I saw an electric engine pulling us and a steam locomotive pushing us. I had never seen a train with two locomotives before.

"This is the *Geislinger Steige*," said the conductor while walking past me. "It's an old trade route since Roman days. Today, it is the most precipitous rail track in Germany."

Our arrival in Ulm was a sad affair. From our compartment window, I saw that, like Kassel, this city was even more damaged than Leipzig. An odd, square-shaped car with the steering wheel on the wrong side awaited us in front of the station.

"This is an English Hillman," explained Hans Eckart, who sat in the driver's seat on the right. The lady next to him was stern Auntie Lily. She didn't smile.

"Let me show you around town a little," he said. We stopped at Ulm Minster, which boasts the highest spire of any church in Germany. The cathedral was horribly damaged. "At least its beautiful windows were evacuated," Lily explained in a café, where *Mutti* handed her the papers needed to register me at the Ulm *Rathaus* (city hall) and at school. *Mutti* then hugged me and walked through the ruins back to the station.

We drove to Hans Eckart's bomb-damaged factory on *Bleichstraße*.

"Our apartment has barely enough space for Uncle Hans, our two daughters, Verena and Heidi, and me," Lily said. "So, for the time being, you will be lodged on the shop floor. As soon as we are allowed to move back into our villa, you will come with us."

The shop floor was one flight up. Hans Eckart showed me around. The place was huge and empty. The damage caused by air raids had only partially been repaired. There was no glass in the windows. I saw a large bed on a carpet. Next to it, the parcels *Omi* and *Mutti* had sent from Leipzig were stacked. This was my new home.

"Where do I wash and do my business?" I asked him.

"You come over to the apartment."

I knew that I wasn't going to do that.

"Dinner is at seven."

Dinner was a horrific experience that I suppressed until I read about it in a memoir by Verena ("Vreni") von Asten, the Eckarts' eldest daughter. She wrote,

"Uwe, the son of a blind prosecutor, who had been a friend of my mother's since her youth, came to stay with us. On that day of all days, she had bought some dried cod . . . But Uwe stubbornly refused to eat the stinky stuff. My mother, a teacher, had raised us lovingly and sternly to be obedient, but with Uwe she bit on granite. Mother remained adamant and forced the poor boy to swallow a few bites. We two girls melted with pity for Uwe, especially when he jumped up, ran into the bathroom, and vomited miserably. I am certain that Uwe, who later became a widely traveled and successful journalist, has never forgotten this horrible story."

The reason I had actually forgotten this dreadful experience was that it was superseded by a more significant discovery I had made about Auntie Lily much later: without telling my parents or me, she had paid my tuition at boarding school for the four years following my brief interlude in Ulm. That she did this so discreetly showed the other, much pleasanter side of her Calvinist upbringing.

Now, though, reading about the dried cod incident in Vreni's book, my recollection of it came back. I had told Auntie Lily of my dangerous fish allergy, but she wouldn't hear it. After throwing up in the bathroom, I left the Eckarts' apartment, but Vreni and Heidi ran after me to tell me how sorry they were about the way their mother had treated me.

"We are on your side," said Vreni. She was already a teenager, whereas Heidi was only one year older than I. I remember how moved I was by their sweet and courageous gesture. From that moment on, we became close friends. Our friendship has endured until this day. Vreni now lives in the German-speaking part of Belgium, and Heidi near Zurich. We telephone frequently, and they often mention the fish dinner on my first day in Ulm. "What an ugly scene!" said Vreni, when we last spoke.

Uwe with Heidi Eckart in whose parents' home in Ulm he found a temporary shelter after his escape from the Soviet zone of occupation. To this day, the two are friends.

As for Auntie Lily, she never tried to force fish on me again. I had won!

Before I went to bed that evening, I walked to my window that had neither glass nor frame, unbuttoned my fly, and relieved myself into the balmy summer night. That done, I said my evening prayers cheerfully, certain that *Omi* would have approved of my little act of reprisal, the vengeance of a Leipzig urchin.

It was a great comfort having Vreni and Heidi on my side. Being several years older, Vreni's interest in me was limited. Heidi and I, by contrast, grew very close. We went to school together by tram and occasionally embraced and kissed when we knew that Auntie Lily was out of the house. I hadn't gone that far with Natasha, but then we were two years younger when we discovered our love for each other.

Auntie Lily had enrolled us in a Rudolf Steiner School, the pedagogical idiosyncrasies of which were not exactly tailor-made for a Leipzig urchin. This was the first of three such schools I had to endure; thank God there were only three, for there are 1,200 around the world! They are named after its founder, the Austrian esotericist Rudolf Steiner (1861–1925), a cognate of Allan Kardec, whose spiritist séances *Omi* used to mock for her superstitious friends during the air war (see chapter 9).

The most unbearable part of the Steiner schools' curriculum is eurythmy, an expressive movement art form compelling us children to mince in flowing garments about the parquet floor.[2] As long as this was done to musical tunes, I could live with it. But God help us if we had to hop to hysterically effusive emissions by so-called *Sprachgestalter* (language framers) whose favorite victims were texts by Johann Wolfgang von Goethe, Germany's greatest poet. Rudolf Steiner thought he was Goethe's reincarnation.

After five years of eurythmy, I needed a recovery period of twenty years to enjoy Goethe again, and I have still not healed from what these people did to archangel Raphael's opening lines of the

---

2 Eurythmy was originated by Rudolf Steiner, in conjunction with Marie von Sivers, in the early twentieth century. Primarily a performance art, it is also used in education, especially in Steiner schools (also known as Waldorf schools) and—as part of anthroposophical medicine—for claimed therapeutic purposes.

"Prologue in Heaven" from *Faust*. In its glorious English translation, it reads as follows:

> The Sun, in ancient guise, competing
> With brother spheres in rival song,
> With thunder-march, his orb completing,
> Moves his predestin'd course along;
> His aspect to the powers supernal
> Gives strength though fathom him none may;
> Transcending thought, the works eternal
> As fair as on the primal day.

Abused by a Steinerian *Sprachgestalter*, the first line of this verse jumps from "The" by an entire octave to "Sun, in," drops down by five notes to "ancient," shoots up another octave to "guise, competing," and then yet another octave . . . you get the drift. I came to loathe eurythmy so much that, to this day, I hold an aversion even against ballet, which, for a lover of the arts, is really unpardonable.

The good news about my school in Ulm was that my eurythmy teacher was a stutterer, which is why he preferred to make us hop to music rather than tortured rhyme and is also why he was spared military service in World War II. Hence he survived the war, unlike his older brother, Field Marshal Erwin Rommel, the Desert Fox, whom Hitler forced to commit suicide. Our teacher's name was Gerhard Rommel.

I didn't last long in that school—nor in Ulm. The weather turned in October 1947, and I caught a cold in my drafty bedroom in the factory. Soon, I coughed as hard as when I had TB in Leipzig. Auntie Lily made space for me in the apartment by moving her two daughters into one bedroom and assigning the other to me. But she warned me, "You won't be able to stay here for long because Uncle Hans' mother has cancer and will soon come to live with us."

My condition grew worse. The Eckarts' family doctor came by and suspected whooping cough. Next, I was bundled off, in their Hillman, to the brand-new Lutheran deaconess' hospital for children in Schwäbisch Hall. Week after week went by. It turned out that I did not have whooping cough after all. Thus I was occupying a bed that was desperately needed for really sick children.

The sisters became increasingly impatient with my absent parents, though never with me. They took turns sitting by my bedside in the evenings to pray with me. They brought me my favorite books from the library, including Luther's Small Catechism and the Lutheran hymnal, which, by the end of my stay, I almost knew by heart.

Then, on the morning of 25 October 1947, my eleventh birthday, the entire deaconess choir, in black cowls and white bonnets, entered my room carrying candles and serenading me with my favorite hymn: "Abide, O Dearest Jesus, among Us with Thy Grace." They reminded me so much of *Omi* I wanted to embrace them all and wished I could have stayed with them.

Shortly before the First Advent, *Mutti* and Auntie Lily appeared, in the Eckarts' Hillman, to visit me.

"How can I show you my gratitude?" I heard *Mutti* ask the mother superior. "How about an Advent concert in your chapel?"

"If you want to do us a favor, please, please take care of your child," Mother Superior answered coolly. "We urgently need his room. We are suffering from no dearth of music because we have a fine organist and a wonderful choir. Uwe will tell you. We gave him a serenade on his birthday."

Lily Eckart drove us to Neu-Ulm, on the Bavarian side of the Danube, where she booked us into an inexpensive inn. At Christmas, *Mutti* rented a second room, which she decorated beautifully. *Vati* joined us. For the last time in my life, the three of us celebrated Christmas Eve together. Suddenly, *Mutti* rose, sent me to bed in the room she and I shared, and said, "Go, sleep; *Vati* and I have something to discuss." Of course, I didn't go to sleep; I pinned my ear to their door and overheard the following conversation, which has remained in my head ever since:

VATI: "The British have offered me a high office in the regional government of Eastern Westphalia, which is where I am from."

MUTTI: "I am happy for you."

VATI: "I will only accept this offer if we reassemble our family. Come back, Ruth—let us get married again! You'll like Detmold. It is beautiful and has one of the most important musical academies in Europe."

MUTTI: "I know about this academy, but, no, I can't, Karl-Heinz! Too much has snapped between us. I have a new life now. I have my music."

VATI: "And Uwe? The court has awarded you custody!"

MUTTI: "*Kommt Zeit, kommt Rat* (Time will tell). For the time being, he will be fine in a boarding school. Lily Eckart has found a good one near Paderborn, a Rudolf Steiner School."

VATI: "Is this your last word, Ruth? I repeat: it would be better if the three of us lived together again."

Uwe ended up in Ulm after escaping from Leipzig. This south German city on the Danube was badly bombed in the last days of the war. Ulm's Lutheran cathedral is the tallest in the world, with a spire measuring 530 feet.

MUTTI: "No, Karl-Heinz, I can't, and I won't. Tomorrow I will return to Leipzig."

VATI: "I won't move to Detmold by myself, even though I could contribute to the reconstruction of our Fatherland if I took the British offer. I have lost my eyesight for my Fatherland, I have lost my home for the Fatherland, and now I have lost my family. You know what, Ruth? I will accept early retirement and my war pension, and then the Fatherland can keep me and kiss my rear."

This was the moment, on Christmas Eve 1947, when I realized that, from now on, I was pretty much on my own.

Postscript
Patience, Hope, and Faith

I FERVENTLY HOPE THAT this volume has not made my readers feel sorry for me. If they do, I have failed in my self-imposed mission. My childhood was short; it ended when I was eleven years old. But seen from the perspective of an octogenarian, it was intense and real and filled with play, wonderment, laughter, and an unshakeable trust in God.

True, I suffered starvation, warfare, and the loss of my home and my family. But so did—and still do—many millions of other children around the world. In my first eleven years, there was also somebody I could trust and look up to, somebody who introduced me to the values and elegance of a bygone era, somebody who taught me the Christian faith, taught me love, respect, and manners. That person was *Omi*, my grandmother.

I was also introduced to the joy of music, which Luther called the greatest thing next to theology. My mother did that. I fell in love with a little black-haired girl and lost her to the Gulag. Stalin stole her. My eyes and ears were opened to recognize courage and decency. Teachers risked their lives to do that. I heard about the evil of rulers who killed millions of innocent people. My blind father told me that. I heard Hitler described as the redeemer of Germany. A pastor in whose home I lived preached this from a Lutheran pulpit. But I also remember with admiration the organist's courageous comment, "He is lying, he is lying. He is betraying our Lord (Christ)." He whispered these unforgettable words into my ears, risking his life for the truth.

If the last scene in this volume were the conclusion of my autobiography, it would indeed be a tragic ending, just as millions upon millions of parental divorces place horrific exclamation marks at the end of their children's lives, leading to their failures at school and in their vocations. But this doesn't have to be so. I am thankful for my early childhood, despite suffering in the years that immediately followed. I dropped out of school, felt abandoned, wondered if I was crazy, but then, still in my adolescence, experienced the beginnings of a stellar career as a journalist.

At home, I had never learned the art of family life but then was blessed by fifty-eight years of marriage (so far). I never thought I would see the inside of a university but ended up with a PhD from Boston University at age fifty-six. I was a millionaire when I was forty, lost everything due to bad investments, and am now a happy, though not rich, old man surrounded by ever-new circles of faithful friends.

I invite my readers to wait for volumes 2 and 3 of my *Urchin Trilogy*. I hope they will show that, in assessing one's own vita, patience, linked with hope and faith, proves a healthy virtue.